POST-SOVIET POLITICAL ORDER

Western countries have sought to promote democracy as the base upon which to build politically stable countries amongst the ashes of the former Soviet empire. *Post-Soviet Political Order* takes a step back from how to build democracy in order to first consider what is shaping the institutional pattern of the post-Soviet political order, both within and among the Soviet successor states. Focusing on the former Soviet Union and Eastern Europe, this study asks what the new order will be like, what patterns of conflict are emerging, and what can be done about stabilizing the region. Using the historical context of other great empire collapses and earlier instances of state formation, the contributors offer a variety of perspectives on the emergence of post-imperial and post-Soviet political institutions. They converge on four common themes that inform the analysis of post-imperial politics: the institutional legacy of empire; the social processes unleashed by imperial collapse; patterns of bargaining within and between states to resolve conflicts arising out of the imperial collapse; and the impact of wider international setting on the pattern of post-imperial politics.

Post-Soviet Political Order broadens the analytical prism through which scholars can view the shaping of post-Soviet political space. It shows that strong state institutions must be constructed from the rubble of the Soviet empire if conflict and political instability are to be avoided.

Barnett R. Rubin is Director of the Center for Preventive Action, Council on Foreign Relations, New York. **Jack Snyder** is Professor and Chair, Political Science Department, Columbia University.

POST-SOVIET POLITICAL ORDER

Conflict and State Building

Edited by Barnett R. Rubin and Jack Snyder

London and New York

First published 1998
by Routledge
11 New Fetter Lane, London EC4P 4EE

Simultaneously published in the USA and Canada
by Routledge
29 West 35th Street, New York, NY 10001

Typeset in Baskerville by Routledge
Printed and bound in Great Britain by Clays Ltd, St. Ives PLC

British Library Cataloguing in Publication Data
A catalogue record for this book is available from the British Library

Library of Congress Cataloging in Publication Data
Post-Soviet political order : conflict and state building / edited by Barnett Rubin and
Jack Snyder.
Includes bibliographical references and index.
1. Former Soviet republics–Politics and government. 2. Former Soviet
republics–Ethnic relations. 3. Post-Soviet–Former Soviet republics.
I. Rubin, Barnett R. II. Snyder, Jack L.
DK293.P67   1998
947–dc21   97–36987
                                                                                CIP

ISBN 0–415–17068–0 (hbk)
ISBN 0–415–17069–9 (pbk)

CONTENTS

CONTENTS

ILLUSTRATIONS

Map

Figures

Tables

CONTRIBUTORS

José Casanova is Professor and Chair of the Department of Sociology at the New School for Social Research. He is the author of *Public Religions in the Modern World* (University of Chicago Press, 1994).

Mark von Hagen is associate professor of history and director of the Harriman Institute at Columbia University. He is the author of *Soldiers in the Proletarian Dictatorship: The Red Army and the Soviet Socialist State, 1917–1930* (Cornell University Press, 1990).

Rajan Menon is Monroe J. Rathbone Professor of International Relations at Lehigh University and a Visiting Scholar at the Harriman Institute. He is the author of *Soviet Power and the Third World* (Yale University Press, 1986) and co-editor of *Limits to Soviet Power* (Lexington Books, 1989). His recent work on security problems in Central Asia and Northeast Asia has appeared in *International Security*, *Survival*, and *The Bulletin of Atomic Scientists*.

Alexander J. Motyl is Associate Director of the Harriman Institute at Columbia University and Editor-in-Chief of *The Encyclopedia of Nationalism* (The Academic Press, forthcoming). He is the author of *Dilemmas of Independence: Ukraine after Totalitarianism* (Council on Foreign Relations, 1993) and *Sovietology, Rationality, Nationality: Coming to Grips with Nationalism in the USSR* (Columbia University Press, 1990). He is the editor of *Thinking Theoretically about Soviet Nationalities* and *The Post-Soviet Nations* (both Columbia University Press, 1992). Motyl is currently compiling a manuscript entitled *This Very Delicate Balance: Empires and Imperial Trajectories*.

Barnett R. Rubin is the Director of the Center for Preventive Action at the Council on Foreign Relations. He was previously Associate Professor of Political Science and Director of the Center for the Study of Central Asia at Columbia University. He is the author of *The Search for Peace in Afghanistan: From Buffer State to Failed State* and *The Fragmentation of Afghanistan: State Formation and Collapse in the International System* (both Yale University Press, 1995), and editor of *Toward Comprehensive Peace in Southeast Europe: Conflict Prevention in the South Balkans* (Council on Foreign Relations and the Twentieth Century Fund, 1996).

Jack Snyder, Professor of Political Science at Columbia University, is the author of *The Ideology of the Offensive* (Cornell University Press, 1984) and *Myths of Empire* (Cornell University Press, 1991). He co-edits the book series on International History and Politics of Princeton University Press, and is chair of the Committee on International Peace and Security of the Social Science Research Council.

Steven Solnick is Assistant Professor of Political Science at Columbia University and Program Coordinator for Russian Studies at Columbia's Harriman Institute. He is the author of *Stealing the State: Control and Collapse in Soviet Institutions* (Harvard University Press, 1997). His current research addresses center–periphery dynamics and state-building processes in post-Soviet Russia and other compound states.

Hendrik Spruyt is Associate Professor in the Department of Political Science at Columbia University and member of the Institute of War and Peace Studies. His book, *The Sovereign State and Its Competitors* (Princeton University Press, 1994) received the Greenstone Prize from the History and Politics Section of the American Political Science Association. He is currently working on issues having to do with territorial distintegration, particularly in empires.

PREFACE

The editors and authors would like to thank the Carnegie Corporation of New York, whose assistance and support made possible the project of which this work was one product. We would also like to thank John Gerard Ruggie, whose leadership of Columbia's School of International and Public Affairs (SIPA) made it possible for us to conceive and fund this project.

The project convened a working conference on 5–6 May 1995, where the authors benefited from comments on several papers by Miles Kahler, Mark Blyth, Karen Ballentine, and Dominique Arel. We would like to thank them for their contributions.

Several students worked as administrative and research assistants on this project. The help of Shahrbanou Tadjbakhsh, Cassandra Cavanaugh, Corinna Snyder, Robin Bhatty, and Mark Suprun enabled us to organize meetings and discussions about drafts. Timothy Crawford prepared the bibliography. Joan Turner, Penny Zaleta, and Diya Bhattacharya of the SIPA dean's office enabled us to track and report on the expenditures. Anya Schmemann and Susanna Campbell of the Council on Foreign Relations assisted in the final preparation of the manuscript.

Finally, a note about transliterations. Since the independence of the former Soviet republics and revival of their national languages, transliteration of place and personal names is evolving away from the Russified versions. As yet, there is no single agreed standard for English transliteration from Ukrainian, Tajik, and so on, and the authors in this volume have made different choices. At the cost of consistency, we have retained the choices made by individual authors.

Commonwealth of Independent States

1

INTRODUCTION

Reconstructing politics amidst the wreckage of empire*

Jack Snyder

When empires come crashing down, they leave hunks of institutional wreckage scattered across the landscape: pieces of bureaucracies, military units, economic networks, administrative districts, as well as demographic and cultural patterns that bear the marks of the imperial past.[1] This detritus of empire constitutes the building blocks of the new political arrangements that are constructed out of the rubble. From these are formed not only new states and nations, but also a whole new system of international and transnational relations among these remnants.

How the rubble of the Soviet empire gets recombined has momentous consequences for the peace and security of the whole world, not to mention the lives of people who inhabit the former empire. The broader international community has consequently shown great interest in shaping the formation of political, economic, and social institutions in the successor states to the Soviet Union. Western governments, international organizations, and non-governmental organizations have all propounded schemes for building democratic institutions, strengthening civil society, establishing markets, and embedding the rule of law in these new states. To a modest degree, they have even deployed resources to these ends. [2]

Building the underpinnings of democracy is a valuable objective. However, this is only one of the dimensions of the reconstitution of political order in the former Soviet empire. In those portions of the former Soviet Union where conflict has been most acute, such as Tajikistan and the Transcaucasus, the more pressing problem is the creation of coherent state institutions, without which the exercise of the democratic franchise has no meaning. Indeed, where effective state institutions are lacking, increased popular participation in politics is likely to be a cause of civil and international strife, rather than an antidote to it.[3]

In this book, we take a step back from the question of how to build democracy in order to ask the prior question of what is shaping the institutional pattern of the post-Soviet political order, both within and among the Soviet successor states. Focusing on Russia, Ukraine, and Central Asia, we ask what the new order will be

---

* I am grateful to Mark Blyth and Miles Kahler for comments on an earlier draft of this chapter.

like, what patterns of conflict are emerging in that order, and what can be done about it. Our analyses of this contemporary problem are set in the historical context of the collapse of other great empires and earlier instances of the formation of national states.

Public discussion of possible futures of the post-Soviet space focuses on three themes: competitive ethno-nationalism, the re-establishment of empire, and the creation of a liberal, democratic zone of peace and co-operation.[4] Many Americans, schooled in a Wilsonian view of world politics, have tended to see the Soviet Union as a "prison house of nations," each naturally wanting to exercise self-determination in the wake of imperial collapse.[5] If so, given the ethnic inter-mingling in the former Soviet space, each nation's demand for self-determination would necessarily conflict with that of others. From this perspective, the supplanting of an archaic empire by ethnically-based nation-states is bound to be a bloody process. A second view, stressing Russia's geopolitical weight and the continuing power of military-imperial interests at the core of the old empire, anticipates the re-emergence of a Moscow-centered informal empire.[6] In this view, the ease of playing the game of dividing, penetrating, and dominating weak states in the former Soviet periphery makes this outcome likely, at least along Russia's southern frontier. The third outcome, perhaps more a hope than a predic-tion, is the notion that a region of liberal co-operation can be institutionalized by creating democratic structures within many of the successor states, and by uniting them in regional and global international organizations to facilitate economic and security co-operation.[7]

These three visions do have some value in organizing our thinking about post-imperial patterns, but reality in this case is more complicated than the pure ideal types. One of the striking features of the post-Soviet order is the incompleteness of the emergence of any of these three patterns. Elements of each pattern are apparent in some corners of the former empire or on some issues. Ethno-national rivalries over sovereignty and self-determination are prevalent in the Caucasus and at lesser intensity in the Baltics, but local clan identities or civic-territorial concepts have often trumped ethnicity elsewhere. Neo-imperial intervention, if not quite domination, has shaped political outcomes in Tajikistan, Georgia, and elsewhere in the South. Normal diplomatic bargaining between more or less democratically elected politicians, sometimes shored up by timely mediation from the broader international community, has led to progress toward settling Russian–Baltic and Russian–Ukrainian differences over the stationing of military forces, sovereignty and citizenship issues, and economic relations.

It is not surprising that the former Soviet space remains indecisively suspended among these different potential outcomes. The circumstances of imperial collapse typically create barriers to the easy emergence of stable patterns of any of these types. The quick emergence of coherent nation-states is hindered by the weakness of governmental institutions in the colonial periphery of the empire and by the arbitrariness of many colonial boundaries imposed by the imperial administra-tion. As was shown in Rupert Emerson's classic work, *From Empire to Nation*, post-colonial nation-building is typically a task of artifice and mobilization carried out by a thin stratum of nationalist elites rather than an inevitable political expression of cultural yearning.[8] Only in the Baltic states and Armenia were pre-formed nations waiting in the wings to occupy the stage after the Soviet collapse. Even at the center of collapsed empires, national identity is problematic, since authoritarian empires, including the Soviet one, typically promote a transnational self-conception to legitimize their domination over other peoples, not a national one. Thus ethno-national rivalries are an uneven and often muted theme in post-Soviet politics.

Democratic outcomes are hindered for many of the same reasons. Among the great empires, only Britain put in place a colonial legacy of democratic institutions, including political parties and a free press, that facilitated the transition to stable democracy in the wake of decolonization.[9] Where administrative institutions are weak, and where the notion of national self-rule is weakly rooted, the preconditions for any statehood, let alone democratic statehood, are shaky.

Yet there are also barriers to the re-establishment of empire. Empires collapse because they become less efficient than their competitors, because their reach exceeds their strength, or because their formula for co-opting or suppressing internal opponents stops working.[10] Unless the imperial center can generate some new source of efficiency or appeal, opponents in the post-colonial periphery and among the great powers will be able to thwart a reassertion, and weary citizens of the post-imperial core may shun its burdens. Bolshevism rather quickly provided a formula for reasserting Russian domination of the "near abroad" in the 1920s. In contrast, as Alexander Motyl's chapter in this volume shows, it took some time until the Nazis could establish an ideological and geopolitical basis for reasserting control over the detritus of the Germanic Austrian and Prussian empires of Central and Eastern Europe. In the Ottoman case, this reassertion never happened, because of geopolitical weakness and the success of a more insular alternative identity based on the Turkish nation-state.

The indecisive evolution of the post-Soviet case reflects the mutually blocking nature of many of the institutional remnants of the Soviet system. On one hand, the legacy of Soviet ethno-federalism loaded the dice towards ethno-national outcomes when the USSR collapsed.[11] With power imploding at the center, people turned if only by default to the administrative structures of the ethnically-titled Soviet republics as the jumping-off points for re-establishing a political order. Since the personnel and symbols of these republican units were ethnically freighted already in the Soviet period, it was natural for many of the post-Soviet state-building elites, whether former Communist or oppositional, to mobilize support based on populist ethnic appeals. On the other hand, any form of mass political participation, whether based on ethnicity or civic democracy, threatened the interests of incumbents in other institutional remnants of empire. For them, transnational elite networks looked like a more attractive alternative to popular support. Former Communist political elites in some republics, for example, had strong incentives to re-establish patronage ties with the imperial center in order to maintain the flow of economic subsidies and military protection against domestic opponents.[12] Likewise, for the Soviet Army, acquiescence to a system of hermetic nation-states would have made borders harder to secure, exacerbated the military housing crisis, and foreclosed illicit business opportunities. Thus the institutional legacy of the Soviet period has helped to create a stalemate, perhaps unstable and temporary, among cross-cutting incentives to adopt ethno-national, democratic, and imperial political forms.

In the short run, this stalemate has mixed consequences for armed conflict in the former Soviet space. On the positive side, transnational connections among neo-imperial elites can provide a basis for political support without relying on the populist enthusiasms of ethno-nationalist movements. They can also provide order in institutional vacuums, like Tajikistan. At the same time, regimes that are nationally-based, yet not highly nationalistic, prevent the need for a reimposition of direct imperial control, which, as in Chechnya, would risk bloodshed and resistance. On the negative side, neo-imperialist circles inject a tone of anti-democratic belligerency into Russian politics, and they have sometimes promoted tension in order to exploit it in the "near abroad."[13]

Thus many post-Soviet relationships of a partly national, partly imperial character have two-edged implications for conflict. In Ukraine, for example, Russian reluctance to part with the Black Sea fleet and other trappings of imperial domination was an irritant to the relationship, yet a commonality of outlook and background between local former Communist politicians in Russia and Eastern Ukraine helps to underwrite political coalitions in both countries that are turning away from the demagogic confrontations of the immediate post-independence period. In Georgia, Russian machinations promoted Abkhazian separatism, which helped to spur a lapse into anarchy that only an invited Russian intervention could reverse. Though Russian policy spurred conflict at the outset, the result, at least temporarily, has been the breaking of militant Georgian nationalism and the stabilization of a moderate, incipiently democratic Shevardnadze regime. In Kazakstan, President Nazarbaev's imposition of sharp limits on democratic parliamentary politics and free speech, though deplored in the West, have arguably helped to contain incipient conflict between local Russians and Kazaks, which could have triggered a larger conflict involving Russia itself.[14] Apart from the Baltic states, where cohesive and moderate national states are well-established, indirect Russian influence through post-Communist elites with interests complementary to Moscow's helps to explain why armed conflict has been so limited in the wake of imperial collapse. The two largest conflicts were in Tajikistan, during the interlude when the transnational nomenklatura's control collapsed, and in Armenian-backed Nagorno-Karabakh, where a mass nationalist movement replaced the Communist-era elites entirely.[15]

This pattern, with its mixed costs or benefits for armed conflict, may not be durable. Only the Baltic states have established a stable equilibrium, based on a moderate ethno-national formula with some guarantees to ethnic minorities, shored up by oversight and backing from the broader international community.

Elsewhere, the stalemate among imperial remnants, truncated democracy, and limited nationalism may have some stabilizing features, but it remains uncertain whether they will be lasting. Social processes unleashed by the collapse of empire and of Communism—increased mass political participation, marketization of the economy, the creation of new bureaucratic state structures, and the competition of elites to mobilize mass support under the banner of nationalism—may gradually erode the institutions left over from the Soviet era. This could be good news, in so far as liberal democratic structures replace those institutions. It could, however, be bad news, in so far as the replacements are more virulent forms of populist nationalism or imperial assertion. Those legacies of empire that are serving to contain conflict may simply be putting post-imperial conflicts on a long fuse.[16]

The contributors to this book offer a variety of perspectives on the emergence of post-imperial and post-Soviet political institutions, but as a group they converge on four common themes that inform the analysis of post-imperial politics in most of the essays: the institutional legacy of empire; the social processes unleashed by imperial collapse; patterns of bargaining within and between states to resolve conflicts arising out of the imperial collapse; and the impact of the wider international setting on the pattern of post-imperial politics.[17] These essays, while developing their distinctive insights, jointly demonstrate what can be gained by analyzing the reconstitution of political order through these perspectives.

The institutional legacy of empire

When a child's edifice assembled from rods and connectors crashes down, the overall structure is destroyed, but tightly interconnected segments of it may retain their shape, though scattered across the floor. When an empire collapses, the still-connected sections may be of several types.

Some of the pieces may be territorial. Administrative units of the old empire may take on political significance because of their state-like bureaucratic structures. All of the Soviet republics, for example, became successor states in the wake of the imperial collapse. In most cases, this was due more to their organizational features than their authenticity as expressions of ethno-national identity. It may be true that ethnic labeling of the republics helped enhance the credibility of these new states as something more than administrative accidents left over from Stalin's divide-and-rule tactics of the 1920s. Moreover, within Russia, as Steven Solnick's chapter shows, regional units that could claim ethnic distinctiveness had a better chance of extracting economic concessions from Moscow. However, since all of the successor states were ethnically diverse except Armenia, ethnic homogeneity cannot explain much about variations in the cohesion of these states. As Barnett Rubin's chapter on Tajikistan shows, and the further examples of Georgia and Azerbaijan confirm, where proto-state structures inherited from the Soviet period were too weak to manage ethnic divisions, they were also too weak to prevent conflict among clans, regions, factions, and mafias. In

Azerbaijan, voters elected the nationalist Abulfez Elchibey on a platform of strengthening the fiscal and war-fighting strength of the state to prevail in the war against the Armenians over Nagorno-Karabakh, but his promises came to naught in the face of Azeri bureaucratic corruption and local loyalties.[18] The institutional weakness of the inherited state explains more about these conflicts and their outcomes than does ethnicity *per se*.

Other institutional remnants of empire are functional, including military organizations, economic networks of supply and production, and the physical infrastructure of communications, pipelines, railroads, and water supply. For some time after the Soviet collapse, Russian units continued to guard the external borders of Central Asian states, the Russian ruble remained the Tajik currency, Ukrainians' main television fare came from Moscow, and Central Asian water resources were controlled by Soviet-era experts operating within a Soviet-created physical and institutional structure.[19] Nationalization of these functions has been a gradual process, which remains incomplete for some of the weaker states.

Another residue of empire is the pattern of patronage ties, including those running from Moscow to the former Soviet republics as well as more local networks within republics. As Rubin's chapter shows, the disruption of these networks as a result of the Soviet collapse did not eliminate their political significance. Patronage networks remained the most cohesive institutionalized structures in places like Tajikistan and Azerbaijan, but the disruption of their accustomed flow of resources forced them to adopt new strategies for mobilizing support and drove them into zero-sum competition for control over a shrinking pie. Sometimes this took the superficial form of ethnic mobilization and clan rivalry, but primordial cultural animosities often had little to do with the resulting conflicts.

Finally, ethnic identity and patterns of ethnic settlement are themselves an institutionalized legacy of empire. The Soviet regime moved Russians into the peripheral states, defined individuals' identities through passport entries, and institutionalized practices that favored titular ethnics in their home republics.[20] Ernest Gellner, among others, has argued that the Soviet collapse left an institutional vacuum and consequently that group formation had to be based by default on race and culture.[21] This not only ignores the fact that many post-Soviet ethnic identities are artifacts of Soviet-era institutions, but also underestimates the extent to which other institutional remnants retained their ability to shape behavioral incentives. Ethnicity was simply one institutional remnant in play along with others in the reconstitution of political order.

These residues of empire—territorial, functional, patrimonial, and demographic—form the static point of departure for post-imperial politics. The political competition among these institutional remnants is made dynamic by the turbulent social processes unleashed by imperial collapse, which shape the strategies for survival of these states, organizations, networks, and ethnic groups.

Social processes unleashed by imperial collapse

Mark von Hagen's chapter in this volume notes that the breakdown of old imperial institutions during the First World War had the effect of speeding up several large-scale processes of social change that are commonly associated with modernization: the transformation of economic and administrative relationships, the undermining of traditional elites, the broadening of political participation, the sharpening of national consciousness, and military mobilization along national lines. The Soviet collapse, he notes, likewise brought a widening of political participation and economic changes that similarly triggered a heightening of national competition and ethnic conflict.

In the wake of collapse, people seek to adapt the institutional wreckage of empire to survive the challenges of social transformation. The first and most pressing of these challenges is the scramble for security in anarchy. As central control over the armed forces, police, and other institutions enforcing imperial order begins to unravel, people's most immediate problem is that of security and physical survival. Facing a situation of potential anarchy, people begin to look for alternative groups to provide security in the new, potentially dangerous circumstances. Barry Posen, in an argument that parallels Gellner's concept of the post-imperial vacuum, contends that the Yugoslav and Soviet collapses created a security vacuum, which caused individuals to race to form state-like self-defense groups based on the default criterion of ethnicity.[22] Several factors, he says, made this a highly volatile strategic situation: intermingled populations, rapidly changing force balances, incentives for preventive attack, and uncertainties about the intentions of potential foes. Posen, like Gellner, exaggerates the degree to which the post-imperial situation was an institutional vacuum and, consequently, the centrality of ethnicity as the criterion for forming self-defense groups. In fact, a variety of institutional forms—territorial republics, clans, military units, and factions based on yet other solidarities—served as nodes around which self-defense groups formed. Making these adjustments, however, Rubin shows that an argument like Posen's can contribute a great deal to understanding the sources of conflict in the institutional semi-anarchy of parts of the former Soviet empire. Thus conflict was greatest in places like Azerbaijan, Georgia, and especially Tajikistan, where conditions came closest to that of an anarchical vacuum; conflict was least prevalent where republics more quickly achieved a state monopoly of force to mitigate the security dilemmas of anarchy.

A second post-imperial challenge is the widening of political participation.[23] The collapse of empire means a weakening of the repressive institutions that kept politics under the control of the ruling elite, in this case, the Communist nomenklatura. While broad participation in well-institutionalized democratic states promotes social stability, an abrupt opening up of politics in the absence of well-established political parties, press institutions, and juridical procedures is more likely to create a clamoring of interest groups and populist movements. With no effective institutional framework to channel and adjudicate this cacophony of demands, political participation tends toward direct action with whatever means the groups have at hand—strikes, coups, and civil war. Hard-pressed elites may resort to some mix of nationalist rhetoric and political repression to manage these rising popular demands. This is an attractive strategy in part because populist demagogy may allow old elites to substitute the rhetoric of national self-rule for the reality of democratic processes, as in Uzbekistan, but also because institutional weakness may leave little alternative, as in the slow drift of Kyrgyzstan from nascent civic democracy towards a more authoritarian, ethnic pattern of politics. Even in states with somewhat better prospects for insti-tutionalizing democratic processes, such as Russia, the armed clashes between the President and Parliament and the Chechen war demonstrate the risk that a weakly institutionalized democracy may degenerate into stalemate, arbitrary administrative rule by the President and so-called "power ministries" like the army and the security apparatus, and the use of nationalist populist rhetoric to cover for the truncation of democratic procedure.

José Casanova's chapter argues that Ukraine may avoid such problems. Although democratic institutions like political parties remain weak, people are disinclined to express their grievances through politics. Thus, the load on even those fragile institutions is bearable.

A third challenge is posed by economic reform. Disruption of patterns of subsidy, the introduction of market relations, the scramble for property rights, and the opening to the international economy create threats and opportunities for indi-viduals and for institutional adjustment. Different successor states, facing a different mix of institutional interests and capacities, have responded variously to this challenge. As Rubin shows, institutional incapacity in Tajikistan to manage the abrupt disappearance of subsidies triggered a Hobbesian struggle for economic survival among a heterogeneous mix of groups. Spruyt and Menon fear that the greater capacity of authoritarian states such as Uzbekistan to delay adjustment to market forces may merely be putting inevitable problems on a longer fuse. In contrast, states with a stronger mandate to legislate a redistribution of property rights and economic reforms through democratic means, most notably the Estonians, made the adjustment more smoothly. In Russia, the association of economic reform with sharply increased inequality and corruption creates a social base for neo-communist and nationalist protest votes, both promising more assertive state control over seemingly capricious markets.[24] Thus, the different institutional capacities of the successor states to manage or suppress economic reform has shaped a variety of economic outcomes with a variety of political consequences.

Building institutional capacity, especially state capacity, is the key to meeting each of these challenges of military security, popular participation, and economic change. Thus, the most central challenges of recreating political order in the wake of imperial collapse are the dilemmas of state- and nation-building. These issues are central to the analyses of all of the contributions to this volume, especially Motyl's, who argues that the tasks facing the elites in weakly institutionalized states in the post-imperial periphery require them to embark on a program of nation-alist mobilization, which is a source of tension with the ethnic minorities in their territory, including the Russian population. However, says Motyl, the different legacy of institutions and discourse at the center of the former empire, combined with the social strains touched off by imperial collapse, are likely to impel not a nationalizing approach to strengthening elite authority, but a program of re-imperialization. He predicts that the dynamic by which political order is recreated after imperial collapse may have a long fuse, but eventually risks a sharp confrontation between the nationalizing periphery and the neo-imperial core. Rubin's concluding chapter, though likewise focusing on state-building, offers more optimistic predictions.

The other authors in this volume offer varied possibilities for recombining the institutional detritus of empire, including nationalist, imperial, federal, and demo-cratic variants in the core, and outcomes ranging from ethno-nationalism to neo-imperial dependency in the periphery. Which outcomes prevail in which parts of the former empire depends, they argue, on differences of economic develop-ment, demographic patterns, resources, geopolitical weight, elite strategies, and the impact of the broader international setting. Though eclectic in the causal factors that they consider, all see the emergence of new forms of institutionalized politics as the key to understanding patterns of conflict and allegiance in the wake of imperial collapse.

Strategies of bargaining and channels for resolving conflicts

The institutional remnants of empire, both territorial and otherwise, engage in bargaining in order to extract the resources that they need to rise out the multiple challenges of popular demands, economic change, and military security. These bargaining games are played out between states, within states, and as Rubin shows, by transnational actors like militaries or mafias whose channels of influence may sometimes evade state control. In many cases, bargaining proceeds between players whose endowments of military power, energy resources, institutional cohe-sion, and ethno-national legitimacy are highly asymmetric. For example, Solnick explains the bargaining maneuvers that stem from differences in taxation of ethnic and non-ethnic federal units within Russia, while Menon and Spruyt examine the consequences of Russia's asymmetric bargaining power in Central Asia.

Motyl's scenario leaves little room for productive bargaining, since the center's drive for reimperialization and the periphery's project of nation-building can lead only to deadlock. Bargaining in these circumstances should center on the efforts of the nationalizing states to co-operate in balancing the power of the neo-imperial center, rather than falling into nationalist squabbles among themselves, which the Russians could exploit. Motyl implies that the common interest in balancing will prevail. Randall Schweller, however, notes that states shun balancing when their combined efforts would fall short of generating the power needed to offset the capabilities of the threatening state. In those circumstances, states are more likely to distance themselves from targets of intervention and appease the unopposable threat.[25] Moreover, Stephen Walt shows that arms races and alliances among small states are directed toward balancing against threats from each other, which they can parry, rather than threats from great powers, which they are incapable of containing. Small states, says Walt, balance against great powers only if they can find a great power to back them up.[26] So far, this pattern seems to hold. Ukraine, which has sufficient weight to try to resist Russia, and the Baltic states, which are counting on diplomatic (if not military) backing from the Western democracies, are balancing sufficiently to maintain their independence from Russian domination. Among the weaker states with fewer diplomatic options to the south of Russia, the more prevalent pattern has been not to balance against Russia, but to recruit Russian support against internal foes or rival neighboring states. Solnick, analyzing the analogous dynamic of alignment among Russia's federal units and the central state, sees neither uniform balancing against the center by the periphery nor uniform centralization. Rather, he finds a pattern of asymmetric concessions to the more cohesive regional units, especially those with a claim to ethnic distinctiveness.

Whether bargaining proceeds peacefully or breaks down into armed conflict depends in part on the availability of institutional channels to facilitate agreement. This is true both within and between states. One of the key differences between peaceful Uzbekistan and war-torn Tajikistan is the centralized management of patrimonial relationships with tribal and regional interests in the former as contrasted with the anarchic struggle of similar groups in the latter.[27] On the interstate plane, most of the institutional mechanisms for coordination are either imperial remnants—like the Soviet Army chain of command or the Central Asian water authority—or they are new and lacking in legitimacy—like the Commonwealth of Independent States. Menon and Spruyt discuss a variety of such mechanisms. In the search for supranational and transnational channels for co-operation, however, the key role of states themselves should not be overlooked. Bilateral bargains between Russia on the one hand and Ukraine and the Baltic states on the other, sometimes helped along by Western involvement, have managed to resolve many knotty issues involving the stationing of armed forces and the disposition of military forces. Where the state has the institutional capacity to make credible commitments, bargains can be struck and maintained with minimal supranational apparatus.

Impact of the wider international setting

Most of the contributors to this volume see the outcome of the institutional restructuring of the Soviet empire as somewhat indeterminate. Though shaped in part by institutional legacies and social pressures generated by the collapse, fundamental choices of bargaining strategy, coalition alignments, institutional design, and ideological orientation remain to be made. Most of the contributors argue that the broader international setting affects the direction of these choices, at least at the margin. In many cases, the international influences may be uncontrollable factors that exacerbate conflicts, such as the cross-border arms flow from Afghanistan to Tajikistan. In some cases, however, the international community may intervene in ways that have a decisive and stabilizing effect on the outcome of post-Soviet bargains, as in the Ukrainian agreement to relinquish its nuclear weapons. Barnett Rubin's concluding chapter addresses the prescriptive insights that follow from our analyses of the impact of the international setting on patterns of post-Soviet political conflict.

The main goal of this volume is to broaden the analytical prism through which scholars and other observers are viewing the shaping of the post-Soviet political space. While the contributors did not seek to converge on a unified outlook, some common propositions emerge from several of the essays.

The likelihood of conflict, in the view of most of the contributors, hinges on the type of regime that emerges at the core of the erstwhile imperial center and on the degree of institutionalization of politics in the periphery. Based on historical comparisons, Motyl is the most pessimistic on these dimensions, arguing that the logic of imperial collapse tends to impel politics in the post-imperial core toward a revolutionary reassertion of empire, while driving elites in the post-imperial periphery towards an uncompromising nation-building program. Rajan Menon and Hendrik Spruyt agree that these are the right variables to examine, but see more room for variation. They argue that conflict is most likely when politics turns authoritarian at the core and unstable at the periphery, and least likely when the core becomes democratic and the periphery establishes coherent, stable state structures. Barnett Rubin's case study of the civil war in Tajikistan provides a vivid analysis of this proposition.

Who prevails in the contest between core and periphery is more a matter of cohesion than of size. The Baltic states and Armenia have established a firm basis for national independence, even to the point of successfully defying the national interests of larger neighbors endowed with greater resources, by virtue of their ethno-national cohesion. Tajikistan, Georgia, and Azerbaijan fell victim to conflict, penetration, and loss of sovereignty because their incoherent state structures failed to knit together internal clans, regions, or "mafia" factions. Likewise, the fate of multiethnic Ukraine, Kazakstan, Uzbekistan, and Russia will depend not so much on their geopolitical size but on whether their central elites can devise the right combination of co-optation and central control to maintain the cohesion of the state. In Ukraine, maintaining this cohesion has required not only the achievement of democratic legitimacy for the government, but also a subtle combination of appeasement of Russophone political interests and an uncompromising assertion of state centralization against Russian separatist forces in Crimea. In Central Asia, elites trying to reconcile strategies of state control and ethnic appeasement have increasingly moved to truncate democratic participation. From the standpoint of the capacity of the state to defuse conflict, democracy is only one means to achieve this, and not necessarily the likeliest in all settings.

In short, the contributors to this book identify a number of circumstances in which the standard recommendations for building a stable post-Soviet political order—for example, strengthening democracy, markets, civil society, bargaining forums—are appropriate. However, their analyses also show that when state institutions are weak, rising political participation, economic transformation, vocal social groups, and bargaining without guarantees of security are causes of conflict, not order. By emphasizing coherent institutional structures—especially state structures—as a precondition for any stable politics, the contributions to this volume provide a wider analytical lens and a more diverse, context-sensitive institutional menu for reconstructing politics from the wreckage of empire.

Notes

1 K. Barkey, "Consequences of Empire," in K. Barkey and M. von Hagen (eds), *After Empire*, Boulder, CO: Westview, forthcoming.
2 L. Diamond, *Promoting Democracy in the 1990s: Actors and Instruments, Issues and Imperatives*, New York: Carnegie Corporation Commission on Preventing Deadly Conflict, December 1995.
3 S.P. Huntington, *Political Order in Changing Societies*, New Haven, CT: Yale University Press, 1968; E.D. Mansfield and J. Snyder, "Democratization and the Danger of War," *International Security*, Summer 1995, vol. 20, pp. 5–38; J. Snyder, "Nationalism and the Crisis of the Post-Soviet State," *Survival*, Spring 1993, vol. 35, pp. 5–27.
4 R. Suny, "Ambiguous Categories: States, Empires and Nations," *Post-Soviet Affairs*, 1995, vol. 11, pp. 185–96.
5 On the practical and legal dilemmas of self-determination, see H. Hannum, *Autonomy, Sovereignty, and Self-Determination: The Accommodation of Conflicting Rights*, Philadelphia, PA: University of Pennsylvania Press, 1990.
6 F. Hill and P. Jewett, *Back in the USSR: Russia's Intervention in the Internal Affairs of Former Soviet Republics and the Implications for United States Policy Toward Russia*, Cambridge, MA: Harvard University, Strengthening Democratic Institutions Project, January 1994.
7 For an evaluation of this idea, see R. Menon and H. Spruyt, Chapter 6 in this volume.
8 R. Emerson, *From Empire to Nation*, Boston: Beacon, 1960.
9 On institutional and other characteristics of successful democratic transitions, see A. Przeworski *et al.*, "What Makes Democracies Endure?" *Journal of Democracy*, January 1996, vol. 7, pp. 39–55.
10 C. Tilly, "How Empires End," in K. Barkey and M. von Hagen (eds), *After Empire*; R. Gilpin, *War and Change in World Politics*, Cambridge: Cambridge University Press, 1981.
11 P. Roeder, "Soviet Federalism and Ethnic Mobilization," *World Politics*, January 1991, vol. 43, pp. 196–232; R. Brubaker, "Nationhood and the National Question in the Soviet Union and Post-Soviet Eurasia: An Institutionalist Account," *Theory and Society*, February 1994, vol. 23, pp. 47–78.
12 See Barnett Rubin's chapter on Tajikistan (Chapter 7) in this volume.
13 T. Goltz, "The Hidden Russian Hand," *Foreign Policy*, Fall 1993, no. 92, pp. 92–116.
14 B. Dave, "Cracks Emerge in Kazakhstan's Government Monopoly," *Transition*, October 6, 1995, vol. 1, no. 18, pp. 73–5; more generally on the relationship between expanding press freedom and nationalist demagogy, see J. Snyder and K. Ballentine, "Nationalism and the Marketplace of Ideas," *International Security*, Fall 1996, vol. 21, pp. 5–40.
15 T. Swietochowski, *Russia and Azerbaijan*, New York: Columbia University Press, 1995.
16 This is Alexander Motyl's imagery; see Chapter 2 in this volume.

17 By institution, I mean a habitual pattern of interaction around which people's expectations converge. For some variations on this basic definition, see W.W. Powell and P. J. DiMaggio (eds), *The New Institutionalism in Organizational Analysis*, Chicago: University of Chicago Press, 1991.

18 E. Fuller, "Azerbaijan's June Revolution," *Radio Free Europe/Radio Liberty Research Report*, August 13, 1993, vol. 2, no. 32, pp. 24–9.

19 B. Rubin in Chapter 7 of this volume; E. Weinthal, "The Politics of Redistributing Resources in the Aral Sea Basin," paper delivered at the MacArthur Consortium Workshop on the Politics and Economics of Development Policy and Institutional Innovation, University of Wisconsin, March 1996.

20 In addition to the works cited above by Brubaker and Roeder, see also R. Suny, *The Revenge of the Past*, Stanford, CA: Stanford University Press, 1993; R. Kaiser, *The Geography of Nationalism in Russia and the Soviet Union*, Princeton, NJ: Princeton University Press, 1994, and K. Ballentine, "The Making of Nations and the Un-Making of the Soviet Union," *The Harriman Review*, December 1995, vol. 8, no. 4, pp. 14–24.

21 E. Gellner, "Nationalism in the Vacuum," in A. Motyl (ed.), *Thinking Theoretically about Soviet Nationalities*, New York: Columbia University Press, 1992, pp. 243–54.

22 B.R. Posen, "The Security Dilemma and Ethnic Conflict," *Survival*, Spring 1993, vol. 35, pp. 27–47.

23 In addition to S.P. Huntington, *Political Order in Changing Societies*, New Haven, CT: Yale University Press, 1968, see Menon and Spruyt, Chapter 6, in this volume.

24 J.F. Hough, E. Davidheiser, and S.G. Lehmann, *The 1996 Russian Presidential Election*, Washington, DC: Brookings, 1996.

25 R. Schweller, "Tripolarity and the Second World War," *International Studies Quarterly*, March 1993, vol. 37, pp. 73–104.

26 S.M. Walt, *The Origins of Alliances*, Princeton, NJ: Princeton University Press, 1987.

27 Compare Rubin's chapter on Tajikistan (Chapter 7) with the discussion by Menon and Spruyt of institutionalized interest-group politics elsewhere in Central Asia (Chapter 6).

2

AFTER EMPIRE

Competing discourses and inter-state conflict in post-imperial Eastern Europe*

Alexander J. Motyl

The collapse of empires is a rare event. When stable imperial systems disappear within a short period of time, we expect the entities that emerge from the rubble to bear the marks of "path dependence." These expectations are not unfounded. As is argued in this chapter, collapse gives rise to conditions that drive a wedge between former imperial cores and former imperial peripheries, increase the likelihood of their engagement in conflict, and push core states toward aggression and expansion.

In particular, the following claims about the likely impact of collapse on post-imperial cores and peripheries can be made. First, they will develop competing legitimating discourses, the language of imperial hegemony in the core and the language of national self-assertiveness in the periphery. Second, both discourses will fixate on, and draw much of their plausibility from, the "abandoned brethren"—former imperial populations turned post-colonial subjects—stranded in the periphery. Third, the distribution of power resources will be skewed in favor of the core, thus providing for geopolitical imbalance and generating genuine insecurity. Fourth, grounds for conflict—above all over abandoned brethren, but also over undemarcated boundaries, intertwined militaries, interdependent economies, and intermixed populations—will be amply available, while institutions and norms for dealing with conflict will not. Fifth, revolutionary elites will come to power in the core while state-building elites will come to power in the periphery, and both will draw on existing discourses to solidify their rule. Finally, all these developments taken together will drive core states toward aggressive behavior.

* Earlier drafts of this paper were presented at a conference on "National Minorities, Nationalizing States, and External National Homelands in the New Europe" at the Bellagio Study and Conference Center, August 22–6, 1994, and at a conference on "Political Order in the Former Soviet Republics" at Columbia University, May 5–6, 1995. For their comments and criticisms, I am thankful to Dominique Arel, Karen Ballentine, Mark Beissinger, Mark Blyth, Ian Bremmer, Rogers Brubaker, Leonid Heretz, Juozas Kazlas, Pal Kolsto, Viktoria Koroteyeva, David Laitin, Rajan Menon, Gusztav Molnar, Laszlo Nemenyi, Zoltan Rastas, Nikolai Rudensky, Oleh Shamshur, Corinna Snyder, Jack Snyder, Raphael Vago, and Veljko Vujacic.

Such an unfolding, it should be emphasized, is only more likely in the aftermath of imperial collapse than under normal international conditions.

This unfolding is illustrated with reference to systems of states that emerged from two instances of bona fide imperial collapse—that of Romanov Russia and the Soviet Union—and from one instance of what is best termed the functional equivalent of collapse—Wilhelmine Germany and the Habsburg empire. Although Kaiser Wilhelm's Reich was not a stable empire according to the definition provided below, its discursive legacy combined with the consequences of Habsburg collapse to produce a state, interwar Germany, that behaved as if it had emerged from collapse. Also discussed below is post-Ottoman Turkey, to illustrate the point that imperial decline by means other than collapse leads to different post-imperial outcomes.

As the above remarks suggest, the argument presented here is structural.[1] In contrast to some of the chapters in this volume, the focus here is not on individuals and their choices, but on the ideological and political forces that produce outcomes irrespective of individual preferences. No epistemological priority is claimed for structural approaches. As Arthur Danto shows, they are different from, but no better and no worse than, methodologically individualist ones.[2]

Because this argument is structural, it claims only to be able to identify facilitating conditions. It does not claim that only imperial collapse generates inter-state conflict, or even that imperial collapse necessarily generates inter-state conflict. As I am not proposing a theory of everything, my aims are far more modest. I merely suggest that, if certain initial conditions are at hand, conflict is more likely to occur in the aftermath of imperial collapse. These qualifications place this approach outside the methodological boundaries of positivism and underline my skepticism about its epistemological utility. They also reflect my belief that the knowledge claims that social science can make are always, at best, provisional and contingent. Having said as much, however, I hasten to emphasize that acceptance of contingency makes it all the more imperative that arguments be conceptually rigorous, logical, and maximally structured along the lines recommended by Carl Hempel.[3] Well-structured arguments are no antidote for the contingency of truth claims, but they can and do ensure the cogency of contingent truth claims.

Triangular relationships

The dependent variable is the "triadic nexus," Rogers Brubaker's concept denoting the relationship among a nationalizing state, a national minority, and an external national homeland.[4] The terms refer, respectively, to a state that promotes its own avowedly national identity, an indigenous group that is perceived, and perceives itself, as foreign, and another state that views itself, and is also viewed by the group, as its "real" homeland. Brubaker holds that these entities can be best conceived of as relational fields defined by discursive contestations and their relationships with other fields.

Brubaker's claim is valid, but only up to a point. As the specific concepts they are, as *fields* of struggle, nations and states cannot logically be thought of as always being in flux. Fields of struggle are not chaotic brawls with no advances or retreats and winners or losers. The very notion of field suggests that the struggle must take place within a bounded space, and not on an infinite plain. The triadic metaphor reinforces this point. Triangles are defined by three distinct points, and not by vaguely delineated and overlapping clusters of points. The three points, and their relations with one another, make the triangle a particular kind of "nexus" with particular kinds of "triadic" properties. Also, like fields, triangles are bounded. Fields of struggle must therefore be defined terrains on which only certain kinds of battles can be fought; and, as the image of battle suggests, there must be losers and winners, even if Pyrrhic ones.

If there are clear limits to the fields or triangles and if there can be outcomes to battles, then several conclusions follow. As the entities under consideration— minorities, homelands, and states—are not always and everywhere "up in the air," we are surely entitled to expect some, if not all, to have more or less defined profiles at various points in time. And if it is legitimate to conceptualize fields as, at times, more or less fixed variables, it becomes equally possible to speak of relations between more or less coherent entities, and not just fields. As is argued below, imperial collapse produces decidedly nationalizing peripheries and imperializing cores, both of which define themselves in terms of the other and in terms of the abandoned brethren. The relations between and among these three more or less clearly defined entities comprise a structure that, in specifically post-imperial circumstances, drives them toward conflict in general and core aggressiveness in particular.

Empires

The independent variable here is imperial collapse, and what that is obviously depends on how empire is defined. As Michael Doyle's definition suggests, an empire must possess the following defining characteristics.[5] First, it must consist of a core and at least two peripheries. Second, both core and peripheries must occupy regionally bounded spaces inhabited by culturally differentiated elites and populations.[6] That is to say, core elites and populations must share certain cultural characteristics and be different from their counterparts in the peripheries.

The concepts of core and periphery—hereafter, the singular form only is used—are central to the concept of empire.[7] A core is defined here as a multidimensional set of territorially concentrated and mutually reinforcing organizations exercising highly centralized authority in a system.[8] These organizations must be:

1   political, economic, and sociocultural (multidimensional);
2   located in a bounded geographic space (territorially concentrated);
3   supportive of one another (mutually reinforcing); and
4   endowed with significant decision-making authority (centralized).

In contrast to cores, peripheries are the territorially bounded administrative outposts of central organizations. There must be at least two peripheries for empires to be distinguishable from bifurcated states, such as the former Czechoslovakia, of which there are and have been many in history.

Core elites staff core organizations; peripheral elites staff peripheral organizations. The highly centralized authority of core elites manifests itself in a variety of ways, some typical of nonimperial states and some peculiar to empires. Thus, core elites, like all state elites, set foreign and defense policy, print the currency, and control borders. But imperial elites also possess several other prerogatives. They control the finances of peripheries; they appoint peripheral governors or prefects; and they are not accountable to the periphery, which has no legal basis for influencing the appointment of core officials and the choice of core policies. While the relationship of core elite to core population may therefore be democratic, that of core elite to peripheral elite is not.[9] Note that, in its exclusive emphasis on the core–periphery relationship, this understanding of empire is unconcerned with the regime of either the core or the periphery.

Self-styled emperors, imperial discourses, and economic exploitation are associated characteristics that are not central to this definition of empire.[10] While they generally go with empires, they need not do so definitionally. Thus, it is not surprising for empires, as peculiarly centralized states, to be ruled by monarchs, emperors, or dictators. Nor is it surprising that they, like all great powers, develop legitimating languages, or what I call imperial discourses;[11] nor is it unusual for organizationally centralized cores to exploit peripheries economically. But these characteristics are likely consequences of empire and not necessary qualities of empire.

Hence, while a species both of multinational state and of dictatorship, an empire is not merely a dictatorial multinational state; it is a peculiar kind of such state. Figure 2.1 situates empires within a family of related polities.

Ethno-territorial federations, such as socialist Yugoslavia and post-Soviet Russia, and possibly Canada, have culturally distinct administrative units, but no core institutions. Such multinational dictatorial states as Franco's Spain and Saddam Hussein's Iraq have cores, but lack culturally bounded administrative

	Core present	Core absent
Culturally distinct administrative units	Empires	Ethno-territorial federations
Not culturally distinct administrative units	Multinational dictatorial states	Multinational non-dictatorial states Territorial federations

Figure 2.1 Types of multinational states

17

units. Multinational non-dictatorial states and territorial federations such as the United States and Switzerland possess neither cores nor distinct cultural subunits. In empires, however, territorially-bounded cores and peripheries are coterminous with culturally distinct administrative units. An empire is, thus, a highly centralized, territorially segmented, and culturally differentiated state within which centralization, segmentation, and differentiation overlap.

Imperial collapse

Because the Persian, Roman, early Byzantine, Mongol, Ottoman, Habsburg, Romanov, French, British, and Soviet empires possessed the defining characteristics of empire, they were identical, but only of course as empires. Thus, in each of these empires the organizations clustered in a culturally distinct region usually centered on a capital city and its hinterland exercised one-way control over the finances and elites of the rest of the empire. Obviously, the degree of cultural distinctiveness, like the degree of control, varied. The Ottomans of Constantinople, Rumelia, and Anatolia shared Islam with most imperial elites; ethnic Germans formed a sizable portion of Tsarist Russia's ruling elite; after 1867, Habsburg control over Hungary declined in a manner reflective of the dynamics of "imperial decay";[12] all elites shared a Soviet Russian culture in Leonid Brezhnev's USSR, while republican elites enjoyed a fair amount of genuine autonomy. In other words, all empires at best approximate the definitional ideal type.

Stable empires—those that have persisted for an extended period of time as durable patterns of rule and not merely as temporary conquests such as those of Alexander the Great, Charlemagne, Genghis Khan, Napoleonic France, Wilhelmine Germany, interwar Japan, or Hitler's Germany—can fall in two ways, by attrition and by means of collapse. As I have argued elsewhere, in both cases a structural flaw, one that pits peripheral elites against the core, produces imperial decay, which in turn undermines the imperial state's ability to withstand internal and external assaults.[13] Attrition involves the more or less gradual loss of accumulated territories and is, as Rein Taagepera has shown, the typical trajectory for most empires.[14] The fall of Rome is the classic example; the decline of Byzantium and of the Ottoman, French, and British empires is also worth citing.

The second type of imperial fall, involving the rapid and comprehensive loss of imperial territory as a result of a life-threatening crisis, is the historical exception. "Rapid" here means perhaps one to four years; "comprehensive" means that the dictatorial relationship between the core and the entire periphery is sundered all at once. According to these criteria, three historically recent empires may be said to have collapsed: the Habsburg realm in 1918, Romanov Russia in 1917–19, and the Soviet empire in 1989–91. As noted above, post-Wilhelmine Germany acted as if its predecessor had collapsed.

After the fall

Consider in this light the theoretical implications of the varieties of imperial fall. Attrition involves the loss of territory, but is premised on the maintenance of the bulk of empire. As a result, the liberated population should be less impelled to become, and see itself as, the bulwark of a nationalizing state because the "other" it confronts, the empire, is still a multinational unit. In turn, the imperial core, as long as it remains the core of a multinational empire, cannot play the role of a national homeland. By the same logic, the settler minority in the liberated territory should be more likely to view itself as a resident group and not as abandoned brethren.

In contrast, collapse lets loose upon the world a whole array of new states, so that the existence and legitimacy of each depends directly on the negation of multinationality and on opposition to the newly nationalized core. These new entities should, as a result, endorse distinctly nationalizing discourses rooted in the language and logic of national oppression, nationalism, and national liberation. These discourses, meanwhile, should identify indigenous ethnic minorities as foreign elements, perhaps even as problems or obstacles.

The sudden loss of empire should also leave the core population's imperial discourse intact at the very moment that the core, having shed its multinational baggage, actually approximates a national state. We would therefore expect a "recontextualization" of the imperial discourse to occur. The hegemony of the core would continue to be emphasized, but within the context of its post-imperial status as a national state. Post-imperial core states should therefore be especially inclined to view themselves as homelands for abandoned brethren, who in turn will become the *raison d'être* of recontextualized imperial discourses and, thus, the *causes célèbres* of core states. Moreover, the vitality of two competing discourses more or less equally fixated on abandoned brethren should incline the brethren to view their territories as irredenta cut off from their natural place of belonging in the imperial homeland.

Collapse has several other noteworthy consequences. As it entails a sundering of formerly stable core–periphery economic relations, the new allocation of resources should mirror the imperial distribution. Because the core figured as the political and, in all likelihood, economic, transportation, cultural, and communications center of the empire—the Austrian core of the Habsburg empire being a partial exception to this rule—the lion's share of post-imperial resources will be concentrated there as well. We therefore expect post-imperial core states to enjoy geopolitical preponderance over their neighbors and, thus, to be inherently capable of greater self-assertiveness.

This imbalance is especially portentous as collapse generates innumerable grounds for conflict. Disagreements, struggles, and altercations are inevitable as new states with new elites try to establish new parameters of life in a setting in which institutional and normative chaos deprives them of recognized procedures for bypassing conflict. Stable imperial relations may or may not be efficient, but they represent clear-cut rules of the game. These rules disappear once the game, the empire, disappears. While post-imperial disarray therefore makes it harder to agree on anything relating to former imperial relations, we expect it to have a particularly unsettling impact on questions involving states and their prerogatives, such as boundaries, military bases, railroads, and the like.

Finally, in contrast to attrition, collapse generates specific kinds of elites— revolutionaries in the core and state builders in the periphery. Although individuals committed to rapid, fundamental, and comprehensive change (i.e., revolution)[15]—regardless of whether the direction of such change is toward or away from a capitalist economy, a democratic polity, or a civil society—are ubiquitous in all contemporary societies,[16] the unprecedented depth and breadth of a post-imperial system's disarray should be especially fertile grounds for their emergence. No less important, post-imperial disarray should enhance both their popular appeal and their mobilizational capacity. Revolutionaries are always able to attract followers more easily in times of stress, if only because institutional and normative fluidity level the "playing field" and permit revolutionaries to compete more effectively with nonrevolutionary elites.

Significantly, the revolutionary impulse should be substantially weaker in peripheral states than in the core. While core elites stand to inherit the imperial state apparatus and much of the empire's resources, thereby having the capacity to embark on systemic transformation, peripheral elites must first transform fragile proto-states—actually, mere agglomerations of post-colonial administrators—into real states under conditions of profound penury and genuine insecurity.[17] Their inclination to pursue revolution should give way (*ceteris paribus* of course) to the impulse to build states as quickly as possible and to secure them against the real and perceived aggressive intentions of the core.

The above factors—competing discourses and elites, resource imbalance, grounds for conflict, and abandoned brethren—are a highly combustible mixture. In the core, we expect revolutionary elites to draw on and revive the imperial discourse in order to enhance their own legitimacy and effectiveness. In the periphery, we expect state-building elites to draw on and promote a nationalizing discourse for the very same reasons. The resource imbalance permits the core to translate imperialist intent into imperialist behavior, as grounds for conflict over borders, interests, and armies abound and the two discourses identify the abandoned brethren as either a sacred cause or a fifth column.

Ottoman lessons

A look at the Ottoman demise is instructive for what it tells us about the aftermath of empires that do not collapse. Here was an instance of imperial decline by means of attrition, as the Ottomans had been losing territory steadily since the late eighteenth century. Alarmed by the transformation of Suleiman the Magnificent's realm into the "sick man of Europe," nineteenth-century Ottoman official and non-official elites began rethinking their security needs as well as the bases of Ottoman identity in the same vein that they promoted the architectural transformation of Istanbul, from an Islamic city into a quasi-European one.[18] In particular, the Young Ottomans and, especially, the Young Turks pushed the Ottoman discourse toward a Westernized Turkish nationalism.[19] No less important, the steady loss of lands— Hungary, Egypt, Greece, and the Balkans—meant that both the newly independent territories and the remnants of the empire could define themselves less in opposition to each other and more in terms of their immediate geopolitical and cultural context. Not surprisingly, the Balkan states became embroiled in regional and/or Habsburg politics as soon as they won independence.

Both developments effectively laid the groundwork for Mustafa Kemal's whole-sale reinterpretation of "Turkishness" in the 1920s. Kemal did not and could not reestablish Turkish imperial power, at least partly because his endorsement of a Turkish national discourse negated a revival of imperial Ottomanism. It was thus no accident that Greece, and not Turkey, initiated hostilities and embarked on land-grabbing in the aftermath of the First World War. While Ankara's subsequent pursuit of population exchanges with Athens must be viewed in the context of the war with Greece, it also attests to Turkey's abandonment of the imperial discourse. The continued presence of Greeks within the Turkish nation-state and of Turks within non-Turkish nation-states was incompatible with Kemalist national identity.

Most significantly perhaps, Kemalist Turkey made no effort to revive the empire in the 1920s and 1930s, even though the imperialist *Zeitgeist* of the age, the availability of pan-Turanist notions, and Kemal's own revolutionary inclinations could have sanctioned such a move. Two obstacles stood in the way: on the one hand, the emergence of an anti-Ottoman discourse removed expansion from the policy agenda, while on the other hand, post-Ottoman Turkey suffered from an unfavorable balance of resources with her neighbors. To the south were territories under British and French mandates; to the east was the Soviet Union; to the west were states that had launched successful national liberation struggles against the Ottomans in the nineteenth and twentieth centuries. Expansion was not an option for the weakened, truncated, and self-consciously Turkish Kemalist Republic.

German puzzles and Habsburg solutions

As might be expected, the Ottoman decline by attrition produced a nonimperial discourse and a nonimperial Turkish foreign policy. Rather more unexpected is the presence of both outcomes in interwar Germany. The loss of a war might be expected to lead to revanchist sentiments, but not to the emergence of a full-fledged imperial discourse and the eventual pursuit of imperialist expansion. Pre-war continental Germany was not an established empire by the definition given here; its African colonies were too recent to qualify as stable, and its wartime gains were transient.[20] So, if little or no stable empire collapsed, how could reimperialization have come to dominate the German political agenda by the early 1930s?

The fall of Austria-Hungary holds the key to the problem. The Habsburg collapse provided post-Wilhelmine Germany with the abandoned brethren on which an imperial discourse thrives. The German-speaking residents of the Habsburg domain had for the most part identified themselves as Germans and not as Austrians at least since the nineteenth century. The end of Franz Joseph's realm put them in the anomalous position of being a German national minority *vis-à-vis* their "real" homeland, Germany, and a disloyal majority *vis-à-vis* the state they proclaimed in 1918, Deutsch-Österreich. After 1918, Wilhelmine great-power ideology could function and thrive as an imperial discourse because inter-war Germany had been transformed into a homeland for post-Habsburg German speakers in Austria, Czechoslovakia, and Poland. Germany's defeat in the First World War and Austria-Hungary's collapse thereby produced the functional equivalent of a German imperial collapse with all the consequences that collapse entails.

Germany's appropriation of Austria's abandoned brethren also helps explain why interwar Austria neither developed an imperial discourse nor toyed with expansion. As two more or less equal parts of the former Habsburg Empire, both Austria and Hungary should have promoted homeland complexes and neoimperial discourses, and should have been equally inclined or disinclined to foreign policy adventurism. On the second count there was agreement, as neither Austria nor Hungary possessed the wherewithal to entertain serious aggression against their more or less equally-endowed neighbors. On the first count, however, there was divergence, as only Hungary adopted expansion myths.

An important intervening variable explains the absence of an Austrian imperial discourse. Because post-Habsburg Austrians actually perceived themselves as the abandoned brethren of Germany, interwar Austrian elites would have been hard-pressed to develop a credible alternative to the discourse propounded by the far more dynamic German elites. The choice before Austrian elites was either to "invent" an Austrian identity or, as Austrian Nazis insisted, to opt for *Anschluss* with the German homeland. Austro-fascism might have succeeded in resolving the dilemma, were it not for the pro-German sentiments of both Austrian Nazis and Austrian Social Democrats and the fact that Austria's economic decline stood in such sharp contrast to Germany's resurgence as a prosperous homeland under the Nazis. It took defeat in the Second World War to break Austria's links with Germany and to permit the creation of a distinctly Austrian nation.[21]

The vitality of imperial discourses

In contrast to the Ottoman discourse, which had been eroding throughout the nine-teenth century, and the remnants of which could be swept away by Kemal, the Wilhelmine, Tsarist Russian, and Soviet Russian imperial myths—and not the legit-imacy and authority of the emperors themselves—were still alive and well at the moment of collapse. As deeper structures, and not just expressions of an ephemeral public opinion, they were able to survive it and, thus, to remain inscribed in the mindsets of most post-imperial German and Russian elites, even those such as Weimar liberals, communist internationalists, and Yeltsinites, who opposed the old regimes and were happy to see them collapse. No less important, imperial assumptions remained central to the worldviews of the populations of these countries, thereby permitting a synergy between elites and masses.

Liah Greenfeld has shown how the German national identity that emerged in the early nineteenth century and that survived more or less intact into the twentieth century was grounded in a restrictive "ethnic nationalism" that glorified German-ness in exclusivist, indeed chauvinist, terms.[22] Wilhelmine understandings of Germany's place in the world also carried over into the 1920s and 1930s. Thus, most interwar Germans to the right of the communists viewed their country's place in Europe in terms of two leitmotifs, *Weltpolitik* and *Lebensraum*, that had also defined Wilhelmine political culture. According to Woodruff Smith, *Weltpolitik* referred to a "foreign policy worldwide in scope, aimed at the protection and expansion of the external connections of the German industrial economy."[23] The second notion encompassed a cluster of ideas based on migrationist colonialism and romantic agrarianism.[24] Together with Germany's exclusivist sense of self, *Weltpolitik* and *Lebensraum* virtually amounted to an imperialist program.

The Tsarist imperial discourse rested on the "theory of official nationality," formulated by Count Sergei Uvarov in the 1830s in response to the perceived threat of French revolutionary and Decembrist ideas. The concepts of Orthodoxy, autocracy, and nationality formed the basis of Uvarov's theory, the first denoting loyalty to the Orthodox Church, the second the unquestioned authority of the Tsar, and the third the primacy of the Russian national heritage.[25] Greatly contested in the mid-nineteenth century, Uvarov's trinity became official doctrine in the last decades of Romanov Russia's existence. Accordingly, good Russian subjects were Russians dedicated to Orthodox ideology and Tsarist power. Panslavism and Slavophilism, although unendorsed by the Tsarist state, complemented these ideas to produce a widespread late-imperial mentality that enthroned Russians within Russia and Russia within the Slavic world. As Mikhail Agursky has persuasively argued, these ideas were recontextualized as National Bolshevism in the 1920s and later provided the conceptual underpinnings for Stalinism.[26]

Of all three discourses, the late Soviet one was most explicit, functioning for many decades as the official ideology of the Communist Party. Central to the explicitly imperial dimension of the Soviet discourse were the "leading role" of the Great Russian people, the primacy of the Russian language as a vehicle of inter-nationality communication, the "friendship of peoples," the continuity between Russian imperial and Soviet history, and proletarian internationalism.[27] In essence, good Soviet citizens were Russians dedicated to Communist ideology and Soviet power, while the USSR was a Russian state with proletarian responsibility for the socialist world.[28] Inasmuch as Soviet ideology sanctioned the USSR's expansion, it was logical for Russians to conclude that Soviet expansion was Russian expansion and, thus, to experience Soviet defeat, as in 1941 and 1989, as

Russian defeat.[29] It was equally logical for post-Soviet Russians to hold on to most of the tenets of Soviet ideology, especially those pertaining to Russia's greatness, its *mission civilisatrice* in the near abroad, and its deserved place in the sun.[30]

The discourses that sustained empire not only survived intact but also acquired enhanced plausibility as a result of the suddenness and comprehensiveness of collapse. Above all, imperial discourses were a balm on the ravaged psyches and cultures of the metropolitan populations. Neoimperialism offered a simple way of getting back at the ungrateful recipients of imperial largesse, the natives who paid their debt by leaving the fold. Imperial discourses also offered a simple, if perhaps simplistic, political solution to post-imperial disarray. Reconquering lost territories, reacquiring lost resources, reestablishing lost bases, and reclaiming abandoned brethren did indeed make some economic, military, and national sense. Finally, neoimperialism served as a discursive substitute for absent or weak institutions. Elites could forge a consensus of sorts by accepting an imperial language that established minimal rules of the game for all political actors.

The triumph of revolutionary elites

In all three cores under consideration, revolutionaries eventually came to power after struggles of varying intensity and length. The Bolsheviks triumphed after three years of a bloody civil war; the Nazis required more than a decade to translate their shock troops and electoral strength into political power; the Yeltsinites had to defeat Mikhail Gorbachev and the putschists of 1991 before they finally got the upper hand. There was, of course, nothing inevitable about their triumph; but neither was it merely fortuitous.

Like all revolutionaries, the Bolsheviks, the Nazis, and the Yeltsinites enjoyed organizational, charismatic, coercive, and instrumental advantages that assumed particular salience in circumstances marked by institutional and normative confusion. All three revolutionary groups were better organized than their opponents, all had relatively charismatic leaders—Vladimir Lenin, Adolf Hitler, and, at least initially, Boris Yeltsin—all had their own fighting units or enjoyed the support of existing ones, and all had access to material resources, be they Tsarist Russia's industrial base, the donations of German industrialists, or Western assistance and Siberian oil and natural gas deposits. Finally, all three elites were committed to programs of revolutionary purism, which inclined them to a ruthlessness and vigor that their more moderate, even reactionary, opponents lacked. Yeltsin's parliamentary opponents, like the German Social Democrats and Russian Mensheviks, were no match for revolutionaries willing to use tanks in the pursuit of their ends.

That revolutionaries enjoy natural advantages which may perhaps enable them to triumph over moderates in times of trouble may be true enough, but it does not explain why they should adopt imperial discourses as their own. The Nazis, of course, exemplified the fusion of revolution with imperialism. Lenin and the Bolsheviks willfully appealed to Russian imperial slogans during the Civil War and the war with Poland. The Yeltsinites acted no differently, appropriating the neoimperial vision traditionally associated with the "Russianists" of the 1960s and 1970s.[31] Although some revolutionaries, such as the Nazis, may have "always" been imperialist, the question of how and why such an amalgamation logically could have come about still needs to be answered.

Three reasons for the revolutionary appropriation of imperial language in general and imperialism in particular come to mind. First, just as post-imperial disarray breeds radicalism, so, too, post-imperial revolutionary extremism invites neoimperialism. According to Theda Skocpol and Jonathan Adelman, revolutionaries generally promote strong states and powerful militaries as instruments of survival and of revolutionary transformation.[32] Both are necessary in order to defend the revolutionary order from attacks by external enemies and to impose the revolution on recalcitrant populations within the country. While increasingly strong states and militaries in the making need not automatically pursue expansion, it is usually in their interest to support such an agenda, especially in the aftermath of the revolutionary seizure of power, when ideological enthusiasm is high and real and imagined enemies abound.

Revolutionary ideologies also possess messianic components that make them highly suitable for export. Knowing the truth obliges revolutionaries to share their knowledge with the whole world: truth, after all, must be always and everywhere true. Its dissemination is thus both a service to humanity and a test of its truthfulness. Accordingly, left-wing revolutionaries feel a genuine need to bring proletarian utopia to the oppressed masses; right-wing revolutionaries, usually more prone to see the world in social Darwinist terms, see expansion as a prerequisite of survival. Free-marketeers and utopian democrats, at least in the twentieth century, feel impelled to build markets everywhere and export democracy to everybody.[33]

Finally, revolutionaries appropriate the imperial discourse in order to enhance their legitimacy and expand their base of support. Revolution, as I have argued in another essay, is always a complex and expensive undertaking.[34] Appeals to imperial glory are a simple way of reducing some of the risks associated with revolutionary change in specifically post-imperial circumstances. Of course, such flirtations are not without their costs, as neoimperial allies may insist on adjustments in the revolutionary program; this happened in Germany in 1933 and post-Soviet Russia in 1994. The Nazis sacrificed Ernst Röhm's *Sturmabteilungen* to the Wehrmacht and large industry, while the Yeltsinites sacrificed Yegor Gaidar to the military-industrial complex.

The triumph of revolutionary elites and their appropriation of imperial language does not guarantee revolutionary success. While the Nazis did revolutionize German society in 1933–4, the Bolsheviks were forced to abandon War Communism and the Yeltsinites discarded shock therapy. Rapid, fundamental, and comprehensive change depends on a variety of factors that cannot concern us here. Suffice to say that revolutionary elites are a facilitating, but perhaps not a necessary and certainly not a sufficient, condition of actual revolutionary change.[35]

The triumph of state-building elites

Although the temptation to pursue radical change was present in all the post-imperial peripheral states of interwar and contemporary Eastern Europe, their elites generally devoted their primary attention to the survival and security of their states. Collapse not only left the periphery bereft of most resources, but it also created a well-endowed, powerful, and discursively menacing former core. Just as Weimar Germany dominated Mitteleuropa, Soviet Russia was infinitely stronger than any of its neighbors, and post-Soviet Russia faced only one potential competitor, Ukraine. It was logical for the imperatives of security, survival, and state building to become paramount.

Virtually no influential revolutionary groups emerged in the peripheral states of post-imperial Eastern Europe. Communists were notoriously weak in the interwar period (one important exception being Czechoslovakia), while right-wing revolutionaries were generally confined to relatively marginal groups such as the Hungarian Arrow Cross, the Polish Falanga, and the Romanian Iron Guard.[36] After 1989–91, revolutionary communists and fascists were almost completely absent, while indigenous revolutionary free-marketeers set the agenda in the Czech Republic and, temporarily, in Poland. Eastern Germany's transformation was a classic instance of revolution from outside, with the role of Lenin being played by none other than the staid Helmut Kohl.[37]

Rather more common, and far stronger, in the post-imperial states of Eastern Europe were the state-building elites. Virtually all East European states adopted authoritarian, militarized regimes in the interwar period (Czechoslovakia again being the exception),[38] and virtually all post-socialist states came under the sway of elites concerned primarily with statehood and its preconditions and prerogatives. Vladimir Meciar of Slovakia, Ion Iliescu of Romania, Abulfez Elchibey of Azerbaijan, Leonid Kravchuk of Ukraine, Nursultan Nazarbaev of Kazakstan, and Eduard Shevardnadze of Georgia have come to typify this kind of leader, but their successors, such as Ukraine's Leonid Kuchma and Azerbaijan's Heydar Aliev, as well as the elites of Estonia, Latvia, Hungary, Poland, and the Czech Republic, were no less preoccupied with questions of citizenship, sovereignty, boundaries, minorities, and security.[39]

The pervasiveness of state builders suggests that they were not transitional elites likely to be supplanted by revolutionaries responding to mounting domestic challenges. Peripheral elites understood that even radical change was premised on statehood. The Czech Prime Minister, Vaclav Klaus, pushed this proposition to its logical conclusion, preferring Czech independence to Czechoslovak integrity as the precondition of reform. Inasmuch as the Russian threat to non-Russian statehood was—and was perceived as—a fact, it was impossible even for policy makers with radical tendencies, such as Kuchma, to disregard the priorities of state building. Indeed, the striking feature of Kuchma's presidency was his fusion of economic reform with the kind of pro-Ukrainian state-building discourse associated with his predecessor, Kravchuk.

Not surprisingly, state builders generally sought to ground their efforts in the language of the nation. In embracing the nation, state builders acquired legitimacy, created a population willing and able to submit itself to the hardships of state building, and found allies. President Tomas Masaryk, Marshal Jozef Pilsudski, Roman Dmowski, Symon Petliura, and Volodymyr Vynnychenko typified the post-First World War state builders who had emerged from and fully accepted nationalist traditions. The democratically inclined Masaryk had no doubts about the supremely legitimate—even if logically confused and arguably anti-Slovak—claims to statehood of the Czechs, just as the more authoritarian Pilsudski and Dmowski agreed that the Polish nation should serve as the basis of the Polish state, and the socialists Petliura and Vynnychenko believed that the Ukrainian peasantry should be the foundation of the Ukrainian state. Chancellor Engelbert Dollfuss and Hetman Pavlo Skoropads'kyi are excellent examples of state builders who came to the nation without any prior commitment to the nationalist cause. Dollfuss promoted Austrofascism as a counterweight to Nazi Germany, while the fully Russified Skoropads'kyi pursued Ukrainization as a means of appealing to Ukrainian nationalism and resisting Bolshevism during his brief tenure as head of state in 1918.

Most prone to accept the nation for reasons of political expedience were the state-building elites who emerged in the post-socialist states in 1989–91. The East Central European state builders with roots in the dissident movements already possessed nationalist inclinations—Vaclav Havel and Lech Walesa come to mind—but virtually all the post-communists, who had traditionally rejected "bourgeois" appeals to the nation, accepted the national discourse in order to avoid marginalization and to compete effectively in the political arena. Even more striking was the behavior of state builders in the formerly Soviet republics. Almost without exception, republican communists adopted the language of the nation so as to forge alliances with nationalist popular fronts before independence, and to maintain their political base among key elites after independence. It was logical that their successors should also adopt the national discourse and promote policies of national revival virtually indistinguishable from those pursued by their ostensibly more nationalist predecessors.

The emergence of irredenta

The neoimperialist agenda promoted by revolutionary elites necessarily transformed diaspora populations into irredenta "longing" for inclusion in the nation. German elites found their constituencies in Austria, the Sudetenland, western Poland, Prussia, Gdansk, and amongst the Volksdeutsche of Eastern Europe. Bolshevik Russia justified its expansionism in terms of the internationalist preferences of the largely Russian proletarian masses in the non-Russian borderlands. Post-Soviet Russia invented a "near abroad" populated by "blood relatives," developed elaborate schemes for protecting their rights, and demanded dual citizenship.

As the former core defined itself as a homeland in relation to irredenta, so too the abandoned brethren came to see themselves as an oppressed minority, an irredenta longing for return to the homeland. This development was hardly automatic, and it was surely historically contingent, being dependent on both discursive and elite developments in the homeland and on ongoing structural changes in the society at large. The economic depression of the 1920s and 1930s, like the economic misery that befell Russia and its neighbors during the Civil War and after the dissolution of the USSR, obviously played a significant role. Even so, homeland rhetoric, in combination with the cultural predispositions of the abandoned brethren, appears to have been decisive in inclining them to seek irredentist solutions to their real and imagined woes.

As already noted, Austria's German-speaking population was remarkably consistent in rejecting the Austrian option throughout the interwar period. The Sudeten Germans, in contrast, were somewhat more fickle. They first supported inclusion in the German state in the immediate aftermath of Czechoslovakia's formation. Their secessionist enthusiasm waned after the Czechoslovak state became an international *fait accompli* and economic conditions in Germany and Austria worsened dramatically. Indeed, in the mid-1920s, they agreed to participate in the official political system. By the early 1930s, however, a historic *Wende* occurred. Political deadlock in Czechoslovakia, the impact of the Depression, the emergence of a dynamic Nazi Germany, and the triumph of *Weltpolitik* and *Lebensraum* propelled the Sudeten Nazis under Konrad Henlein to political dominance. By 1938–9, as Hitler openly expressed annexationist intentions toward Czechoslovakia, the preferences, perceptions, and stances of the Sudeten Germans became academic, except insofar as the imminence of a German takeover swelled the ranks of Henlein's movement.[40]

The behavior of Russians resident in the borderlands was strikingly similar in 1918–21.[41] Russian abandoned brethren invariably supported the imperial option, whether Red or White, and, when faced with no choice between Reds or Whites, preferred Bolshevik occupation to the non-Russian elites. Central Asia may have been the most egregious example of the fusion of Russianism with Bolshevism, as local Russian Bolsheviks adopted explicitly chauvinist slogans and pursued outwardly racist policies toward the indigenous peoples. Although the Bolsheviks may have claimed to be acting as proletarians, and not as Russians, for most Russians and non-Russians, Russian meant worker and worker meant Russian, just as non-Russian meant peasant and vice versa.

Almost all ethnic Russian communities in the near abroad—especially in Estonia, Latvia, Belarus, Moldova, Ukraine, and Kazakstan—developed secessionist longings in the course of 1991–5.[42] Those of southeastern Ukraine were typical. Among the most Sovietized and least nationally conscious of the ethnic Russian population in the former USSR, Ukraine's Russians actually voted for the country's independence in late 1991, overwhelmingly in the industrial Donbas and with a slim majority in the Crimea. Within two years, however, despite Kiev's commitment to an inclusive program of nation-building, their political discourse began changing, with many coming to identify themselves with the increasingly strident homeland in Russia. Secessionist tendencies grew apace, as did calls for *vossoedinenie* with Russia. The election in early 1994 of Yuri Meshkov as Crimean President seemed to make secession the order of the day until homeland elites, worried by the impact on Russia's own national minorities of a unilateral border adjustment, refrained from pressing for the peninsula's annexation.[43] As the triadic relationship would suggest, the imperial core's (possibly temporary) redefinition of itself as a homeland manqué perforce redefined both the nationalizing state and the national minority, inclining both to seek accommodation in late 1994. The Chechen crisis may have resolved the issue by diverting Russia from the Crimea and permitting Kiev to crack down on Meshkov.

The push toward expansion

It is at this point in the analysis that geopolitical realities assert themselves with full force. Consider what has transpired. Former cores adopt neoimperial discourses, enjoy geopolitical preponderance over their neighbors, defend abandoned brethren, and are led by self-styled revolutionary-imperialist elites committed to iron rule. Former peripheries adopt anti-imperial discourses, are weaker than the core, view abandoned brethren as fifth columns, and are led by state-building elites in search of legitimacy. Uncertainty and power imbalances abound, mutual perceptions are hostile, and core elites are in muscle-flexing, risk-taking moods, while grounds for conflict are ubiquitous and barriers to conflict, such as common norms and institutions, are absent.

Most theories of international relations predict that, under conditions such as these, core states will engage in aggressive behavior *vis-à-vis* peripheries. Neorealist theories emphasize the gross imbalance of power; their competitors might point to the absence of appropriate institutional mechanisms or international norms or to the presence of "myths of empire."[44] In turn, because the imperial discourse earmarks them for possible absorption, we expect peripheries to respond to perceived core aggression, not by starting bandwagoning, but by balancing—thereby radicalizing their own nationalizing discourses, underlining the foreignness of abandoned brethren, and adding fuel to the fire of imperial discourses.

As a structural perspective suggests, aggressive behavior need not be automatic, and core–periphery conflict need not appear everywhere and with equal intensity. However, attempts at reimperialization, sometimes intentional and planned, sometimes unintentional and contingent, may be well-nigh inevitable. Actual historical developments do not invalidate these expectations. Interwar Germany seized the Rhineland, the Sudetenland, and Austria, and eventually initiated the Second World War. Soviet Russia reconquered the vast majority of Tsarist Russia's territories by 1924.

Will post-Soviet Russia follow in its predecessors' footsteps? A closer look at Bolshevik Russia and Nazi Germany may give us some clues. Despite their dire economic straits, the Bolsheviks could reconquer the Tsarist borderlands because, in comparison to the resources held by the non-Russian "incipient states," they possessed overwhelming military, industrial, communications, and organizational advantages.[45] They met their match in Poland, where a well-endowed opponent and their own strategic overextension produced defeat on the Vistula. Nazi Germany also enjoyed geopolitical preponderance over its neighbors and could therefore embark on imperial expansion, but it too could not sustain the expansionist effort once American involvement in the war tipped the balance. In both instances, the imbalance of power resources was a necessary, but not sufficient, condition of expansion.[46] It was for this reason that interwar Austria could not, as suggested above, even entertain the notion of expansion.

Although it is not logically necessary for post-Soviet Russia to embark on a forcible ingathering of former Soviet territories, the empirical evidence—so far at least—suggests that it may be going in this direction. By mid-1995, as Jack Snyder points out in this volume, Russia had succeeded in re-establishing hegemony, if not quite empire, over much of the former Soviet Union.[47] Its economic dominance was unchallenged and unchallengeable, its political meddling was on the rise, and its military power was undisputed. Belarus appeared to have become a Finlandized outpost of Russian rule, Georgia was coerced into joining the Commonwealth of Independent States after Russian support of Abkhazia almost destroyed the country, Moldova remained home to the 14th Army, Tajikistan continued to be occupied by Russian troops, and Chechnya fell victim to genocide.[48] Last but not least, Central Asia seems destined for, as Rajan Menon and Hendrik Spruyt suggest, vassalage.[49] Only the Baltic states, which enjoyed Western support, and Ukraine, which was strong and confident enough to withstand Russian pressure, still remained outside the Russian sphere of influence.

Russian neoimperialists welcomed Russia's hegemonic involvement in much of the former Soviet Union, but the consequences of actual reimperialization will probably be less welcome. Sooner or later, an expansionist post-Soviet Russia will, like Nazi Germany and Bolshevik Russia, meet its limits, and these limits are likely to be near rather than far. Unlike Nazi Germany, post-Soviet Russia is not an economic powerhouse; nor in light of the uncertainties associated with its economic transition, is it likely to become one soon. And unlike Bolshevik Russia, contemporary Russia does not face economically and politically undeveloped states in the near abroad.

Successful reimperialization is therefore improbable. Attempted reimperialization, however, will in all likelihood transform the triadic nexuses within which Russia is embedded from relatively loose conglomerations of fields into almost reified sets of mutually incomprehensible discourses and mutually hostile entities. Peripheries invariably acquire a profound sense of national identity after bloody confrontations with the imperialist other—as in Eastern Europe or, after the Second World War, in much of the Third World.

While attempted reimperialization may actually consolidate the non-Russian peripheries, it will place an enormous strain on Russia itself. One possible consequence may be an intensification of centrifugal forces, as Russia's own autonomous units make greater demands on a weakened center.[50] It is for this reason that the war with Chechnya assumes special significance. If, as may well be the case, this event portends the end of Russia's encounter with democracy, then Russia's own transformation from an ethno-territorial federation into an empire would appear to be imminent.[51] But, as suggested above, exhausted empires are not stable creatures. Besides possessing a structural flaw that impels regions to assert their interests against those of the center, decaying empires disintegrate when subjected to massive crises, such as enervating wars or civil wars. If so, Russia's collapse may be the unavoidable consequence of the post-imperial pursuit of imperial glory.

Notes

1 For excellent discussions of structure, see D. Easton, *The Analysis of Political Structure*, New York: Routledge, 1990, and K. Waltz, *Theory of International Politics*, New York: Random House, 1978.

2 A. Danto, *Narration and Knowledge*, New York: Columbia University Press, 1985, pp. 257–84.

3 See D.-H. Ruben (ed.), *Explanation*, Oxford: Oxford University Press, 1993; E. Sosa and M. Tooley (eds), *Causation*, Oxford: Oxford University Press, 1993; M.H. Salmon, "Explanation in the Social Sciences," in P. Kitcher and W.C. Salmon (eds), *Scientific Explanation*, Minneapolis: University of Minnesota Press, 1989, pp. 384–409.

4 R. Brubaker, "National Minorities, Nationalizing States, and External National Homelands," unpublished paper, 1994. See also R. Brubaker, "Rethinking Nationhood," *Contention*, Fall 1994, vol. 4, no. 1, pp. 3–14.

5 According to Doyle, "Empire ... is a relationship, formal or informal, in which one state controls the effective political sovereignty of another political society." M. Doyle, *Empires*, Ithaca, NY: Cornell University Press, 1986, p. 45.

6 I employ here the concept of culture developed in C. Geertz, *The Interpretation of Cultures*, New York: Basic Books, 1973.

7 See J. Gottmann (ed.), *Centre and Periphery: Spatial Variation in Politics*, Beverly Hills, CA: Sage, 1980.

8 I speak of organizations, and not institutions, for two reasons. One is that my definition of core thereby echoes Max Weber's classic definition of the state. The other is that "institution" currently denotes virtually everything and has therefore become almost useless as a concept. For a striking example of how broadly the concept is used, see D. North, *Institutions, Institutional Change and Economic Performance*, Cambridge: Cambridge University Press, 1990.

9 I discuss this relationship in "From Imperial Decay to Imperial Collapse: The Fall of the Soviet Empire in Comparative Perspective," in R.L. Rudolph and D.F. Good, (eds), *Nationalism and Empire*, New York: St. Martin's, 1992, pp. 15–43.

10 On defining and associated characteristics, see G. Sartori, "Guidelines for Concept Analysis," in G. Sartori (ed.), *Social Science Concepts*, Beverly Hills, CA: Sage, 1984, pp. 15–85.

11 Legitimating ideologies are discussed in S.N. Eisenstadt, *The Political Systems of Empires*, New York: The Free Press, 1963, and S.N. Eisenstadt, "Center–Periphery Relations in the Soviet Empire," in A.J. Motyl (ed.), *Thinking Theoretically about Soviet Nationalities*, New York: Columbia University Press, 1992, pp. 205–21.

12 On imperial decay, see Motyl, "From Imperial Decay to Imperial Collapse."

13 For a discussion of attrition and collapse, see A.J. Motyl, "Imperial Collapse and Revolutionary Change," in J. Nautz and R. Vahrenkamp (eds), *Die Wiener Jahrhundertwende*, Vienna: Böhlau, 1993, pp. 813–19.

14 R. Taagepera, "Patterns of Empire Growth and Decline: Context for Russia," unpublished paper, March 1995.

15 I discuss different definitions of revolution in "Concepts and Skocpol: Ambiguity and Vagueness in the Study of Revolution," *Journal of Theoretical Politics*, January 1992, vol. 4, no. 1, pp. 93–112.

16 M. Rejai and K. Phillips illustrate this point in *Leaders of Revolution*, Beverly Hills, CA: Sage, 1979.

17 On the connection between imperial collapse and revolution in the post-Soviet context, see A.J. Motyl, *Dilemmas of Independence: Ukraine after Totalitarianism*, New York: Council on Foreign Relations, 1993, pp. 51–70.

18 Z. Celik, *The Remaking of Istanbul*, Berkeley, CA: University of California Press, 1986.

19 B. Lewis, *The Emergence of Modern Turkey*, 2nd edn, London: Oxford University Press, 1968 [first edition 1961].

20 See H.-U. Wehler, *The German Empire, 1871–1918*, Leamington Spa: Berg, 1985.

21 G. Stourzh, *Vom Reich zur Republik*, Vienna: Edition Atelier, 1990.

22 L. Greenfeld, *Nationalism*, Cambridge: Harvard University Press, 1992, pp. 277–395.

23 W.D. Smith, *The Ideological Origins of Nazi Imperialism*, New York: Oxford University Press, 1986, p. 53.

24 Ibid., pp. 83–93.

25 M.T. Florinsky, *Russia: A History and an Interpretation*, New York: Macmillan, 1953, vol. 2, pp. 797–800.

26 M. Agursky, *The Third Rome: National Bolshevism in the USSR*, Boulder, CO: Westview, 1987.

27 A.J. Motyl, *Will the Non-Russians Rebel?*, Ithaca, NY: Cornell University Press, 1987, pp. 71–87.

28 F.C. Barghoorn, *Soviet Russian Nationalism*, New York: Oxford University Press, 1956.

29 A.J. Motyl, *Sovietology, Rationality, Nationality: Coming to Grips with Nationalism in the USSR*, New York: Columbia University Press, 1990, pp. 161–73.

30 Roman Szporluk discusses this syndrome in "Reflections on Ukraine after 1994: The Dilemmas of Nationhood," *The Harriman Review*, March–May 1994, vol. 7, nos. 7–9, pp. 1–9.

31 See F.C. Barghoorn, "Russian Nationalism and Soviet Politics," in R. Conquest (ed.), *The Last Empire*, Stanford, CA: Hoover Institution Press, 1986, pp. 30–77.

32 T. Skocpol, "Social Revolutions and Mass Military Mobilization," *World Politics*, January 1988, vol. 40, no. 2, pp. 147–68; J.R. Adelman, *Revolution, Armies, and War*, Boulder, CO: Lynne Rienner, 1985.

33 See, for instance, J. Sachs, *Poland's Jump to the Market Economy*, Cambridge, MA: MIT Press, 1994.

34 A.J. Motyl, "Reform, Transition, or Revolution?," *Contention*, Fall 1994, vol. 4, no. 1, pp. 141–60.

35 For a forceful statement of this position, see T. Skocpol, *States and Social Revolutions*, Cambridge: Cambridge University Press, 1979.

36 H. Rogger and E. Weber (eds), *The European Right*, Berkeley: University of California Press, 1966; E. Nolte, *Die faschistischen Bewegungen*, Munich: Deutsche Taschenbuch Verlag, 1966.

37 See Helmut Kohl, *Deutschlands Zukunft in Europa*, Herford: Busse und Seewald, 1990.

38 On Czech exceptionalism, see E. Gellner, "The Price of Velvet: Tomas Masaryk and Vaclav Havel," in *Encounters with Nationalism*, Oxford: Blackwell, 1994, pp. 114–29.

39 See T. Colton and R. Tucker (eds), *Patterns in Post-Soviet Leadership*, Boulder, CO: Westview, 1995.
40 J. Rothschild, *East Central Europe Between the Two World Wars*, Seattle: University of Washington Press, 1974, pp. 73–135.
41 The best treatment of this issue is still R. Pipes, *The Formation of the Soviet Union*, New York: Atheneum, 1974 [first edition 1954].
42 C.D. Harris, "Ethnic Tensions in Areas of the Russian Diaspora," *Post-Soviet Geography*, April 1993, vol. 34, no. 4, pp. 233–8.
43 See *Developments in Crimea. Challenges for Ukraine and Implications for Regional Security*, Washington, DC: American Association for the Advancement of Science, 1995.
44 Current international relations theories are discussed in R. Keohane (ed.), *Neorealism and Its Critics*, New York: Columbia University Press, 1986; S.D. Krasner (ed.), *International Regimes*, Ithaca, NY: Cornell University Press, 1983; and J. Snyder, *Myths of Empire*, Ithaca, NY: Cornell University Press, 1991.
45 On incipient states, see Motyl, *Sovietology, Rationality, Nationality*, pp. 103–18.
46 This, in essence, is the argument of Paul Kennedy; see P. Kennedy, *The Rise and Fall of the Great Powers*, New York: Vintage, 1987.
47 J. Snyder, Chapter 1 in this volume.
48 V. Baranovsky, "Conflict Developments on the Territory of the Former Soviet Union," *SIPRI Yearbook*, Stockholm: SIPRI, 1994, pp. 169–203.
49 R. Menon and H. Spruyt, Chapter 6 in this volume.
50 For a more hopeful interpretation, see S. Solnick, Chapter 4 in this volume.
51 See G. Starovoitova, "Democracy in Russia after Chechnya," *The East & Central Europe Program Bulletin*, May 1995, vol. 5, no. 4, pp. 1, 3–4, 7.

3

THE GREAT WAR AND THE MOBILIZATION OF ETHNICITY IN THE RUSSIAN EMPIRE

Mark von Hagen

As the Soviet bloc entered into a process of disintegration, nationalist politics and ethnic conflict appeared as part of the momentous transformations. Nationalism and violent conflict waged in the rhetoric of ethnic antagonisms caught most observers and participants by surprise. The most popular explanation that emerged has been caricatured as the "deep freeze" theory; communism, in this version taken for once as some sort of internationalist or non-nationalist ideology, kept the subterranean, primeval nationalisms in the region in a deep freeze. Anthropologist Katherine Verdery has insisted that this is ideology cloaking itself as analysis, and a dangerous ideology at that, for it legitimates a stance of non-intervention by assuming the primacy of irrational forces that are beyond the control of any political actors. Instead, she argues, contemporary nationalist politics did not come out of nowhere. Communist regimes perpetuated ethnic divisions through a variety of policies and structures; indeed, communism, as practiced in the former Soviet Union and Eastern Europe, had made considerable accommodation with local nationalisms. But although this historical analysis might help explain the persistence of ethnic identities in post-Soviet nations, it does not yet explain how those ethnic identities have been mobilized in often violent conflicts. Equally important to her argument, then, is her insistence that much of today's ethnic conflict is a consequence of specific policies of the exit from the Old Regimes, including marketization and democratization. Above all, Verdery reminds us of the importance of agency and historical processes in explaining contemporary conflict and warns of the dangers of treating nationalism as a social actor in its own right rather than as a set of symbols over which diverse groups compete in varying contexts.[1]

The confusion, surprise, and readiness to resort to explanations that gave primacy to irrational forces in the wake of the end of the Soviet system bear striking parallels with the responses of elites in the Russian Empire in 1917 to an analogous "explosion" of the national question. The Georgian Menshevik Iraklii Tsereteli later acknowledged that the central democratic parties had been blind on the national question;[2] clearly the radical demands made by non-Russian political actors were as unexpected as the rejection of polite society's authority by the end of 1917. The new elites and many ethnic Russians generally shared liberal and socialist expectations that the national question was a consequence of Tsarist oppression and would disappear with the collapse of the autocracy. Faced with the "national awakenings" of 1917, they had to find explanations of why this issue not only persisted but even became exacerbated with each passing month. The new elites had been conditioned by years of conspiracy theories; in their more generous moods, they viewed the emergence of movements for national autonomy, federalism, and national liberation as artificial and superficial phenomena, and otherwise as treason and the direct result of the machinations of the German, Austro-Hungarian and Ottoman Empires designed to foment national discontent within the borders of the Russian Empire. In other words, what was considered by the elites to be a reasonable form of political analysis was actually a masked form of ideology. The elites confidently expected that the impersonal forces of "democracy" or the "Revolution" would neutralize the irrational power of another impersonal force, nationalism. Accordingly, the Provisional Government pursued a politics of procrastination and postponement with regard to the claims for greater autonomy and self-rule by the "borderlands," in the hopes that greater democracy would "solve" the national problem on its own terms.

What the new elites overlooked in their "blindness" on the national question was the degree to which the politics of the Great War had raised and altered the stakes of national identity and given those identities much more urgency, indeed often life and death urgency, than had been the case before 1914. But, as Verdery would remind us, equally important in explaining the dramatic rise of radical nationalist politics during 1917 were the conditions of exit from the Old Regime, specifically, the policies of the Provisional Government as it sought to destroy the institutional pillars of the legitimacy of the Romanovs' dynastic autocracy. The policies that offer the most explanatory power for the rapid radicalization and spread of nationalist politics center on the decision to continue to pursue the war against the Central Powers, now in the name of "the Revolution," and the Provisional Government's appeals to "society" to organize itself in defense of the revolution, contrasted with its appointment of its "own" people as commissars to local governments, in effect setting up alternative power bases against the Old Regime local and municipal administration.[3]

This chapter proposes an explanation for the emergence of national conflict in the disintegrating Russian Empire by focusing on state and elite policies and their intended and unintended consequences during the years of the Great War. Although the focus here is on the rise of the Ukrainian movement, the dynamics of that particular movement can only be understood in the greater context of the mobilization of ethnicity in the conditions of war and revolution. A discussion of the conditions of exit from the Old Regime, properly speaking, requires separate treatment and will be the subject of a future article; in an important sense, however, the wartime policies already represented a break with previous policies. Certainly for the population of occupied Galicia, but even for those subjects of the

Russian Empire who found themselves in martial-law regimes in the front-line provinces, the transformations of their lives were equivalent to revolutionary change. In Galicia, a foreign government extended its reach into local politics and society; for the subjects of the Russian Empire, authorities speaking in the name of the Old Regime intruded into areas and upset communal life in vastly different ways from the peacetime autocracy. Even before 1917, the rules of everyday life had changed dramatically.

The war was a watershed in relations between Russians and non-Russians and among non-Russians as well. It was not just the war per se, but (1) the character of the regimes waging that war, especially the multinational dynastic empires of Austria-Hungary, the Ottomans and Russia; (2) the character of the war, with Russia locked in combat with its three powerful neighbors to the west and south (no war since the Napoleonic invasion so directly involved the transfer, destruction, and occupation of the densely populated European provinces of the Empire); and (3) very specific policies pursued by those regimes in military manpower, wartime propaganda, occupation and evacuation and even refugee aid. The consequences for Russia of these policies were nothing less than the internationalization and militarization of the Empire's "national questions."

What the war changed was the politics of identity that had prevailed in the Russian Empire in the last decades of the autocracy. In everyday practice, the minority communities of the Empire combined adherence to local languages, religions, and cultures with loyalty to the Tsar and Imperial state. With varying degrees of qualifications, Baltic Germans, Jews, Tatars, Ukrainians, and Poles formed a cosmopolitan elite whose loyalties were focused on the transnational state and the autocrat. The Imperial administration tried to ignore ethnic categories in its public documents in favor of traditional categories of religion and estate.[4] Accordingly, Jeffrey Brooks has argued that Russian popular literature revealed a relatively more tolerant and cosmopolitan attitude toward non-Russians, especially when contrasted to contemporary American and British popular fiction, after the turn of the century.[5] Similarly, Paul Bushkovitch observed that Russian national politics at the end of the Old Regime remained backward vis-à-vis its Western and Central European variants, where a more militant and chauvinist politics was becoming the norm before the outbreak of the Great War.[6] However, a somewhat less benevolent view can be taken of inter-ethnic relations in the empire on the eve of the war. After all, Russification policies dating from the reign of Alexander III had provoked protest movements which expressed themselves in clearly national and religious language. After the concessions to the non-Russian communities of 1905, the Stolypin counter-reforms and gentry reaction once again disadvantaged many vocal non-Russian communities.[7] In this view, then, the war exacerbated many already existing tensions in prewar Imperial society and politics, but definitely effected a qualitative change in relations among the peoples of the Empire.

The politics of the Great War had as their consequence the narrowing of the choices available to many communities and the raising of the stakes for choosing or having attributed to them the "wrong" national identity. Within the cosmopolitan Imperial elites themselves, the wartime policies and the ways in which the war was inserted into other political conflicts had the effect of polarization along national lines. The result of these changes and the policies which shaped them was the politicization of ethnic differences and the overlaying of an ethnic or national dimension to many otherwise non-national political, economic and social conflicts. This is not to say that by 1917 the various communities had been converted to the nationalist causes to which they would eventually lend their support over the course of the next several years. However, ethnic communities were polarized, more communities had become accustomed to thinking of themselves in more exclusively ethnic or national terms, and more came to view current and future conflicts as involving these ethnic and national identities.

Norman Stone, in the one recent history of the Russian involvement in the Great War, has argued that the war had the effect of a rapid modernization process on the Russian Empire's economy and administrative structure.[8] Although he does not extend the argument to ethnicity, as is described below, new forms and media of patriotism and national identities emerged and were provisionally consolidated during the war, partly as a consequence of state policies and their often unintended consequences, but also as a result of the "unofficial" activities of elites especially after the abdication of Nicholas II. Among the war's consequences was a speeding up of the reconfiguration of identities—itself part of the longer-term shift in the way Imperial society was structured—from traditional dynastic, confessional, and estate categories to ones of class and ethnicity. Wartime policies, furthermore, had economic and social consequences that amounted to a dramatic undermining of the position of many traditional elites, especially that of the gentry.[9] Indeed, when the Provisional Government abolished Imperial estate and rank distinctions in March 1917, it was acknowledging a fact already largely accomplished.

But the war did more than achieve a demographic turnover; as the focus of national attention, it became a testing ground for social privilege, especially Old Regime social privilege. The war was waged with patriotic appeals to national sacrifice; exemption from wartime service, for example, became a constant source of resentment among those who were serving or who had relatives on the fronts. The autocracy's performance in the war became more than ever a test of its legitimacy. In other words, the diminished importance of traditional anchors of identity such as estate and dynasty opened considerable space for heightened emphasis on national and ethnic ones, on the one hand, and class ones, on the other.

The propaganda war: internationalization of imperial national politics

In the Russian Empire, the war was greeted most enthusiastically by the propertied classes and intelligentsia. The common peasant or working-class recruit, on the other hand, had little sense at the beginning of the war as to who precisely the enemy was. From the start, Russian military propaganda tried to answer that question with a version of the pan-Slavic expectation of a clash between Slavic and Teutonic civilizations, and the expectation that all Slavic peoples would welcome the liberating Russian Army and join the struggle against the Austro-Hungarian oppressors.[10] Such liberationist hyperbole became typical for the major belligerent powers against their enemies, but such rhetorical games carried a grave risk of encouraging the disgruntled peoples of one's own empire. Indeed, the war had the undesired consequence for the imperial elites of "internationalizing" the Empire's nationalities problems.[11] The Entente waged its war, among its other proclaimed aims, in the name of self-determination of nations. Of course, Britain, France and Russia in particular had in mind the disintegration of the Habsburg and Ottoman Empires, but the Russian nationality problem also became a sensitive area in Allied relations. The Germans and Austrians, for their part, sponsored conferences and publishing activities by several anti-imperial national groupings from the Russian Empire, especially the Poles, Ukrainians, Lithuanians, Finns and eventually the Muslims. They also waged propaganda campaigns, at first rather primitive, to appeal to potential anti-Russian feelings among the non-Russians.

The Russian Empire countered these moves with occasional rhetorical gestures that were meant to appeal to certain non-Russian national groups who might be thereby persuaded to support the Russian cause. The most notable and controversial was Grand Duke Nikolai Nikolaevich's announcement on 14 August 1914 that the Russian state might finally recognize an autonomous Poland within the Russian Empire after the war; in fact, the government made no firm commitments, nor did it ease restrictions on Polish subjects during the war. On 5 November 1916, the Germans stepped up the propaganda war by announcing their intention of uniting Polish lands after the war in an independent Polish state. Whatever their motives, the belligerent powers inadvertently gave hope to more than just the Poles that their national dreams would be realized at the end of the war.[12]

For the Ukrainian national movement, the war years promised new trials and opportunities. On the eve of the war, Ukrainians of the Russian Empire had no official parliamentary representation in the State Duma; as such, they were denied the opportunity to pledge loyalty to the war effort as other nationalities had done. Moreover, because of the suspicious attitude of the authorities toward the Ukrainian movement as agents of the enemy, a new series of bans were imposed on Ukrainian cultural, educational, and political life. In the Habsburg lands, by contrast, the prewar situation had been more favorable for the Ukrainians. At the end of 1912, the three major Ukrainian parties there issued a joint declaration of loyalty to the Austrian Empire in the event of a war against Russia, and formed a Ukrainian Information Committee to agitate on behalf of the Ukrainian cause in western Europe. With the outbreak of the war, the three parties joined forces as the Supreme Ukrainian Council (Holovna Ukrains'ka Rada), once again declared their hostility to Russia and announced the creation of the Ukrainian Sich

Sharpshooters (Ukrains'ki Sichovi Stril'tsi) as a distinct unit within the Austrian Army. Shortly thereafter the Ukrainian Information Committee became the Union for the Liberation of Ukraine (Soiuz Vyzvolennia Ukrainy, or SVU).[13] When the Russians began their successful invasion of Galicia, the émigrés quickly moved to Vienna and founded a branch in Berlin as well, where they enjoyed the limited financial and political support of both Germany and Austria. The SVU, like many other organizations devoted to national liberation, conducted furious diplomatic activity with the Central Powers throughout the war.[14]

Militarization of ethnic relations

The sanctioning of the Sich Sharpshooters as a part of the Austrian Army was part of the dangerous escalation of imperial competition that would later pit armies of national minorities against an enemy that also counted large numbers of those minorities among its own population. It was only a small step from forming special units from among one's own conscript pool, as was the case with the Sich Sharpshooters, to organizing volunteer detachments made up of exiles from the enemy camp. The first steps toward militarizing the ethnic discontents of the Russian Empire were taken when the Germans formed corps of Finnish officers and the Austrians sponsored the Polish Legion on their territory to fight against the Central Powers' enemies.[15]

Yet another step was taken when Imperial authorities resolved to permit national agitation among prisoners of war. The SVU began to conduct propaganda among Ukrainian prisoners, the second largest group of prisoners of war held by the Central Powers, in German and Austrian camps; they sought to reduce illiteracy and raise soldiers' national consciousness for the struggle against the Russian Empire and for Ukrainian independence with Austrian sponsorship and protection.[16] In the spring of 1915 they won from the German and Austrians permission to separate Ukrainian prisoners out into separate Ukrainian camps; such separate prisoner of war camps had already been approved for Finns and Poles and other separate camps were later approved for Georgians and Muslims of the Russian Empire.

The very process of separating out prisoners of war by nationality provoked conflicts in the camps.[17] Any discussion of the Ukrainian issue, especially in the extremely anti-Russian variant proposed by the SVU, typically ended in a fistfight in the barracks, with Russians insisting that they would never permit Little Russia to be torn from Russia, while some particularly emboldened Ukrainians asserted that they would achieve freedom for Ukraine whether Russians permitted it or not. Several Ukrainian soldiers told the SVU delegates privately that they had feared contact with them and hid their nationality because of the intimidation campaign by the Russians. Generally, the observers were surprised at the militancy of the Russians' patriotism. In response to the SVU's efforts at separating out Ukrainians into special barracks, in several camps the "Russophiles" formed their own barracks, which included Russian patriots of all possible nationalities. The Russian soldiers and officers monitored the political behavior of all *inorodtsy* and threatened with execution by hanging all those who dared enter into relations with Austrian authorities; they kept blacklists of "nationally conscious" Ukrainians, and threatened to release these to the Russian police upon their return home.[18] Despite such threats, not only Ukrainians, but Poles, Jews, and Muslims began to form their own "national" organizations in the camps. The intrusion of the SVU and its agenda clearly contributed to a sharper sense of ethnic politics and a polarization along ethnic lines in the camps.[19] A very similar dynamic unfolded in 1917, when Ukrainians began pursuing Ukrainization in the Russian Imperial Army.

Russian officials may have actually outpaced the Central Powers in forming national military units from among prisoners of war. The Russian Army, during the years 1914–17, captured a large number of prisoners of war, nearly two million according to postwar statisticians. The largest contingent of the prisoners, more than 400,000, were concentrated in the Kiev Military District.[20] The Russian military, motivated in part by the utopian pan-Slavic ideals shared by a considerable part of their ruling elites, began experimenting with national military units even before their opponents. Convinced that the Slavic brethren nations were groaning under Habsburg oppression and eagerly awaiting their moment to join the Russian cause of liberation, as early as 6 August 1914, the General Staff was seriously discussing the formation of Czech, Slovak, and Polish units, and also considered Finnish and Latvian ones.[21] The Czech, Slovak, and Polish units were to be formed from among the large and rapidly growing population of Austro-Hungarian soldiers in Russian captivity, tens of thousands of whom were held in a camp at Darnitsa, near Odessa. An All-Russian Society for the Care of Slavic Prisoners was authorized to conduct charity and propaganda work among these groups, which eventually added Slovenes, Serbs, and Croatians to their concerns.

Émigré Czech societies volunteered to help form the units with the express aim of fighting against Austria-Hungary, fomenting uprisings there among their compatriots and "liberating their motherland from Austrian enslavement." The War Ministry won unanimous approval from the Council of Ministers on 30 August for the formation of two infantry regiments in the Kiev Military District. The War Ministry acknowledged that because these units were being authorized primarily out of political considerations, they needed to be treated differently in matters of staffing. The Czech volunteers, for example, were not likely to have much military training since they were largely political exiles. At first Russian officers would be assigned to the units, but the eventual aim was to create a Czech officer corps as well.[22]

After the Ottoman Empire entered the war on the side of the Central Powers, the initial appeals of Slavic brotherhood were embellished and transformed into a campaign of Christians against Muslims. The immediate object of the new appeals was the Armenian population, which was caught between the two belligerent powers of Russia and Turkey and briefly pursued a policy of neutrality. After turning down an offer from the Young Turks for autonomy in exchange for aid against Russia, the Dashnaks unwisely aligned themselves with the Russians in expectation of a quick Entente victory. The Dashnak leaders organized volunteer detachments of Armenians to fight alongside the Russian army and prepared uprisings in the rear of the Turkish lines.[23]

Thus by the eve of the February 1917 revolution, the principle of military formations organized along national or ethnic lines with the express intention of national liberation—albeit in the enemy camp—was firmly established, and Ukrainian activists would point to that firmly-established precedent when they demanded, almost immediately after the revolution in Petrograd, that the Provisional Government and General Staff permit the formation of Ukrainian units to secure national autonomy and rights. In addition, a Ukrainian fighting force (the Sich Sharpshooters) did exist and would play an important role in the unfolding of revolutionary politics in 1917. On both sides of the war, the experiments in national military units waged in the name of inter-imperial struggle contributed to the disintegration of the Imperial Armies and the monarchies themselves.[24]

"The Russian army-liberator is approaching": the occupation regime in Galicia

The Great War proved especially destructive for the peoples of the territories on the western frontier of Russia, where most of the fighting occurred: Germans, Jews, Ukrainians, Belorussians, Poles, and the Baltic peoples.[25] In nearly all cases, large numbers of the Imperial minority populations were fighting on both sides of the war and suffered psychological and material consequences of conflicting loyalties.[26] Wartime policies in these borderlands exacerbated ethnic tensions by targeting specific national communities. Discriminatory legislation on both sides either privileged or disadvantaged one ethnic group over another in matters of language and schooling, religious practice, military service obligations, property rights and other economic warfare measures.

The formulation and evolution of wartime policy is well illustrated from the initial campaigns of the war, especially the invasion of Galicia on the Southwest Front, and the capture and occupation of Lemberg (L'vov/Lviv) during the fall and winter 1914–15. Directly after the invasion, the Governor-General of Kiev, Trepov, had brief jurisdiction over the region and appointed several of his officials to Galicia. For some time, the occupation forces had difficulty in establishing a firm and systematic policy. After first appointing a pro-Polish governor, Colonel Sergei Sheremet'ev, anti-Polish forces among the local Ukrainian elites and Russian nationalists who had descended upon occupied Galicia achieved Sheremet'ev's replacement with Count Georgii Bobrinskii.[27] His martial-law commander was General Nikolai Ianushkevich, who exercised arbitrary and brutal authority, ordering the deportations of Germans, Jews, Poles, and Ukrainians.[28] An extensive report compiled by Bobrinskii's staff after the fall of L'vov to the enemy in June 1915 outlines the occupation regime's priorities and some of the ideas that guided their actions.[29]

Bobrinskii immediately turned to the Russophiles for help and had in his immediate entourage several officials known for their Russophile sympathies. For all
that, however, the occupation regime was staffed overwhelmingly by bureaucrats
transferred from Kiev, Podolia, Volynia, and Warsaw. The Russian nationalist
organizations, especially the Union of Russian People, were stronger in the southwest region than nearly anywhere else.[30] They brought with them to Galicia their
politics of Great Russian imperialism and anti-Semitism. But beyond the more
extreme manifestations of Russian nationalist and imperialist politics, the liberationist rhetoric that accompanied the Russian Army's invasion of Galicia and the
firm, peculiarly irredentist conviction that the Russian Army was "restoring" to
Russia its long-lost brethren was shared by a far larger part of the patriotic political
and intellectual leadership of the Empire. Even those liberals who were critical of
the Russophile orientation, such as Pavel Miliukov, attacked them not for the
substance of their mission but for employing the wrong means.

What made these political views so important for developments in Galicia was
the new situation created by the martial law regime. The occupation regime was
supposed to operate according to a law of 16 July 1914 on military zones, that
decreed the supremacy of military commanders over all civilian authorities and
allowed considerable space for arbitrary actions by low-ranking officers in large
regions of the country. The military authorities had broad authority over censorship, detention of suspected spies and other politically unreliable persons, and
general movement in and out of the military zones. They began introducing a
security regime that was intended to control the movement of people, goods and
ideas in their zone. The primary concern was to prevent spies from carrying out
their work in the region or from infiltrating from outside.[31]

All foreign citizens and politically unreliable persons were to be deported to the
interior provinces of the Empire, while an extensive system of surveillance was
erected to keep track of large groups of less unreliable persons. The most obvious
targets were clearly Germans and those who might be perceived as harboring
sympathies toward the German and Austrian cause. In a wave of Germanophobic
hysteria, and in coordination with their British and French allies, the Russian
government decreed the alienation and sale of certain properties of persons
related to subjects of Austria-Hungary and Germany.[32] The Ministry of Internal
Affairs resolved to liquidate German colonization in the Empire. German
colonists were deported from Volynia very shortly after the outbreak of war; in
southern provinces, other German colonists were expropriated and, fearing
deportation too and attempting to preempt expropriation, sold all their property in
a panic.[33]

The theme of ominous German influence and conspiracies (*nemetskoe zasil'e*)
everywhere became a commonplace in popular politics. The front-line newspaper
carried a regular rubric devoted to German machinations at home as well as
German barbarities on the front, linking the two in highly explosive fashion, while
military censors developed a category to keep track of all such anti-German
sentiments that might also undermine loyalty for the imperial family. German-

language publications were ordered closed. All correspondence, gatherings, and public conversations in German were banned. Most explosive for the Army, given the considerable number of prominent military men of Baltic German origins, was the linking of the German question with the Baltic question.[34] Military men with German surnames began to worry seriously about their future, as even liberal Russians appeared to be infected with the chauvinist (*kvasnoi*) patriotism that the war had made acceptable.

The authorities mistrusted the Germans above all, but the largest group of "political unreliables" was the Jews, who became equated with foreign subjects in many of the occupation and evacuation instructions.[35] The Galician Jews in particular, who had enjoyed legal equality under the Habsburg monarchy, were viewed with considerable suspicion by Russian nationalist circles, and those suspicions served as a pretext for a particularly energetic anti-Jewish campaign from the very beginning of the occupation. Many Galician Jews had indeed chosen to flee the occupied zone; their land and property was confiscated and designated for "poor peasants," who translated here as Ukrainians. Under the military regime, the press and the Russian benevolent societies that descended upon Galicia to organize relief aid incited poor Ukrainian peasants against wealthier Jewish landowners. Virtually all Galician Jews were viewed as potential spies or traitors, and a particularly vicious policy of censorship, arrest, and deportation was implemented.[36] In the early months of the war, Jews had been particularly visible among the agents who were supplying the army in Galicia; on the pretext of the threat of widespread espionage on the part of these merchants and suppliers, in February 1915 the commander of the Southwest front decreed a ban on the entry of any further Jews into the zone as well as a ban on movement from one province within Galicia to another.

By the winter of the first campaign this anti-Semitic wave extended to Jews who were Russian subjects and serving in various civilian support agencies, such as the *zemstvos* and the Red Cross. General Alekseev ordered that Jewish officials be removed from *zemstvo* organizations on the grounds that they were either avoiding military service or disseminating party propaganda.[37] Generals Ianushkevich and Ivanov also began to raise the sensitive question of Jews serving in the Army itself, and advocated their exclusion. In any event, officers were ordered to follow closely the attitudes of Jewish soldiers toward the war and to monitor their performance during combat.[38] In this atmosphere of heightened suspicion toward Jews, the Southwest Command received numerous reports of units, especially forts, either refusing to accept Jewish soldiers who were sent as replacements or transferring Jewish soldiers out of the region into the interior provinces, all without express authorization.[39]

The attitudes and policies of the occupying regime toward other peoples of Galicia, primarily Slavic peoples, varied in their severity. Considerable attention was devoted to the preparation of special propaganda for Poles and other Slavic peoples of Austria-Hungary. The Ministry of Foreign Affairs counseled their military counterparts to exercise a particularly humane policy toward the civilian population of Galicia, as well as toward prisoners of war, many of whom were Slavs. They even proposed—and this on 11 August 1914—that the military authorities consider the possibility of releasing all prisoners who were Russians, Poles, Serbs or other Slavs.[40]

The Poles in Galicia presented a complicated picture. They too were split into at least two camps, one still hoping for a change in Russian Imperial policy and indeed collaborating with the Russian occupation authorities, the other casting its fate with the Central Powers. After Galician Jews, it was the Poles who attracted the most attention from counter-intelligence, which suspected every Pole of being a potential spy. Agents kept lists of Poles suspected of espionage and delivered regular reports on the Polish revolutionary movement. Russian authorities were well aware that the Austrian High Command had allowed Jozef Pilsudski to form Polish Legions on Austrian soil, among whose recruits were Polish exiles from Russia. Thousands of Galician Poles were deported out of the rear zones of the Southwest Front, especially priests who persisted in delivering sermons "in a sep-aratist spirit" and members of illegal Polish political parties and organizations.[41]

The overriding goal of the occupation regime was the unification of Galician Rus with the Russian Empire, and here the focus of attention was on the Galician Ukrainians, or, in the categories of the Russian authorities, the Galician Russians. The Foreign Ministry, in a note to the War Ministry, recommended reopening the Russian-language newspaper *Prikarpatskaia Rus'*, which had been closed down by Austrian authorities. The Russian authorities were encouraged to take advantage of the aura of popular resistance that the Russophile party had recently come to enjoy after many of them were arrested by the Austrians, detained in prison in Hungary and even executed.[42] The Foreign Ministry expected that the majority of Uniates in Galicia actually were inclined to prefer the Orthodox Church, but recognized that they would need to be handled with tact. At the same time, all social and cultural organizations were to be shut down until their political orienta-tion could be determined, the local *sejm* ought not to be convened, and no concessions were to be made to the Ukrainian separatist movement because of its intention to "undermine the unity of the Russian tribe" (*russkogo plemeni*). Nor was any mention to be made of a separate Ukrainian language.

These views were nearly identical to those expressed by Count Georgii Bobrinskii in his summary of the first occupation regime. Bobrinskii saw his primary task as the fusion of the region with the Empire in both "the political and national senses."[43] Following from these views, the occupation authorities arrested and deported thousands of Ukrainian political, religious, and cultural leaders and banned the posting and distribution of all materials in Russian or Little Russian *narechii* that had been published beyond the frontiers of the Russian Empire, as well as materials printed in other languages, "if the content of these books was hostile to the Russian government and Russian people." Furthermore, all Ukrainian bookstores had to be closed "because of the tendentious, anti-Russian character of the publications that were being sold."[44]

The victory of the Russian Army was accompanied by a political-cultural occupation that was marked by the symbolic triumph of the Russian language as the "expression of the Russian spirit." This new linguistic order was presented as the "restoration" of the Russian language, previously debased by the perfidious Austrian authorities.[45] During the takeover of the urban administration, the occupying authorities required the use of the Russian language by all officials, which made for considerable difficulties for many of the Galicians, and for the dismissal of all Jews from responsible positions.[46] Schools were identified early on as a major instrument for the planned Russification of the population. In mid-September all schools were temporarily shut down, then reopened on the condition that Russian-language instruction be introduced. Special Russian-language courses for teachers in eastern Galicia and Bukovina were organized with official encouragement.[47]

It was religious policy, possibly more than anything else, that turned once loyal Russophiles and perhaps neutral Galician peasants against the Russian occupiers. According to Bobrinskii, with the advance of Russian forces into Galicia, many Roman and Greek Catholic priests, primarily "Mazepists" in Bobrinskii's characterization, fled their parishes and departed with the Austrians. Once the local population was assured that the Russian forces were not hostile to them, they began, according to Bobrinskii, to return to their parishes and request the appointment of Orthodox priests. Bobrinskii saw his task at this time as the prevention of any re-Catholicization of the local population, which translated into surveillance of the remaining Catholic and Uniate clergy, and several arrests and deportations to interior Russia, the most notable being the arrest of the Greek Catholic Metropolitan Andrei Sheptits'kyi. He announced an official policy of religious tolerance—as least far as Christians were concerned—and urged the local and arriving Orthodox clergy to exercise extreme caution in their dealings with the local population. Bobrinskii's announced policy required that a 75 percent Orthodox majority of the local population of a village or town be established by voting before an Orthodox priest would be sent.[48]

Unbeknownst to Bobrinskii or to the Southwest Front Commander, the Holy Synod appointed Archbishop Evlogii to leadership of the Orthodox Church in Galicia.[49] Evlogii arrived in L'vov and began to order dismissals, transfers, and appointments of Orthodox clergy from the interior provinces of the Empire to Galicia, often in violation of the 75 percent majority policy. In any event, Evlogii made no effort whatsoever to coordinate his behavior with the hierarchy of the military chaplaincy, ostensibly the superior spiritual authority in the occupation regime. Such arbitrary actions provoked violent conflict in many parishes and, according to Bobrinskii, had even more alarming consequences during the evacuation, when tens of thousands of Galicians were compelled to flee with the departing Russian forces out of fear that they would be persecuted by the reoccupying Austrian forces or by local fellow parishioners.[50] But the primary result of these arbitrary actions was widespread discontent with Russian authorities in the occupied territory. Despite the entreaties of both Bobrinskii and Brusilov to the Synod and the General Staff, Evlogii was allowed to pursue his independent policy and to threaten the peace of the military regime that local military and civilian authorities tried so hard to preserve.

Retreat and evacuation

After Germany's General August von Mackensen came to the rescue of Austria and launched an offensive in mid-April 1915, the Russian armies began the Great Retreat (mid-April to mid-September 1915), losing large numbers of prisoners and suffering from shortages of arms and ammunition. The year 1915 generally brought military disaster and political crisis to Russia; all of Russian Poland and a large part of the Polish-Russian borderlands were lost, and troop morale plummeted during the months of sustained retreat. The Russian high command ordered the evacuation of L'vov and the rest of Galicia on 20 June. Two days later the Austro-Hungarian Army entered the Galician capital. As they retreated from the territories, Russian military officials commanded a policy of "scorched earth" and forced mass population evacuations to deny the Germans any further advantages from the occupation.[51]

The evacuation of L'vov and Galicia served to further antagonize nearly all the peoples who had fallen under Russian rule, from the Jews who bore the worst of the disastrous mismanagement to the Galician Russophiles, who by that time had fallen into disfavor as well. In so far as one can write of conscious policies, they too were very ethno-specific. During the evacuation of Galicia, Russian authorities refused to give Jews the transit passes all evacuees were expected to carry, whereas, true to their continued faith in the unity of the Russian people, "Galician Russians" of Orthodox faith had the usual five-year residence requirement for Russian citizenship waived if they declared an intention to resettle in Asian Russia.[52] Most of the Germans evacuated during late 1914 and early 1915 from the Russian-Polish frontier had resettled in the province of Volynia. But during the Great Retreat, Ianushkevich demanded that Volynia be cleared of all Jews and Germans (14 June 1915) on the grounds that nearly all of them were eager to collaborate with the German invading armies. During the summer of 1915, hundreds of thousands of Jews, Germans, and Poles were brutally evacuated or deported from the war zone eastward as spies or collaborators.[53]

The flood of refugees clogged the path of the retreating armies and added to the confusion. The government fought with *zemstvo* and town organizations for jurisdiction over the refugee crisis, but the predictable result was institutional stalemate while the number of refugees continued to grow. By spring 1916, the Tatiana Committee estimated the total number of refugees settled in Russia at 3,306,051. Even the non-governmental relief organizations that formed to aid the refugees entered into the emerging politics of nationality; each major national group raised funds for refugees who were determined to be co-nationals and, predictably, denied aid to those who could not demonstrate their belonging.[54] These inter-ethnic tensions were often exacerbated by the official government relief agencies' preferential policies for one nationality over another.[55] Every one of the several evacuations between 1914 and 1918 brought with it increasing numbers of incidents of rape, pillage and wanton destruction. The refugees themselves, powerless in their homeless condition, were ever more inclined to respond favorably to the appeals of radical parties, while the populations that were forced to receive them also struck out in riots and violence against the intruders.[56]

The barbarism of the occupying (and evacuating) authorities provoked a range of responses from concerned citizens, victims, and eyewitnesses. Part of the government expressed its disapproval of the military's rule, but appeals from the Council of Ministers to the Emperor to rein in the military authorities were in vain. The Duma emerged as another forum for critics of the excesses allowed under martial law. Reports about the Galician occupation regime brought protests even from some of the conservative deputies in the Duma, but it was primarily the center and left parties who spoke out most vociferously and demanded an end to the persecution of non-Russians.[57] The demands, though approved by the Duma, did little to mitigate the repressive activities of military authorities. The government, however, underwent some significant changes, including the dismissal of the now notorious Ianushkevich, who since his triumphant career in Galicia had been promoted to the post of Chief of the General Staff. Toward the end of 1916 the Russian government began to make some belated concessions to the public protests. In November it authorized a new Ukrainian monthly journal to be published in Moscow, and in a conciliatory tone declared that the editors could use current Ukrainian orthography and not that which was allowed during the occupation regime. The Russian government then relented on the schools question and permitted the opening of schools in Galicia and Bukovina in all native languages except German.

But the retreats and failures of the first year of the war had other unfortunate consequences for the tone of political discussions among the ruling elites. They set in motion a dynamic of suspicion and a veritable obsession with treason and traitors that focused on ethnic identities. Jews, Germans, and ethnic "others" generally came under suspicion for profiting from the war and abetting the enemy. Rightist Duma deputies regularly articulated anti-Semitic sentiments during discussion of wartime legislation, including the expulsion of Jews from military service. Within the army, rumors of German treason were behind several investigations of military failure and a heightening lynch-mob atmosphere against Russian officers with German-sounding names.

The Russian nationalist radical right viewed the war as an opportunity to rebuild and revive their organizations under the slogans of patriotism. The Union of Russian People remained the prominent nationalist movement, and sought to exploit the population's discontent with the economic hardships that the war brought down upon them. Since city and provincial *dumas* and *zemstvos* had taken over much of the economic activity, the right targeted civilian institutions as well as foreign and domestic "aliens" and enemies. The Union continued to find considerable moral and financial support among key government officials, such as Interior Minister Protopopov. Although Jews and Germans were the primary targets of these "patriotic" groups, the loyalty of all non-Russians was regularly questioned and all efforts to remove legal and administrative disabilities for non-Russians were blocked by intensive lobbying from the right.

The mobilization of the Russian nationalist right and the harsh policies of the military authorities had the further unintended consequence of encouraging the consolidation of more radical anti-Russian movements throughout the Russian Empire. Even before the catastrophic evacuation of the summer of 1915, the occupation policies of the Galician regime had begun to make their impact felt in other parts of the Empire. The continual deportations of politically unreliable individuals and large groups was transforming Kiev, among other major cities, into a cauldron of conspiratorial societies and revolutionary circles. The Director of a Kiev gymnasium wrote a concerned letter to the Kiev Military District in which he complained of the increasing dangers of refugees and deportees and the "considerable numbers of exiles and administrative exiles [arriving] more or less daily in Kiev." [58] In response to similar concerns, a commission considered the need to conduct a registration of the population of Kiev and its environs.[59]

Finally, there is considerable evidence that for many ethnically Ukrainian soldiers who had not previously attached much political significance to their differences from the Russians, the barbarism associated with the Galician campaign began a process of reorientation of their identities. From the contradictory evidence that is available, this reorientation did not follow any one particular pattern. SVU activists devoted special attention to the attitudes of prisoners of war and information about Galicia in the extensive questionnaires that they filled out for each soldier and recorded the answers in their reports from the camps.[60] The most positive signs that the SVU was able to ascertain from the prisoners was their enthusiasm for Ukrainian literature and culture.[61] Soldiers told of arriving in "Moscophile" villages during the 1914 campaign, where the army was greeted with curses on Poles, Jews, and Ukrainians, but the curses were spoken in Ukrainian. Others told how, in several villages, the inhabitants held back any expressions until the officers had left and only soldiers remained. When they discovered Ukrainians among them, they rejoiced and brought them tobacco, bread and other gifts. Many prisoners claimed that when they entered Galicia, they refused to fire a single bullet, so as not to kill their "brethren"; one young Ukrainian claimed he had wanted to shoot himself so as not to have to witness this "terrible drama," but instead deserted his unit and gave himself up to the enemy.[62] Still another told how his officer, upon arrival in a Galician village, asked where the reading room was, then ordered the soldiers to remove all the books and newspapers and set fire to it. The vehemence with which the military authorities prosecuted the anti-Ukrainian campaign in Galicia and the overall privileging and disfranchising of the population along ethnic lines awoke soldiers and NCOs to the risks they faced in articulating a Ukrainian identity that might be perceived as challenging Russian hegemony.[63]

Conclusion

Ironically, the Russian Empire's wartime policies contributed in important ways to the emergence of nationalist mass politics and ethnic conflict by 1917. Those non-Russian national elites who had tried to "build" their national movements in the brief period between the Revolution of 1905 and the outbreak of war through primary schooling, publishing activities, and co-operative societies may not have succeeded nearly so well as the Imperial elites' own politics of occupation and evacuation, however unintended the consequences may have been. And in several instances, the policies of politicization of ethnic difference were all too obviously intended to pit one ethnic community against another.

The very fact of a war waged among multinational empires raised new issues and the potential for new conflict among the subject peoples; wartime policy was inextricably tied up with ethnic politics and the intensification of already existing hostilities as well as the insertion of several new confrontations through the execution of occupation, evacuation, and resettlement policies. The national liberation propaganda of the belligerent powers undermined the transnational pretensions of the Old Regime dynasties and their cosmopolitan elites and exacerbated tensions among the confessional and ethnic communities with those elites. The principle of national military units also extended those tensions to the soldiers, a major social group that had not been the target of most prewar national movements. Occupation policy, conducted in the name of national security, changed the stakes of ethnic identity when the consequences could be privileging for the "correct" groups and property confiscation, deportation, arrest, or execution for the "wrong" ones. Evacuation policy and refugee relief efforts all served to reinforce the new "nationalized" politics of the war. Many earlier social and political tensions had an ethnic element overlaid on them, while ethnicity became a weapon and policy instrument for all the belligerent powers. When Nicholas II abdicated in early 1917, many educated citizens still expected social and ethnic tensions to abate. In fact, their utopian hopes were quickly and tragically dashed.

Notes

1 K. Verdery, "Nationalism and National Sentiment in Post-socialist Romania," *Slavic Review*, Summer 1993, vol. 52, no. 2, pp. 179–203. Verdery's argument about the accommodations of communist regimes with nationalism is made at greater length in her *National Ideology under Socialism: Identity and Cultural Politics in Ceausescu's Romania*, Berkeley, CA: University of California Press, 1991; Yuri Slezkine has made a similar argument about the Soviet state's perpetuation of ethnic differences in his "The USSR as a Communal Apartment, or How a Socialist State Promoted Ethnic Particularism," *Slavic Review*, Summer 1994, vol. 53, no. 2, pp. 414–52.
2 See his discussion of the national question in I. I. Tsereteli, *Vospominaniia o Fevral'skoi revoliutsii*, Paris and The Hague: Mouton and Co., 1963, vol. 2, pp. 69–161. That blindness has been shared by most of the major historians of 1917 as well. With the exception of Richard Pipes, *The Formation of the Soviet Union*, Cambridge, MA: Harvard University Press, 1964 [first edition 1954] and R. Grigor Suny, *The Baku Commune, 1917–1918: Class and Nationality in the Russian Revolution*, Princeton, NJ: Princeton

University Press, 1972, most non-Soviet and especially Soviet chroniclers of the revolutions have emphasized non-national social factors and preconditions, especially the role of the working class and peasantry in revolutionary politics. The two major histories of soldiers in 1917, however—A. Wildman, *The End of the Russian Imperial Army*, Princeton, NJ: Princeton University Press, 1987, and M.S. Frenkin, *Russkaia armiia i revoliutsiia 1917–1918*, Munich: Logos, 1978—are exceptional in their attention to non-Russians.

3 In a similar way, Mikhail Gorbachev appealed to the intelligentsia to consolidate his reformism from the top and devolved large powers to local "commissars" in an effort to break the hold of the central bureaucracies on the Soviet Union's political and economic life. The sense of surprise and confoundment that Gorbachev and his closest advisors expressed at the explosion of the national question and their rapid loss of control over the reform process bears uncanny similarity to the Provisional Government's and Petrograd Soviet's response to developments during 1917.

4 See, for example, government employment documents, *formuliarnye spiski*; curiously, more "modern" ethnic categories were delineated by the military statisticians who drew the security maps that were used in the General Staff schools, but these remained exceptions and, notably, classified. See A.M. Zolotarev, *Zapiski voennoi statistiki Rossii. Tom I: Teoriia statistiki. Obshchee obozrenie Rossii. Vooruzhennye sily*, St. Petersburg: A.E. Landau, 1885.

5 See his *When Russia Learned to Read*, Princeton, NJ: Princeton University Press, 1985, ch. 6.

6 P. Bushkovitch, "What is Russia? Russian National Consciousness and the State, 1500–1917," unpublished conference paper presented at Columbia University, November 1994.

7 On the policies of the autocracy in the last decade before 1917, see V. Conolly, "The 'Nationalities Question' in the Last Phase of Tsardom," in E. Oberlaender (ed.), *Russia Enters the Twentieth Century, 1894–1917*, New York: Schocken Books, 1971; and A. Kappeler, *Russland als Vielvoelkerreich*, Munich: C.H. Beck Verlag, 1992, chapter 9.

8 "There was, in other words, a burst of economic activity between 1914 and 1917 that brought as much change to Russia as the whole of the previous generation. It was, indeed, the economic 'take-off' that men had been predicting for Russia, that had, in a sense, caused the First World War, since German apprehensions of it had led Germany's leaders into provoking a preventive war. The First World War provoked a crisis of economic modernisation, and the Bolshevik Revolution was the outcome" (N. Stone, *The Eastern Front, 1914–1917*, London: Hodder & Stoughton, 1975, p. 285).

9 For example, most scholars have agreed that the heavy losses in the army contributed to a democratization of the officer corps, resulting in a sharp decline in the weight and power of the gentry in that institution.

10 From the first days of the war the official organ of the Southwest Front, *Armeiskii vestnik*, declared that "Russia seeks nothing but the restoration of right and justice. To you, peoples of Austria–Hungary, she now brings freedom and the realization of your national aspirations." *Armeiskii vestnik*, 16 September 1914, p. 1.

11 Marc Ferro, "La politique des nationalités du gouvernement provisoire, fevrier–octobre 1917," *Cahiers du monde russe et sovietique*, 1961, vol. 2, p. 136.

12 During the initial campaigns on the Caucasian Front, the Caucasian Viceroy Vorontsov-Dashkov, who was widely known as sympathetic to the cause of establishing an Armenian nation, provoked conflicts with his field commander, General Iudenich, over the former's strategy of forcing a rapid offensive. Several Caucasian deputies to the Duma, notably Nikolai Semenovich Chkheidze, also criticized Vorontsov-Dashkov for taking such politically motivated strategic risks. A.N. Iakhontov, *Prologue to Revolution: Notes of A. N. Iakhontov on the Secret Meetings of the Council of Ministers, 1915*, trans. and ed. M. Cherniavsky, Englewood Cliffs, NJ: Prentice-Hall, 1967, pp. 36–7. For the dilemmas

of Turks and Muslims in the Russian Empire after the entry of the Ottoman Empire into the war on the side of the Central Powers, see S.A. Zenkovsky, *Pan-Turkism and Islam in Russia*, Cambridge, MA: Harvard University Press, 1967, pp. 123–9.

13 On the political activities, see K. Levyts'kyi, *Istoriia politychnoi dumky halyts'kykh ukraintsiv 1848–1914*, 2 vols, L'viv: published by author, 1926, pp. 720–2; on the Sich Sharpshooters, see S. Ripets'kyi, *Ukrains'ke sichove strilets'tvo: Vyzvol'na ideia i zbroinyi chyn*, New York: 1956, pp. 17–76.

14 On the Union, Austria and Germany during the war, see O.S. Fedyshyn, "The Germans and the Union for the Liberation of the Ukraine, 1914–1917," in T. Hunczak (ed.), *The Ukraine, 1917–1921: A Study in Revolution*, Cambridge, MA: Harvard University Press, 1977, pp. 305–22; O. Fedyshyn, *Germany's Drive to the East and the Ukrainian Revolution in World War I*, New Brunswick, NJ: Rutgers University Press, 1970, esp. chs 1–3; and H. Grebing, "Österreich-Ungarn und die 'Ukrainische Aktion' 1914–18," *Jahrbücher für Geschichte Osteuropas*, N.F., vol. 8, no. 3, Munich: Priebatsch's Buchhaldlung, 1959, pp. 270–96.

15 Finnish youth groups decided to prepare for the Finnish liberation struggle by taking military training in Germany. The first group of Finnish patriots arrived in Germany 22 February 1915. One year later they were formed into the Royal Prussian Jäger Battalion and during May 1916 saw their first service on the Riga front. K. Tiander, *Das Erwachen Osteuropas: Die Nationalitätenbewegung in Russland und der Weltkrieg*, Vienna and Leipzig: Wilhelm Braumuller, 1934, pp. 66–9.

16 O. Terletskyi, *Istoriia ukrainskoi hromady v Rashtati*, Kiev–Leipzig: Ukrainska nakladnia, 1919. Terletskyi was a teacher in the POW camps. By the end of the war, the Russian Army had lost nearly four million officers and soldiers to the enemy, primarily held captive in Germany and Austria, but also in Turkey and Bulgaria. N.N. Golovin, *Voennye usiliia Rossii v mirovoi voine*, Paris, T-vo obedinennykh izdatelei, 1939, vol. 1, p. 142.

17 For a series of reports by SVU members in POW camps, see National Archives of Canada, The Andry Zhuk Collection, MG 30, C 167, vol. 12.

18 "Zvit z Somorii," Zhuk collection, vol. 12, file 2. Several Russian soldiers protested to the SVU delegates and to the camp commandant against the distribution of literature that was expressly forbidden in Russia, especially the pamphlet "Tsari, pany i liudy." One drill sergeant even took upon himself the role of camp censor (Zhuk collection, vol. 12, file 3). On Russians volunteering to control the camp population, see also "Zvit-Raikhenberg," Zhuk collection, vol. 12, file 7, p. 17. Russian soldiers began to spread rumors that Ukrainians had surrendered voluntarily to the Austrians and hinted that they were traitors ("Zvit z Kliainminkhen/kolo Linz,", December 1914, Zhuk collection, vol. 12, file 5, p. 2).

19 Incidentally, it was not only Russians who protested against the Ukrainophile activities in the camps. Analogous reports concern Polish NCOs who refused to let soldiers identify themselves as Ukrainians, insisting that they were really Poles. The Poles in the camps, however, reserved most of their hostility for Russians ("Zvit z Kliainminkhen/kolo Linz," Zhuk collection, vol. 12, file 5). A constant concern of the SVU activists was to rid the Ukrainian barracks of "Black Hundred" elements who were disrupting the agitational program ("Pershi organizatsiini zbory suspilno pros'vitnoho hurtka,", 20 August 1915, Zhuk collection, vol. 12, file 17).

20 Golovin, *Voennyia usiliia*, vol. 1, p. 118.

21 Gosudarstvennyi voenno-istoricheskii arkhiv Rossiiskoi Federatsii, hereafter GVIARF f. 2003, op. 2, d. 323. On the formation of Polish *druzhiny*, see also f. 2000, d. 3882; f. 2003, op. 2, d. 691, l. 35. The first request, from Chelm province, to form Polish volunteer detachments for the Russian Army dates 20 August 1914. *Armeiskii vestnik*, 9 October 1914 announced that Polish Legions had been formed on the Russian side with the permission of the Supreme Commander-in-Chief.

22 GVIARF, f. 1759, op. 3, dd. 461, 477.

23 G. Korganoff, *La Participation des Arméniens à la Guerre Mondiale sur le Front du Caucase, 1914–1918*, Paris: Massis, 1927. In 1915 the Commander in Chief of the Caucasian Army was granted permission to form an Armenian rifle battalion, but was denied permission to form cavalry units until 1916. The first Armenian battalion was established 21 May 1916 (GVIARF f. 2003, op. 2, d. 325, l. 1).

24 On the impact of the war on the Habsburg armies, see I. Deak, *Beyond Nationalism: A Social and Political History of the Habsburg Officer Corps, 1848–1918*, Oxford: Oxford University Press, 1990, ch. 11.

25 At a Council of Ministers meeting, Prince V. N. Shakhovskoi criticized the military for its rapacious practices, "The systematic devastation of the front-line territories of the southwest forces one to think that the Supreme Command does not hope to recover this area for Russia and wants to leave the enemy a total desert." Iakhontov, *Prologue*, pp. 121–2.

26 According to Tiander (*Das Erwachen Osteuropas*, p. 137), nearly eight million Poles were fighting for the Central Powers, while another two million were serving in the Russian Army. Ingeborg Fleischhauer (*Die Deutschen im Zarenreich: Zwei Jahrhunderte deutsch-russische Kulturgemeinschaft*, Stuttgart, Deutsche Verlags-Anstalt, 1986 p. 461) estimates that well over 300,000 ethnic Germans served in the Tsar's army against their co-religionists and co-nationals on the German and Austrian side. Heinz-Dietrich Loewe, in *Antisemitismus und reaktionäre Utopie: Russischer Konservatismus im Kampf gegen den Wandel von Staat und Gesellschaft, 1890–1917*, Hamburg: Hoffmann und Campe Verlag, 1978, p. 146, estimates that nearly one-tenth of the Jewish population, or about 500,000 Jewish soldiers, fought in the ranks of the Russian Army.

27 Archbishop Evlogii speculates that Bobrinskii was chosen to head the occupation regime because of the popularity of his cousin, Vladimir Alekseevich. See Evlogii, *Put' moei zhizni: Vospominaniia Mitropolita Evlogiia*, izlozhennyia po ego rasskazam T. Manukhinoi, Paris, YMCA Press, 1947, p. 253. Vladimir Bobrinskii, 1867–1927 served as marshal of nobility for the *zemstvo* in Bogoroditsk district; then was elected to the second, third, and fourth Dumas where, as vice-chairman of the Nationalist Fraction, he advocated the liberation of the Slavs and the annexation of Eastern Galicia to the Russian Empire; in June 1910 he conducted an agitational tour of Galicia that was underwritten by Stolypin to the tune of 70,000 rubles. Tiander, *Das Erwachen Osteuropas*, p. 50; Vladimir I. Gurko, *Features and Figures of the Past: Government and Opinion in the Reign of Nicholas II*, Stanford, CA: Stanford University Press, 1939.

28 Ianushkevich was reputed to have been one of the most pathological anti-Semites among Russia's leaders. See W. Bruce Lincoln, *Passage through Armageddon: The Russians in War and Revolution*, New York: Simon & Schuster, 1986, pp. 141–2; Major-General Sir Alfred Knox, *With the Russian Army, 1914–1917*, London: Dutton, 1921, I, p. 290. As Chief of Staff, Ianushkevich was among the most vocal military officials who regularly denounced Germans, Jews, and Ukrainians as agents of the Central Powers and spies.

29 "Otchet kantseliarii voennogo general-gubernatora Galitsii v period vremeni s 28/VIII. 1914 po 1/VII. 1915," GVIARF f. 2003, op. 2, d. 539, ll. 1–85; and "Otchet vremennogo voennogo general-gubernatora Galitsii po upravleniiu kraem za vremia s 1-go/IX. 1914 g. po 1-go/VII. 1915 g.," ll. 1–26. For other accounts of the Russian occupation, see F. Przysiecki, *Rzady rosyjskie w Galicyi wschodniej*, Piotrkow: Wiadomosci Polskich, 1915; J.B. Cholodecki, *Lwow w czasie okupacji rosyjskiej, 3 wrzesnia 1914–22 czerwca 1915*, Lwow: Nakladen Towarzystwa milosnikow przeszlosci, 1930; B. Janusz, *Dokumenty urzedowe okupacyi rosyjskiej*, Lwow: Nakladen Towarzystwa Milosnikow Przeszlosci, 1916; B. Janusz, *293 dni rzadow rosyjskich we Lwowie*, Lwow: Nakladen Towarzystwa Milosnikow Przeszlosci, 1915; *Odezwy i rozporzadzenia z czasow okupacyi rosyjskiej Lwowa, 1914–1915*, Lwow: 1916; I. Petrovych, *Halychyna pidchas rosiis'koi*

okupatsii: serpen' 1914–cherven' 1915, L'viv: Politychna Biblioteka, 1915; A. Cholovskii, *L'vov vo vremena russkago vladychestva*, Petrograd?: 1915; M. Chlamtacz, *Lembergs politische Physiognomie während der russischen Invasion*, Vienna: R. Lechner, 1916.

30 R. Edelman, *Gentry Politics on the Eve of the Russian Revolution: The Nationalist Party, 1907–1917*, New Brunswick, NJ: Rutgers University Press, 1980. Among the prominent Kiev organizations was the Carpatho-Russian Liberation Committee, *Karpato-Russkii osvoboditel'nyi komitet*, whose chairman was Iulian Iavorskii. For a list of Bobrinskii's closest staff appointments, see "Otchet kantseliarii," GVIARF f. 2003, op. 2, d. 539, ll. 1–85. Most of the appointees came from the chancellery of the governor-general of Kiev, Podolia, and Volynia. Local administration was staffed with *zemstvo* activists, marshals of the nobility, *zemstvo* land captains, and officers transferred from Army ranks. Local notables were admitted to administrative service if they demonstrated the requisite loyalty.

31 Those areas under the military's formal jurisdiction included the capital, Transcaucasia, and the western borderlands, the latter inhabited by large non-Russian populations. See "Polozhenie o polevom upravlenii voisk v voennoe vremia," St. Petersburg: 1914, described in D. Graf, "Military Rule Behind the Russian Front, 1914–1917: The Political Ramifications," *Jahrbücher für Geschichte Osteuropas*, Neue Folge, Band 22, 1974, Heft 3, pp. 390ff. "O vvedenii v Kievskoi gubernii voennoi tsenzury," GVIARF f. 1759, dop. op., d. 1406. For special instructions on the administration of territories of Austria–Hungary occupied by Russian troops, see "Vremennoe polozhenie ob upravlenii oblastiami Avstro–Vengrii, zaniatymi po pravu voiny," GVIARF f.2003, op.2, d. 691, ll. 26–8. See also procedures for arresting spies and for deporting all Chinese merchants from the border region to the interior of Russia.

32 R.W. Coonrod, "The Duma's Attitude toward War-time Problems of Minority Groups," *American Slavic and East European Review*, 1954, vol. 13, pp. 30–8. Elsewhere in the Empire, anti-German riots shook Moscow in June 1915. Conservative and rightist deputies from the Duma called for the annihilation of the Baltic nobility. On the confiscation of German property and discriminatory economic measures during the war, see Fleischhauer, *Die Deutschen*, pp. 479–522.

33 See *Armeiskii vestnik*, 16 October 1914, p. 4; and D. Rempel, "The Expropriation of the German Colonists in South Russia during the Great War," *Journal of Modern History*, 1932, vol. 4, pp. 49–67. During the summer of 1915, Headquarters presented Agriculture Minister Krivoshein with a proposal to award soldiers who distinguished themselves in battle with land endowments from, among other sources, the confiscated estates of German colonists and enemy subjects. The measure was not enacted. See Iakhontov, *Prologue*, p. 22.

34 *Armeiskii vestnik*, 2 November 1914. The censors' reports were full of the following sentiment, "We are fighting against the Germans, but our leadership in Russia is all Germans. Who commands the Russian soldiers? Germans. You know very well that the Germans are winning everywhere without a fight" (GVIARF f. 1759, op. 4, d. 1846, l. 88). This particular report is dated 1916. During the fall of that year the censor reported, "They do not cease writing about the German preponderance" (f. 1759, op. 4, d. 1870, l. 255 ob).

35 See "O poriadke vyseleniia inostrannykh poddannykh i evreev vo vnutrennie gubernii Rossii i vyezde za granitsu inostrantsev," GVIARF f. 1759, dop. op., d. 1421.

36 On the deportations of the Jews, see "Iz 'chernoi knigi' russkago evreistva, materialy dlia istorii voiny, 1914–1915," *Evreiskaia Starina*, 1918, vol. 10, pp. 231–53; also "Dokumenty o presledovanii evreev," in I.V. Gessen (ed.), *Arkhiv russkoi revoliutsii*, vol. 19, Berlin: Terra, 1928, pp. 245–84. Because the military censor's office had no specialists in Yiddish, a ban on all publications and correspondence was implemented ("Prikaz

No. 389," 19 September 1914. GVIARF f. 1759, op. 4, d. 1843, ll. 9, 219–22). The censors' files are full of confiscated letters in Yiddish.

37 Loewe, *Antisemitismus*, p. 149; GVIARF f. 2003, op. 2, d. 950. From the archival evidence, military authorities spent much of their time compiling lists of Jews in various branches of the civilian and military administration.

38 GVIARF f. 2003, op. 2, dd. 701–2. The military authorities even devised a special questionnaire to ascertain the loyalty of Jewish soldiers (GVIARF f. 2067, dd. 3784, 3786; f. 2003, op. 2, d. 701, ll. 10–2). Ivanov wrote that "without fail at the end of the war we shall have to most seriously discuss the possibility of keeping Jews in the ranks of the army, or, in any case, the diminution of their numbers in combat units."

39 GVIARF f. 2003, op. 2, 701, l. 4. As of 20 March 1915, the Southwest Command reported 180,000 Jews in the army.

40 On 31 July 1914, all Austrian and German male subjects between the ages of 18 and 45 were declared prisoners of war and designated for deportation, except Rusyns, Czechs, and Serbs (GVIARF f. 1759, op. 3, d. 1420, l. 1). These measures were gradually refined to appeal to all potentially loyal Slavs among the Ottoman and Habsburg Empires. The archives reveal a fascinating conflict over the designation of who could be considered a foreign subject in wartime conditions and what sorts of differentiated policy could be developed to take advantage of the complicated sets of loyalties; see f. 1759, op. 3, d. 1420. See also a reference work for military officers published by the Commander-in-Chief of the Southwestern Front in July 1914, *Sovremennaia Galichina. Etnograficheskoe i kul'turno-politicheskoe sostoainie eia, v sviazi s natsional'no-obshchestvennymi nastroeniami.*

41 "Vypiska iz spiska poliakov neblagonadezhnykh v politicheskom otnoshenii i vrazhdebnykh russkoi Gosudarsvtennosti, prebyvanie koikh v tylu armii Iugo-Zapadnogo fronta nezhelatel'no i vredno," GVIARF f. 1759, op. 3, d. 1410, l. 24.

42 During the retreat of the Austrian Army, troops, especially Hungarian Honveds, unleashed a wave of terror on the local population. Hundreds of Galicians of all political persuasions were arrested and interned in concentration camps, the most notorious one at Talerhof in Styria. Talerhof and the Austrians' repressive policies served as a potent symbol for the Russian national and military press. See *Voennye prestupleniia Gabsburgskoi monarkhii 1914–1917 gg.: Galitskaia golgofa*, Trumbull, CT: Peter S. Hardy, 1964.

43 Bobrinskii's speech to the notables of occupied Lvov on 10 September 1914. An important symbolic moment in Bobrinskii's campaign for integration was the inauguration of direct rail service between Kiev and L'vov. See *Armeiskii vestnik*, 8 November 1914, p. 4, for the announcement and commentary on its significance. *Armeiskii vestnik* carried regular feature articles of Russian visitors to Galicia who marveled at how similar were the natives to their Russian brethren. See, for example, "Iz galitskikh vpechatlenii," 27 November 1914, or a series of articles written under the pseudonym of El'-Es' (real name Leonid Zakharovich Solov'ev) about the "restoration" of the lands to Russia. The Emperor himself visited L'vov to reaffirm the "historic ties" of Galicia to Russia, 9 April 1915.

44 "Otchet," GVIARF f. 2003, op. 2, d. 539, p. 21; p. 23. The bookstore of the Shevchenko Society was closed on 22 September 1914.

45 The lead editorial of *Armeiskii vestnik*, 18 September 1914, described a tumultuous "rehabilitation" of the Russian language: "The streets, public buildings and hotels of Lvov are covered in Russian signs; on the squares and street corners, the Russian newspaper *Prikarpatskaia Rus'*, recently closed by the Austrian government, is being sold; displayed in the windows of book stores is *The Grammar of the Russian Literary Language*, for which the author, S. Iu. Bendasiuk, sat in an Austrian jail for two years. Poles, Jews, Germans, and Armenians, all are studying Russian." Bendasiuk and Iuliian Iavorskii,

emigres from Galicia, arrived from Kiev with the occupying army to "restore" the Russian language to a prominent position.

46 "Otchet," GVIARF f. 2003, op. 2, d. 539, p. 40.

47 Tiander, *Das Erwachen Osteuropas*, p. 50; "Otchet," GVIARF f. 2003, op. 2, d. 539, l. 22. The Russian Ministry of Enlightenment opened only ten elementary schools during the occupation; the Synod, however, was far more active and opened nearly fifty schools during the same period. Much of this activity was coordinated by the Galician–Russian Benevolent Society, with its branches in Petersburg, Moscow, Kiev, Odessa and other cities. The local affiliates raised funds for "our Russophile comrades" in Galicia and stipends for students who were willing to attend Russian-language universities and institutes. Besides the *Galitsko–russkoe blagotvoritel'noe obshchestvo*, several other ideologically allied organizations were active in occupied Galicia: *Slavianskoe blagotvoritel'noe obshchestvo*, *slavianskie komitety*, and several *tserkovnye bratstva*. At the head of all of them stood Vladimir Bobrinskii. "Halychyna i Bukovyna," Zhuk collection, vol. 9, file 24.

48 Bobrinskii's policy was criticized by the conservative Russian newspaper *Novoe vremia* as too liberal to defend the interests of Orthodoxy. *Armeiskii vestnik*, 2 October 1914, p. 4.

49 Evlogii had been archbishop in Volynia and Zhitomir, served fifteen years as the bishop of Cholm, and had a long history of contacts with the Russophiles. The *Oberprokurator* of the Synod responsible for the appointment was V.K. Sabler. See also Evlogii's memoirs, *Put' moei zhizni*, p. 253; Evlogii claims that Sabler was against his appointment, but Tsar Nicholas intervened in Evlogii's favor.

50 O.W. Gerus, "The Ukrainian Question in the Russia Dumas, 1906–1917: An Overview," *Studia Ucrainica*, 1984, vol. 2, pp. 165–6. Grand Duke Nikolai Nikolaevich complained that the Russian officials in the newly occupied territories were so zealous in their efforts at the forcible conversion of Ukrainian Uniates to Orthodoxy that they commandeered desperately needed ammunition trains to transport priests to the region. Bruce Lincoln, *Passage through Armageddon: The Russians in War and Revolution, 1914–1918*, New York: Touchstone, 1986, p. 97, quotes Maurice Paleologue, *La Russie des Tsars pendant la Grande Guerre*, Paris: Plon, 1921, vol. 1, pp. 222–3.

51 General Polivanov defended the scorched earth policy before the Duma by appealing to the historical precedent of the 1812 campaign, but the Council of Ministers, including Polivanov, saw little wisdom in this decision by the Supreme Commander and much impending disaster. Iakhontov, *Prologue*, pp. 38–9. SVU activists protested against the Russian destruction in Cholm and Volynia provinces and against Bobrinskii's order of 7 May 1915. See Omelian Bachyns'kyi's editorials in *Vistnyk SVU*.

52 On the Jews, see "Otchet" GVIARF f. 2003, op. 2, d. 539, p. 20. On the waiver for Galician Russians, see *Armeiskii vestnik*, 21 June 1915, p. 3.

53 See Knox, *With the Russian Army*, vol. 1, for reports of an execution of a Jew as a spy for the Germans, p. 120; for violence between Jews and Cossacks, p. 171. On the eve of the departure from Warsaw, the military authorities ordered the arrest of "a whole mass of people—Poles and Jews—on suspicion of pro-Austrian sympathies." The arrested people, including minors, were sent to the rear and put into prisons. Iakhontov, *Prologue*, pp. 122–3.

54 Refugee aid organizations formed for Estonians and Latvians in Petrograd and for the flood of Polish refugees in Moscow (Tiander, *Das Erwachen Osteuropas*, pp. 51–2). The Polish *obywatelskie komitety*, for example, often refused to accept and treat Jewish refugees; see Sh. Anski, pseudonym of Sh. Z. Rapoport, *Gezamelte shriftn*, Warsaw: Ansky, 1928, vol. 5, pp. 32–3, cited in M. Stanislawski, "Refugees in Russia 1914–1916: The Institutional Stalemate," unpublished paper, p. 29. For Jewish communal life, see S.J. Zipperstein, "The Politics of Relief: The Transformation of Russian Jewish Communal Life During the First World War," in J. Frankel (ed.), *The Jews and the European Crisis, 1914–21*, vol. 4 of *Studies in Contemporary Jewry: An Annual*, Oxford: Oxford Univeristy

Press, 1988, esp. pp. 22–4. On the mechanics of refugee relief, see P.P. Gronskii, "The Effects of the War on the Central Government Institutions of Russia," unpublished manuscript, Hoover Institution Archives; T.I. Polner, V. Obolenskii, and S.P. Turin, *Russian Local Government During the War and the Union of Zemstvos*, New Haven, CT: Yale University Press, 1930. Gronskii, p. 52 lists the following national relief committees that formed during the war: the Polish Central Citizens' Committee, the Armenian Central Committee for Relief of War Sufferers; the Central Jewish Committee for the Relief of War Sufferers; the Committee of Baku Moslems Benevolent Society for Relief of War Sufferers on the Caucasian Front; the Lettish Aid Committee; the Central Committee of the Lithuanian Society for Relief of War Sufferers; the Chief Administration of the Georgian Society in the City of Tiflis, "and others."

55 Evgenii Nikol'skii, who served as the regional plenipotentiary of *Severopomoshch'*, reported that his predecessor in Riga had concerned himself overly with Polish refugees, thereby arousing discontent among all non-Polish refugees. See his typed report, "Bezhentsy v Velikuiu voinu," Hoover Institution Archives, p. 77. He also reports that an organization called "Rodina" took care of only Lithuanian refugees in Riga. The Benevolent Committee, *Blagotvoritel'nyi komitet*, headed by Vladimir Bobrinskii and several other prominent Russophiles, was the most active organization for relief to Galician peasants who had suffered during the destruction of the recent invasions.

56 Among the dilemmas created for the Imperial Government, the mass flight of Jews effectively breached the Pale of Settlement for the first time. Local governors in the inner provinces were overwhelmed with the arrival of so many refugees and warned that they could not be responsible for the safety of the new inhabitants, "because the people are worked up and there is agitation for pogroms, particularly on the part of soldiers coming back from the front." Iakhontov, *Prologue*, p. 58; also p. 102.

57 In the spring 1915 session of the Duma, the Kadet spokesman Miliukov attacked the "centrifugal tendencies" of the regime, the press policies, and above all the nationality policies of the occupying forces. He singled out the Jewish, Ukrainian, and Polish populations for special attention. The Social Democrats and *Trudoviki* proposed legislation eliminating all disabilities and discrimination based on nationality, but the Kadets were constrained by their allies in the Progressive Bloc from supporting so radical a measure. The Progressive Bloc that formed in August 1915 demanded an end to the persecutions in Galicia and the restoration of the Ukrainian press in all of Russian Ukraine. "Kadety v dni Galitsiiskogo razgroma 1915 g.," *Krasnyi arkhiv* 59, , pp. 112f., Loewe, 156n; see also the interpolation of Duma deputies Chkheidze, Menshevik, Kerenskii, Socialist-Revolutionaries *et al.*, protesting "the illegal actions of the government regarding the Jewish population in the theater of military operations," 20 July 1915, in *Prilozhenie k stenograficheskim otchetam-Gosudarstvennaia Duma*, 1915, p. 2.

58 He warned that far more attention to the loyalty of these refugees was needed. In particular, he noted that on the one hand, Stepan Borsuk, a convinced Russian patriot and active member of the Russophile party languished in jail and should be released immediately, while others of the "Mazepa party" were at large in Kiev, such as Timofei Starukh and his son. Starukh had been a noted member of the Viennese Parliament and Galician Sejm and had "the imprisonment and excution of many Russian people in Galicia on his conscience." Letter dated 30 June 1915, GVIARF f. 1759, op. 3, d. 1420, l. 318.

59 9 September 1915. GVIARF f. 1759, op. 3, 1420, l. 351.

60 "Pytannia iaki maiut' buty postavleni brantsevi," Zhuk collection, vol. 12, file 10. Among the questions were: 12.a. How did the people react to the mobilization and war and what did they think about them? b. What did the people think about those powers against whom the war was being waged? 13. How did the soldier himself react to a. and

b., previous question? 14. What did the leadership [*nachal'stvo*] tell the population and soldiers about [these matters] and about Austria-Hungary and Germany and Galicia? ... 16. How did the population of Galicia, Ukrainians, Poles, and Jews react to the Russian Army and, on the contrary, how did the army react to the population? 17. Had the soldier heard anything about Galicia before the war? 18. How did the population in Kingdom Poland react to the Russian, and how to the Austro-Hungarian and German armies?

61 After the arrival of the Russian Army in L'vov, many Ukrainian soldiers reported that they bought up as many books as they could, especially Shevchenko's *Kobzar*, some saying they wanted to die with Shevchenko near their hearts.

62 "Zvit," May 1915, Zhuk collection, vol. 12, file 8, p. III.

63 Mykola Kulish, the prominent Ukrainian playwright of the 1920s, first came into contact with the Ukrainian national movement in 1915 while serving in the ranks of the Russian army on the Austrian front in Galicia. G.S.N. Luckyj, *Literary Politics in the Soviet Ukraine, 1917–1934*, New York: Columbia University Press, 1956, p. 130.

4

WILL RUSSIA SURVIVE?

Center and periphery in the Russian Federation[*]

Steven Solnick

When Russia became independent in 1991, many Russian and Western observers predicted that the fragmentation that had doomed the USSR would not stop at the borders of the Russian Federation.[1] By the close of 1991, most of Russia's own autonomous republics had declared themselves "sovereign"; since each of these entities was the designated homeland of a different non-Russian ethnic group, the threat of ethnic conflict was real. In Tatarstan, for instance, radical nationalists calling for independence from Russia were drawing large crowds; in Chechnya, a secessionist movement succeeded in disarming and expelling Russian troops sent to quell the revolt.

More than four years later, however, many observers see the Russian Federation advancing inexorably toward a restoration of Soviet-style unitary centrism. Despite the military debacles that have trapped federal troops in Chechnya, separatism has not spread to the other ethnic republics. On the contrary, presidents of many of these republics have consolidated power at home and thrown in their lot with the "Party of Power" in Moscow. Meanwhile, governors of most of the predominantly Russian oblasts and krais were still appointed and dismissed directly by President Yeltsin until late 1996.[2]

This chapter examines the dynamics of federal state-building in Russia and seeks to explain why the expected conflagration has not occurred. In the course of this examination, some previous assumptions about Russia in particular, and about multi-ethnic federations in general, are questioned. If we portray center–periphery relations as the search for a federal "bargain" over distributional and jurisdictional issues, then asymmetries among sub-national units may be seen playing a more ambiguous role. In particular, the role of ethnicity in Russian federal bargaining may be less divisive than first thought: rather than pitting one ethnic group against another, the institutional inheritance of ethno-federalism may have served to unite a block of states capable of bargaining collectively with the center. The asymmetries produced by this block have, in turn, given Moscow some important room for maneuver as it seeks to consolidate central powers and

* The author is grateful to Stepan Titov and Kate Blumenreich for research assistance, and to Karen Ballentine and Hendrik Spruyt for constructive comments on an earlier draft.

prevent fragmentation. In other words, ethno-federal distinctions in Russia may have created more cohesion than division.

Before discussing the Russian case, the chapter first sketches out the nature of bargaining in a proto-federal state and the types of strategies available to national and sub-national actors. It then provides an overview of the Russian state structure as it has evolved since 1990, and discusses how the bargaining strategies pursued by federal and regional authorities have influenced the evolving Russian state structure. In particular, it examines how the ethnic republics effectively preserved their privileged status in an asymmetric federation, frustrating efforts by Moscow and the predominantly Russian oblasts and krais to either remove or universalize these benefits. Also considered here is how events since the end of 1995 have begun to erode this structural asymmetry. The chapter concludes by reviewing the implications of this analysis for our understanding of post-Soviet state-building.

The strategic environment of post-Soviet Russian domestic politics

As will be argued later in this paper, the actors in the Russian center and periphery are engaged in serious, protracted negotiations over the future shape of the Russian state. This section discusses how we might begin to model those negotiations.

State-building as a center–periphery bargaining game

In the state-building phase of any system containing regional and national levels of government, we can portray the center–periphery struggle as an ongoing bargaining game over the ultimate distribution of powers in the future state. In the post-Soviet Russian case, the actors are the federal authorities in Moscow and regional authorities in the eighty-nine "subjects" of the Russian Federation. Three features distinguish this N+1 player bargaining game:

1   The national government is bargaining with each of the federation subjects simultaneously, so the results of one negotiation can affect each of the others. The outcomes of any negotiation are important not merely for substantive policy decisions (over taxes, or personnel, or status), but also for the information they convey to other regional actors about the strategy and resources of the center. This information is especially important, since the bargaining process is not a one-shot episode, but rather is ongoing.
2   Since there is no external enforcement authority, any constitutional structure emerging from this bargaining game must be self-enforcing.[3] In other words, solutions to the center–periphery struggle must be perceived by the players as beneficial to all sides, unless the center is clearly (and unequivocally) prepared to employ force.

3   Not all actors are equal. Rather, sub-national units are almost always defined prior to the beginning of any state-building negotiations. In the Russian case, an asymmetrical federal structure was defined by the Soviet state for its own purposes (that is, ethnic policy) and these definitions created sub-national units with wide disparities in resource endowments, population, ethnic composition, and so on. While the bargaining process might be simplified if all sub-national units were more similar, the disparities among units becomes an important focus of the negotiations themselves. State structure, in other words, is highly "path dependent," with potential future outcomes highly constrained by decisions made in an earlier period.[4]

Though the term "federal" has been used loosely until now, it is useful to define it more precisely. According to Riker, a federal state consists of two levels of government ruling the same land and people, each having at least one area of action in which it is guaranteed autonomy.[5] The federal "bargain" therefore, must determine an acceptable and lasting division of authority between levels of government.[6] In a centralized federal state, most functions are performed by the federal authorities; in a peripheralized federal state, the federal center is sharply constrained. Centralized federal systems are more likely to survive centrifugal pressures, but are also more likely to see regional autonomy trampled by expanding federal authority. Peripheralized federal states, on the other hand, are more likely to succumb to regional conflict or even civil war. Different state structures have very different distributional consequences: centralized federalisms are more likely to be able to redistribute resources to poorer subjects, while regional disparities (and, consequently, inter-regional tensions) are likely to be greater in peripheralized systems.

Centralization or peripheralization are not the only potential outcomes of this bargaining game. A hybrid result—an asymmetric federation—is also possible, in which certain units (or groups of units) enjoy higher status and greater powers and privileges.

Federal and regional strategies

What determines whether a federal "bargain" can be reached, and what shape it may take? Different strategies adopted by federal and regional authorities may promote, or erode, different bargaining equilibria. This analysis presented here focuses on whether the center deals with sub-national actors collectively or individually, and whether these regional actors are themselves capable of collective action.

Federal strategies

In any iterated game in which one established actor faces multiple challengers, the established player may choose to invest in reputation in order to deter future aggression. This may involve bearing heavy costs to deter early aggression, in order to signal future challengers that no concessions will be made and therefore no further challenges should be attempted.[7]

In the context of center–periphery bargaining, a reputation-building strategy by the center amounts to establishing uniform and transparent rules for intergovernmental relations and then punishing all transgressions from stated rules. The World Bank, for instance, has been a strong proponent of "transparent" revenue-sharing arrangements and has been critical of a provincial contracting scheme employed by Chinese authorities. According to a recent World Bank study, the Chinese scheme has permitted the provinces to "bargain down" their contributions to the center, leaving the national government severely under-funded, and has exacerbated boom-bust cycles at the regional level.[8]

Transparent rules need not dictate identical treatment for all regional actors, nor does it dictate greater centralization. Rather, the critical element is that jurisdictional and distributional issues are fixed and not subject to *ad hoc* bilateral renegotiation. Sub-national actors, in other words, cannot gain special treatment from the center by virtue of unilateral changes in strategy or behavior. Though rules may favor some territories over others, they apply equally to all of them.

A critical problem with transparent and clearly delineated rules is that the reputation of the national government is just as likely to be eroded by such an arrangement as it is to be enhanced. If, for example, revenue-sharing norms are firm and not open to *ad hoc* renegotiation, open regional defiance can quickly undermine the center's credibility. If the central authorities are weak, it may be better for their weakness to remain partly obscured by a veil of "ad hocery."

Federal authorities fearing that they might not be able to impose universal rules, therefore, might prefer to employ independent bilateral negotiation as an alternative bargaining tactic. According to this strategy, different regions could negotiate different deals with federal authorities. Under such a system, federal authorities would essentially be offering side-payments to specific regions in return for their acceptance of a specific jurisdictional and distributional deal.

A selective negotiating strategy could be used, for instance, to reward regions that have shown particular loyalty to the federal regime; this has been the hallmark of Chinese regional policy.[9] Conversely, a similar strategy could be used to "buy" the consent of separatist regions; this is more commonly the route that produces ethno-federal arrangements. Daniel Elazar has coined the term "foralistic" federalism to describe such an incrementally negotiated state structure, deriving it from the Spanish practice of granting special privileges (*fueros*, or exceptions) to individual regional groups.[10]

Provincial strategies

As labor unionists have demonstrated, actors bargaining with a common central authority can realize potential gains from bargaining collectively. In the case of federal bargaining, a block of territories that is able to act together can make a far more credible threat of disrupting state affairs than any single territory acting alone; at the same time, agreement with a block of territories will strengthen the center in future negotiations with unaffiliated regions.

Collective action is difficult to achieve, however, especially among territories with different economic and social bases. Ideally, a bargaining bloc should be large enough to exact concessions from the center, yet small enough to discourage free riding.[11] In federal bargaining, the problem of coordination is especially acute: the short-term distributional game is likely to appear to be zero sum, and stronger regions will face constant temptations either to seek a better bilateral deal with the center or at least to ignore transgressions by the center against weaker coalition members.[12] Ultimately, the viability of any bargaining coalition will depend upon whether sub-national actors distrust each other less than they each distrust the center. The presence or absence of effective inter-regional coordination mechanisms will be an important factor affecting the degree of inter-regional trust, and hence collective action.

Naturally, the center will not watch passively as sub-national collective action emerges or dissolves. Under some circumstances, federal authorities may prefer dealing with a few large blocs rather than a diverse set of unruly territories. However, since stronger regions implies a weaker center, we might expect federal authorities to seek to limit regional coordination. For instance, they may offer the more powerful regions special deals in order to lure them away from emerging regional coalitions. As discussed below, this tactic has been an important tool in the center's management of both regions and republics.

Potential bargaining outcomes

The preceding discussion suggests that national and sub-national strategies are likely to be interdependent. More significant for the purposes of this discussion, the ultimate likelihood of conflict or coordination, and the ultimate shape of the state itself, will be strongly affected by the strategies chosen. Figure 4.1 portrays the relation between bargaining strategies and structural outcomes.

If territories are unable to bargain collectively, the center can attempt to impose transparent and universal rules, resulting in a unitary state (southwest quadrant of Figure 4.1). If, however, the center engages in *ad hoc* bargaining with individual regions, it runs the risk of triggering a cascade of escalating demands, as regions respond to inter-regional inequalities (northwest quadrant). In extreme cases, this scenario could lead to open conflict—either among sub-national units, or between them and the center—or to a quasi-feudalistic structure based on personal networks linking elites at various levels.

If some regions are able to form coalitions for bargaining with the center, they may be able to exact concessions from federal authorities. At the same time, unaligned regions may seek to strengthen the federal center as a safeguard against domination by emerging blocs. This scenario could lead to a federal bargain incorporating a strong center and/or asymmetrical treatment of regional groups (this corresponds to the central area of Figure 4.1).

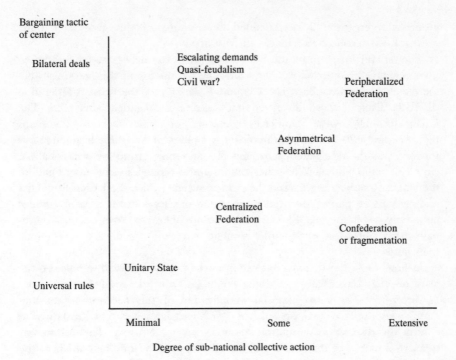

Figure 4.1 Potential outcomes of federal bargaining

If, however, regional coalitions become stronger and more comprehensive, the role for the center may diminish. With little bargaining leverage left to federal authorities, this scenario could lead either to a peripheralized federal state or to a confederation (as in the northeast and southeast quadrants of Figure 4.1). In extreme cases, like that of the Soviet Union, regional blocs may break away from the federal state altogether.

The remainder of this paper will apply this preceding model to post-Soviet Russia. As argued below, the path-dependent character of post-Soviet federal bargaining facilitated collective action for one subset of sub-national actors—the ethnic republics. As a consequence, the options available to federal authorities in Moscow have been highly constrained. Whether ongoing center–periphery nego-tiations produce conflict or a lasting federal bargain will depend, in large part, on whether the center can remove some of these constraints. Before exploring these issues, however, I must detour to provide some historical background.

Soviet and Russian state structure: 1990–6

The Soviet Union was a multi-ethnic federation in which major ethnic groups were associated with particular national "homelands." This linkage of ethnic groups with territorial divisions defined the structure as "ethno-federal," and the present Russian constitution retains this distinction.

The federal structure of the Soviet state was extremely complex and based upon a detailed hierarchy of federal sub-units. At the top of this hierarchy were the fifteen Union Republics, like Ukraine, Kazakstan or the Russian Federation (RSFSR). Each of these fifteen republics became independent after 1991. The Union Republics were themselves composed of some twenty autonomous republics and 120 territorial-administrative oblasts or krais. Each autonomous republic was the designated homeland of one ethnic group (or occasionally a cluster of nationalities). While these autonomous republics were subordinate to the Union Republics and lacked the right to secede (which the Union Republics had, at least on paper), they did have certain privileges in the area of cultural autonomy and home rule. Eighteen autonomous oblasts or okrugs, each subordinate to an oblast or autonomous republic, constituted a third tier of ethnic homelands.

In June 1990, the Russian Federation's newly elected legislature followed the lead of the Caucasian and Baltic republics and declared Russia to be "sovereign."[13] The most important implication of this declaration was that Russia's laws were to take precedence over Soviet laws, and that Russia was to control the disposition of natural resources on her territory. This action was quickly mimicked by the sixteen autonomous republics within the borders of the Russian Federation, eager to seize the opportunity to gain greater control over their own affairs. By October of 1990, eleven of these sixteen republics had passed their own sovereignty declarations.[14]

Though initially wary of the long-range implications of these developments, Boris Yeltsin quickly decided to enlist the autonomous republics in his more pressing struggle against Mikhail Gorbachev. Noting that Gorbachev's opposition to republican declarations of autonomy were futile, Yeltsin told the leaders of his autonomous republics to "take as much autonomy as you can swallow."[15] When the Soviet Union disintegrated in December 1991, Yeltsin had to scramble to make good on his pledge while consolidating the new state. Many observers expected him to fail, and Russian commentators in early 1992 were fond of punning "razvivatsiia Rossii" (Russia's development) into "razviazatsiia Rossii" (Russia's unraveling).

Yeltsin attempted to secure the allegiance of the restive autonomous republics by offering to sign a "federation treaty" with them that would serve as the basis for a new, post-Soviet constitution. According to this treaty, the republics were acknowledged to be "sovereign republics within the Russian Federation" with property rights over land and natural resources on their territory.[16] The gambit backfired, however, when the remaining oblasts of the federation objected to being permanently relegated to second-class status. As one analyst in *Moscow News* observed: "Twenty three million Russian subjects will live in a federation, and another 124 [million] will live in a unitary state."[17]

Hoping to stave off a revolt from the oblasts but still eager to reach consensus on at least a provisional state structure, Yeltsin signed three similar treaties in March 1992: one with the autonomous republics (and four autonomous oblasts elevated to republic status—Adygea, Gorno-Altai, Karachai-Cherkassia, and Khakassia); one with the lesser autonomous okrugs; and one with the non-ethnic oblasts and krais (and the "federal cities" of Moscow and St. Petersburg, which essentially received treatment as oblasts). These federation treaties recognized two different classes of "subjects of the Federation": twenty-one ethnic republics and sixty-eight administrative-territorial regions.[18] Territories in the former group, which here are called simply "republics," were recognized by federation treaty as "sovereign states" and were promised expanded rights over their natural resources, external trade, and internal budgets. Two republics, Tatarstan and Chechnya, insisted on a fuller statement of their independence from Moscow and refused to sign the treaties. The non-republic territories—which here are simply called "regions"—received few enhanced rights beyond their designation as "subjects of the Federation," the same term used to describe the republics.

Subjects of the Federation soon found themselves in the middle of the ongoing struggle between Yeltsin and the Russian parliament. In the national referendum of 25 April 1993, Boris Yeltsin's showing in Russia's regions was significantly stronger than in her republics. On the first question on the ballot, inquiring about "trust in the President," Yeltsin failed to carry ten of the twenty republics participating in the vote (no balloting was held in the Chechen Republic); he failed to carry just sixteen of the sixty-eight regions.[19] Following Yeltsin's overall success in the referendum, attempts to devise a new constitutional foundation alternated between courting the intransigent republics and moving to strip them of their privileges.

In July, a specially convened Constitutional Assembly was initially reluctant to preserve the republics' "sovereign" status in the new draft of the Russian constitution; the remaining federation subjects demanded equal rights. The draft ultimately approved by the Assembly, however, embodied the essential clauses of the federation treaty, including republican "sovereignty." Nevertheless, this draft received the support of representatives from just eight of these twenty-one republics, and ultimately failed to generate much political support among provincial leaders of either stripe.[20]

Yeltsin made one final attempt in August 1993 to win the support of provincial leaders for a draft constitution that could break his increasingly bitter deadlock with the Russian parliament. Yeltsin met with regional and republican representatives in Petrozavodsk and proposed the creation of a Federation Council that would be staffed, *ex officio*, by representatives of the eighty-nine provincial governments, and would serve as the upper house of the new Russian Parliament. The proposal, however, was seen as by regional leaders as a short-term ploy to circumvent the Supreme Soviet, then controlled by Yeltsin's political enemy, Ruslan Khasbulatov. In the longer term, there was no guarantee a similar ploy would not be used to undermine the Federation Council itself. Republic leaders, meanwhile, objected to the proposal's equal treatment of all Federation subjects, which would have left them badly outnumbered by the predominantly Russian oblasts.[21]

After the Federation Council scheme was finally rejected by regional and republican leaders in mid-September, Yeltsin launched his decisive attack on the old Parliament. His victory on 3–4 October was achieved with little help from provincial leaders. Many had declared his move unconstitutional—and a majority of provincial leaders had even attempted to seize power at the expense of both the President and Parliament by establishing a short-lived "Council of the Subjects of the Federation."[22]

In the wake of the "October events," republics began to lose many of the privileges accumulated in earlier agreements, and the role of the center *vis-à-vis* the provinces was strengthened. The new constitution, ratified on 12 December, treated republics and regions essentially as equals and dropped earlier references to republican sovereignty. Predictably, the new constitution was not well received in the republics: voters in nine of the twenty-one opposed it outright, while another half-dozen either boycotted the referendum or failed to attract the required 50 percent of registered voters.[23] As 1994 began, only two republics— Chechnya and Tatarstan—refused to acknowledge the legitimacy of the new constitution.

On 15 February 1994, Yeltsin signed a bilateral treaty with Tatarstan defining the respective roles of federal and republican authorities. Though the treaty actually granted Tatarstan few real rights beyond those granted to republics in the new constitution, the move satisfied Kazan's long-standing demand to be treated as an equal by Moscow. Having just concluded a protracted exercise in constitution-drafting, Yeltsin thus re-opened the door for other subjects of the federation to demand special treatment. Despite repeated avowals that no more bilateral "treaties" would be signed, by the end of 1995, Moscow had signed similar documents with six other republics: Kabardino-Balkaria, Bashkortostan, North Ossetia, Sakha/Yakutia, Buryatia and Udmurtia. In 1996, Yeltsin began to offer similar bilateral treaties to the oblasts and krais, concluding deals with Sverdlovsk, Orenburg, Kaliningrad, Krasnodar, and Khabarovsk, as well as the Republic of Komi.[24] Still more treaties with both republics and oblasts/krais were signed during the 1996 Presidential campaign.

From this quick overview, Russian federal policy appears to be essentially *ad hoc*, determined largely by the personalities of particular leaders at the national and sub-national level. How can we begin to analyze the broader systemic of forces pushing Russia toward greater centralization or decentralization?

National and sub-national bargaining strategies in Russia

Is Russian federal bargaining "real"?

The preceding account offers some justification for portraying post-Soviet constitutional politics as a set of ongoing negotiations between center and periphery over jurisdictional and distributional issues. Russian regions (or at least some of them) apparently have the power to frustrate the state-building process by with-holding their consent. Given the "sham" nature of Soviet federalism, it is worth pausing to consider how the regions and republics of post-Soviet Russia acquired this power.

The leverage of the regions and republics has not been limited to their influ-ence over the abortive constitution-drafting process. During 1992 and again in 1993, up to thirty subjects of the federation withheld their contributions to the federal budget and demanded special tax regimes or new federal subsidies. Partly as a consequence of these actions, and partly as a result of deliberate devolution of social policies to the provincial level, the percentage of overall government expen-ditures at the federal level dropped from 65 percent in 1992 to 35 percent in 1994.[25] The massive privatization program begun in 1992 was largely conducted at the provincial level, with State Property Funds in each republic or region deter-mining the terms of regional privatization.[26] Control over the levers of privatization put massive resources under the direct control of regional leaders. And, finally, Yeltsin's initial pursuit of a Federation Treaty established the impor-tance of regional consent for the implementation of any constitutional plan.[27]

The preceding catalogue of provincial bargaining assets suggests that Moscow was not free to dictate its desired outcome; it does not imply, however, that Moscow was wholly at the mercy of its provinces. Since the Soviet state had been highly centralized, most administrative, communication, transportation and information networks flowed to and from Moscow. Any talk of regional autarchy was mostly fantasy; even states as large as Belarus and Ukraine have discovered that their economic and infrastructural dependence on Moscow was deep and complex. More important, Yeltsin had the power to appoint and dismiss the heads of administration ("governors") of the oblasts and krais, though not of the republics. In the wake of the October 1993 presidential coup, Yeltsin ordered all provincial legislatures disbanded until new elections could be held; he did not, however, take any systematic action against governors who had failed to support him.

It is not immediately obvious, therefore, that either Moscow or her provinces held the decisive hand in the ongoing bargaining process. As suggested earlier, outcomes of this bargaining game were highly sensitive to the particular strategies chosen by the respective actors, which are now considered below.

Moscow's options: transparent rules vs. selective rewards

Figure 4.2 plots the development of Russian federal negotiations within the frame-work developed earlier in this paper. In 1990, the Russian Federation was still essentially a unitary state, run from Moscow with few inter-regional coalitions of any real significance. By 1994, it had developed into a highly asymmetrical federa-tion, with Moscow engaged in extensive selective bargaining with subjects of the federation, and sharp distinctions between the treatment of ethnic republics and non-ethnic regions. The following section traces movement along the vertical axis

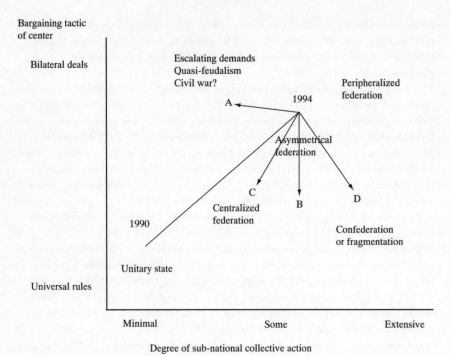

Figure 4.2 Paths of Russian federal negotiations

of Figure 4.2, the federal strategies; sub-national strategies are dealt with in subsequent sections.

Moscow's abandonment of universal rules to guide regional policy came swiftly after the Soviet collapse. Several republics won special deals in return for their acceptance of the 1992 federation treaties. Bashkortostan, for instance, demanded a special appendix granting it additional control over its foreign trade.[28] The Republic of Sakha, a major gold and diamond center occupying a vast territory in Siberia, won the right to retain a significant share of its mining revenues.[29]

Russian regional fiscal policy has also featured both overt and covert tactics for selectively favoring certain regions. In the most explicit variant, preferential tax retention rates or even direct subsidies are granted to some regions as the result of bilateral negotiations. More difficult to assess are those cases in which Moscow simply acquiesces in the unilateral decision of some regions to withhold higher than normal shares of tax revenues.

Poorer agricultural or industrial regions have begun to complain openly about the preferential treatment accorded to certain resource-rich republics. The fiscal picture is further complicated by the nature of simultaneous transactions involved in the overall budgeting process: provincial tax remittances to the federal budget are frequently offset by transfers and subventions from the center into local budgets or by high levels of expenditures on the region out of the federal budget. These complex cross-flows have led to no small share of confusion over exactly who is benefiting and who is suffering from the current fiscal regime.[30]

One dominant theme that has clearly emerged, however, is that the system in place at the beginning of 1992 was inequitable.[31] According to one analyst, only 10 percent of subsidies of regional budgets from the center went to territories facing severe environmental or climatic hardships (that is, to regions where the center should be expected to offset natural disadvantages). The remaining 90 percent went to republics like Sakha, Tatarstan and Bashkortostan, whose per capita incomes are above the national average. The resulting sense of injustice, a direct consequence of the center's selective benefits strategy, is captured in one analyst's rhetorical climax: "Why should Ulianovsk oblast have to pay back one-quarter of its legal revenues, if as a result its per capita budget is two-thirds that of neighboring Tatarstan?"[32]

On closer examination, however, it is difficult to be sure who is actually winning and who is losing from Moscow's manipulation of fiscal policy. Attempts to sort out the chief beneficiaries of Moscow's largesse (or weakness) are highly sensitive to the choice of indicator. For instance, if we consider the percentage of total tax revenues collected that are forwarded to the national level, then 1992 figures ranged from over 60 percent to less than 30 percent.[33] If we look instead at the net revenue transfers to the regions (subsidies and subventions minus tax remittances), we get a different set of winners and losers.[34] Yet another picture emerges if one considers not just federal subsidies, but also preferential tax sharing arrangements; in this case eight territories with per capita regional budgets above the national norm emerge as net recipients of federal subsidies while ten territories with per capita regional budgets below the national average emerge as net donors.[35]

Such conflicting signals invite charges of discrimination from many regional leaders. One fact seems little in dispute, however: predominantly Russian regions emerged by any measure as the most consistent losers under the revenue-sharing schemes in effect during 1992–5, while the ethnic republics emerged as consistent winners. One analyst, reflecting on the center's strategy, suggested that the pattern of selective distribution of benefits may be less a program to distribute political rewards than an effort to conceal political weakness: "Perhaps this is happening because some of the republics comprising Russia have decided not to pay any taxes to the center, and the center, rather than use force, decided to shift the tax burden to others?"[36]

Only once, after the violent disbanding of Parliament in October 1993, did Moscow seriously attempt to impose a universal and transparent set of fiscal rules. On 27 October 1993, Yeltsin signed a Presidential decree ordering the Council of Ministers to impose harsh sanctions against any regions or republics delinquent in the payment of tax revenues to the center, including suspending all federal financing of activities within the region, embargoing centrally distributed goods (including imports), and confiscating regional accounts in the Russian Central Bank.[37] The move was effective, prompting all but Tatarstan and Chechnya to resume paying taxes to the federal budget, and it gave teeth to the new constitution's declaration of equality among federation subjects.

With the signing of the February 1994 treaty with Tatarstan, however, *ad hoc* bilateral deals were once again the chief mechanism for establishing constitutional order. The treaty granted both republican and federal authorities rights to set and levy taxes, but left unclear whether the revenue-sharing formulas applied to Russia's other territories would automatically apply in Tatarstan. The subsequent deal with Bashkortostan was more explicit in granting that republic the right to operate a "single-channel" tax system, whereby a single lump-sum payment would be sent to Moscow by republic leaders.

The bilateral "treaties" signed in 1994 and 1995, like the special tax regimes before them and the federation treaties before that, were concluded only with ethnic republics. The Federation could credibly claim, therefore, that such deals were the exclusive prerogative of republics, and not available for oblasts and krais. In January 1996, however, Yeltsin signed similar treaties with Sverdlovsk, Kaliningrad and Orenburg oblasts and Krasnodar krai. The floodgates were again open, and all of the remaining fifty-six predominantly Russian subjects of the federation began demanding their own treaties to clarify center–periphery distributional and jurisdictional questions. The following two sections consider the sources of the republics' monopoly on formal agreements with Moscow, and why it took so long for the Russian regions to be able to break it.[38]

Regional collective action: republics vs. regions

Collective action at the sub-national level has been substantial since 1994, but certainly not universal. To be more precise, Russia's twenty ethnic republics (excepting Chechnya) maintained a *de facto* coalition that has worked to preserve their privileges. The Russian regions, on the other hand, were unable either to strip the republics of their special status, or to unite to bargain effectively for comparable privileges for themselves.

The success of the Russian republics points to an interesting role for the "ethnic factor" in the Russian federation. In more conventional settings, ethnic organization can serve as a means to facilitate collective action.[39] Ethnicity offers a mechanism for coordinating activity in pursuit of distributional benefits, while facilitating the selective exclusion of benefits from non-group members. From this perspective, ethnicity serves too conveniently to divide one group from another; for this reason, ethno-federal systems are held to be dangerously unstable.

In the Russian federal bargaining game, however, ethnic republics were initially accorded privileged status as a consequence of the Soviet imperial heritage. While this status is linked to their designation as ethnic "homelands," it is important to note that most are not minority enclaves, nationalism-based claims have been muted, and the republics have little in common. On the contrary, Russians constitute a majority or plurality in twelve of the twenty initial ethnic republics, and the titular minority group represents an absolute majority of the population in just six of them. In the Republic of Sakha (Yakutia), recipient of the most generous revenue sharing deal in 1992, just 33 percent of the population is Yakut; Bashkirs constitute just 22 percent of the population of Bashkortostan. Paradoxically, the most "indigenous" republics—Dagestan, Chuvashia, Tyva—have yet to receive special bilateral "treaties."[40]

Rather than relying on the force of ethnic and nationalist demands, the leaders of the ethnic republics have focused on preserving the republics as a privileged class of sub-national actors. While this distinction has been justified by reference to claims of cultural autonomy, its force has derived from the united front presented by all twenty republics, resource-rich and resource-poor alike. Ethnic claims, in other words, serve as a coordinating mechanism across different ethnic republics, distinguishing them from the Russian regions. Any proposal to eliminate the distinction between regions and republics, in other words, can be recognized immediately by each of the republics as a direct threat to its own interests.

Early in the constitution-drafting process, Moscow officials attempted to eliminate the emerging asymmetries in the federation by reorganizing the republics and oblasts into equal "*zemli*" (lands, patterned on the German *länder*) having equal status in the federation.[41] The proposal failed to attract the expected support of the Russian oblasts, however, since it called for a nationwide redrawing of the map that would have unseated regional and republican elites alike. Deprived of the support of the Russian regions, the proposal was subjected to furious attack by the ethnic republics. The republics—led by gold and diamond-rich Sakha and oil-rich Tatarstan—threatened to leave the federation if the proposal was not dropped. The Congress of People's Deputies refused to even consider the plan. Its author, Oleg Rumiantsev, later observed that the word "*zemli*" acted as a "red flag to the autonomies [republics]."[42]

Throughout 1993 and 1994, regions complained in vain about the political and economic privileges enjoyed by the republics. In May 1993, for instance, during another constitution-drafting round, leaders of five oblasts in the Urals revived the idea of merging regions and republics into "guberniias formed not on an ethnic, but on a territorial principal."[43] A year later, another proposal to reconstitute the federation into fourteen economic zones was motivated by the observation that "administrative-territorial divisions are in an unequal position with respect to the other members of the Federation" despite the fact that "the majority of Russia's population lives in the territories and provinces."[44]

In response to these critiques, republic leaders perpetually cite the "special concerns" of the ethnic homelands. Typical is the justification offered by Muraza Rakhimov, President of Bashkortostan, for his bilateral treaty with Moscow:

> I feel that if we actually want to have a truly federative state, Russia must sign bilateral treaties with all the republics forming the Federation. Because it is not the krais and oblasts that form the Federation. The Federation is made up of all the republics . . . .

> There are those among us who want to make the republics, oblasts and krais completely equal politically. That cannot be allowed. Economically they must all be identical . . . . But there are questions that arise, for instance, in Bashkiria and Tatarstan, that do not arise in the oblasts. In Sverdlovsk oblast, for example, the nationality question does not arise.[45]

The effectiveness, and limitations, of the coalition of republics was evident after the invasion of Chechnya. Opposition to the war was much more vocal from the ethnic republics than from the Russian regions.[46] Citing opposition to the war from Karelia, which lacks any Muslim population, one political geographer noted that "the factor of status is also important, not simply religious and ethnic kinship."[47] Seizing the opportunity to revitalize their coalition, a meeting in Cheboksary of seven republic presidents called for the re-establishment of the "Council of Heads of the Republics," which had been abolished in the aftermath of the October 1993 presidential coup.[48] Most dramatically, the President of Chuvashia signed an unconstitutional decree permitting Chuvash soldiers to refuse duty in Chechnya.[49]

Opposition to the war was more muted, however, from Tatarstan and Bashkortostan, Muslim oil republics, like Chechnya, but signatories to their own bilateral deals with Moscow in the previous year.[50] Though leaders of these republics attended the Cheboksary meeting, they have responded to the invasion not with threats but with offers to mediate. Given the parallels between their republics and Chechnya, the lack of a more forceful reply has been surprising to many. Indeed, Nationalities Minister Nikolai Yegorov acknowledged that the Chechen invasion would have triggered a civil war had it occurred three years earlier; he speculated that the Chechen President, Dzhokhar Dudaev, had failed to realize that the situation had changed radically.[51]

From this perspective, then, Moscow's strategy in pursuing *ad hoc* regional treaties might be seen as serving a dual purpose. In addition to placating restive republics, the center may have also weakened the coordinating mechanism that had permitted the republics to act collectively since 1990. If Tatarstan, for instance, derives its special benefits from its bilateral treaty rather than from its status as a republic, then perhaps it will be less likely to incur costs to preserve the distinction between regions and republics. If this is the case, the latest calls for the establishment of "guberniias" or "economic regions" may well have some chance of success.

Regional responses to asymmetries

The previous section suggests that homeland status served as an effective coordinating device for the ethnic republics, enabling them to act collectively to preserve their privileged status and exclude significant benefits to non-republics. Why were the Russian oblasts and krais unable to devise any of their own effective mechanisms to coordinate their bargaining with federal authorities, and what caused the center to finally acknowledge their equal right to bilateral treaties?

Several efforts were made in recent years to form regional associations that might be able to bargain more effectively with Moscow and serve as an alternative to the exclusive "club" of republics. Few of these have amounted to much more than regional trade associations. The most durable and successful of these ventures, the so-called "Siberian Agreement," served briefly as a conduit for regional opposition to Yeltsin. In the long run, however, the capacity of member regions to deal collectively with the center was undermined by inter-regional economic differences and Moscow's manipulation of the status of autonomous okrugs within the Siberian oblasts.[52] The potential benefits of collective action, in other words, were outweighed by the selective benefits controlled by Moscow.

In the wake of the signing of the asymmetric federation treaties, several oblasts began plotting to unilaterally elevate their own status to match that of republics. While several regions, including Vologda, Primorskii Krai, and Krasnoiarsk, issued grand declarations, the most serious effort came in Yeltsin's old home oblast of Sverdlovsk. The fate of the short-lived "Urals Republic" demonstrates both the obstacles to regional integration, and the wide range of options available to federal authorities in Moscow. In 1990, five oblasts in the Urals region (Kurgan, Orenburg, Perm, Cheliabinsk, and Sverdlovsk) formed a "Greater Urals" associa- tion to promote regional development.[53] In 1993, these five oblasts criticized the ongoing constitution-drafting process for preserving the distinction between oblasts and republics.[54] The first proposals began to circulate for converting the Grand Urals association into a "Urals Republic."

At roughly the same time, federal authorities began seeking to disrupt the unity of the "Urals Five." Prime Minister Chernomyrdin visited Orenburg oblast, bearing a draft decree "On the Socioeconomic Status of Orenburg Province." Such decrees were the standard format for the center to deliver economic rewards (tax breaks, subsidies, investments, free enterprise zone status, and so on) to indi- vidual regions. Not long afterward, the governor of Orenburg was heaping scorn on the Grand Urals scheme, claiming that "as soon as the first signs of glorious Yekaterinburg's [Sverdlovsk's] bid for leadership were apparent, the other members of the association lost interest in their offspring."[55]

Undeterred by the defections of its neighbors, on 1 July 1993, Sverdlovsk oblast declared "that it is upgrading the status of Sverdlovsk oblast to a republic within the Russian Federation (the Urals Republic)."[56] The move was described as a direct response to dissatisfaction with the "existing asymmetrical federal model"; no secessionist claims were advanced. The Sverdlovsk declaration invited other Urals oblasts to join the republic, but their immediate reactions were guarded.[57] The governor of Perm complained about the ethnic republics' "unjustified advan- tages and privileges" and declared "ideally our aim is . . . exactly the same status the republics have."[58] The Speaker of the Cheliabinsk soviet agreed that "the important thing is for us to get rid of discrimination."[59] Neither region moved to join, however. The governor of Orenburg, not surprisingly, was more openly skeptical, declaring: "The formation of individual republics will lead to nowhere."[60]

The response of the republics to the Urals Republic was predictably hostile. Murtaza Rakhimov, soon to become President of Bashkortostan, saw the hand of Moscow behind the declaration from Sverdlovsk: "Who gave them the right to call themselves a Urals Republic? The Bashkirs, Tatars, Chuvash, Maris, Mordvins, and Udmurts lived in the Urals long before the coming of the Russians."[61] Perhaps reflecting his confidence in the ability of republics to reject this challenge, Rakhimov concluded by shrugging off the entire episode: "Many stupid things are being done today."

By mid-July, it was becoming clear that the Urals Republic was not serving to promote collective action among the Urals oblasts. Cheliabinsk officials began planning for a "South Urals Republic."[62] By September, however, as the political crisis in Moscow was coming to a head and the wave of tax withholding was beginning to crest, the Urals Five again pledged to consider political integration.[63] According to Aleksei Vorobiev, an advisor to Eduard Rossel, Sverdlovsk's governor and godfather of the Urals Republic scheme, neighboring regions supported political integration, but "as soon as it came down to signing memoranda of intentions people would get up from the negotiating table. . . . You would have had to have been there to understand just how awkward it felt sometimes."[64] Undeterred, the Sverdlovsk soviet drafted a "constitution" for the new Republic.

According to Vorobiev, Sergei Shakhrai warned the Sverdlovsk leaders that Yeltsin would not approve any Urals Republic scheme unless it included several regions. After the subsequent disbanding of Parliament that month, however, "all the rest [of the Urals regions] felt extremely intimidated, and our agreements collapsed."[65] On 27 October the Sverdlovsk soviet, acting alone, approved a "constitution" for the Urals Republic which went into force on 31 October.[66] Coming in the wake of the presidential victory over parliament, Sverdlovsk's initiative presented Yeltsin with an unconventional avenue for achieving his stated goal of equalizing all subjects of the federation. Indeed, Yeltsin's initial reaction to the Ural Republic seems to have been mildly supportive.[67] At the very least, reports in the press suggested that he had refused to "unreservedly condemn" the move.[68] On 9 November 1993, however, Yeltsin climbed off the fence and dissolved the Urals Republic as well as the Sverdlovsk parliament, citing gross violations of the constitution. On the following day, he fired Rossel.

The question of why Yeltsin's reaction was so ambivalent remains a mystery, though the timing of events provides a clue. During early November, Yeltsin's team was busy creating the draft of the constitution that would be presented for ratification the following month. The move by Sverdlovsk gave him a choice of mechanisms for "equalizing" subjects of the federation: he could allow all the regions to follow Sverdlovsk's lead and declare themselves republics, or he could preserve the distinction between regions and republics while declaring them to be "equal."

In November 1993, the coalition of republics was still quite strong. Yeltsin probably concluded that the Urals Republic model would be more likely to provoke a hostile response from the republics, from whom he still needed some minimal level of support to gain ratification of his constitution. Since Sverdlovsk was acting alone, dissolving the Urals Republic would have alienated just one region, not twenty. Furthermore, even if the Ural Republic survived the opposition of the ethnic republics, the result would have been a new "parade" of upgraded republics, independently advancing a new set of distributional demands. Since Moscow had only just coerced all the recalcitrant regions into paying their taxes, there was probably little support for reopening the jurisdictional question, at least between Moscow and the Russian regions.

Thus, Yeltsin's team opted for preserving the distinction between region and republic but declaring all to be equal; once this decision was taken, the Ural Republic was dissolved. The chosen strategy was less risky for Yeltsin precisely because it was perceived as less of a threat to the republics and therefore provoked a milder reaction. The return to special treatment of republics in 1994 suggests that the republics' perception was probably accurate. Had Yeltsin really wished to equalize regions and republics, he could have given Sverdlovsk a green light and capitalized on his newly enhanced reputation to establish clear guidelines for regions to "upgrade."[69]

Rossel did not let go of the Urals Republic, however. His dismissal by Yeltsin made him a folk hero among the region's voters, and in May 1994 he was elected chairman of the oblast Duma. He continued to press for the creation of a Urals republic until, one year later, Yeltsin agreed to Rossel's demand that gubernatorial elections be scheduled in the oblast. On 20 August 1995, Rossel was elected governor of Sverdlovsk oblast, defeating the Yeltsin-appointed incumbent who had replaced him almost two years earlier. He promptly announced his intention to seek a power-sharing treaty with Moscow, and declared that such a treaty would remove the need for Sverdlovsk to upgrade its status. The Urals Republic was finally dead, traded away by Rossel for his political resurrection and a bilateral treaty. In return for these concessions, Yeltsin was able to remove the final significant challenge (outside of Chechnya) to Russia's asymmetrical federal structure. Yeltsin's chief concession, however, was to acknowledge the federal center's willingness to negotiate bilateral treaties with oblasts as well as with republics.

By the beginning of 1996, three developments were putting further pressure on Yeltsin to extend equal treatment to the Russian regions. First, gubernatorial elections were held in a number of oblasts and krais, providing more governors with job security on a par with that of republican leaders. Collective action among these elected leaders may prove more difficult to disrupt, especially since the newly reorganized Federation Council provides a forum for their regular assembly. Second, the presidential elections in the summer of 1996 ignited a new round of distribution of federal benefits to regional governors. Finally, the growing institutionalization of regional economic associations may also promote regional collective action that replaces status cleavages (that is, oblast–republic) by regional cleavages. To date, however, the political impact of these economic associations remains slight.

Conclusions

The analysis developed in this chapter suggests that the ability of sub-national actors to sustain coalitions—in other words, to bargain collectively—has been a critical factor in determining the contours of the emerging Russian state. Republics coordinated their demands in order to preserve their privileges (political and distributional) and to deny these privileges to other sub-national units. Ethnic differences among the republics were apparently far less important than the salience of ethnicity as a "marker" of higher status. Ultimately, however, the federal center's own need to disrupt republics' collective action led to an extension of similar privileges to the oblasts and krais; this recent development represents the most serious challenge since Russian independence to the elevated status of the ethnic republics.

What does this analysis suggest for the future of center–periphery relations in Russia? Figure 4.2 indicates several potential paths of development. If Russia pursues the path of "foralistic" federalism—negotiating an endless series of bilateral treaties with subjects of the federation—it may see the present asymmetry give way to an anarchic scramble for benefits (arrow A). The dangers of this path suggest that Moscow must be seeking means to regularize center–periphery relations (arrow B).[70] Movement along this path would almost certainly provoke a reaction from the provinces. It could finally provide the non-ethnic regions with incentives to combine into regional blocs (arrow D). Alternatively, the center might succeed in cutting off the flow of bilateral treaties, successfully splitting the republics' coalition into more and less privileged groups (arrow C). This path might then lead to a Spanish or Indian style federal structure, in which the center is strong enough to redistribute resources, but a few territories enjoy special privileges.

Notes

1 See, for instance, "How Close is Russia to Breaking Up?" *Current Digest of the Soviet Press (CDSP)*, 25 March 1992, vol. 44, no. 8, p. 1.

2 Despite the direct election of thirteen governors in 1995, Yeltsin continued to exercise his prerogative to dismiss and replace governors in regions where elections have not yet been held. In the first half of 1996, for instance, he replaced half a dozen governors.

3 The self-enforcing nature of constitutions is a basic tenet of recent work on the positive theory of constitutions. See, for example, R. Hardin, "Why a Constitution?," in B. Grofman and D. Wittman (eds), *The Federalist Papers and the New Institutionalism*, New York: Agathon, 1989, pp. 100–20; P. Ordeshook, "Constitutional Stability," *Constitutional Political Economy*, 1992, vol. 3, no. 2, pp. 137–75; and B. Weingast, "Constitutions as Governance Structures: The Political Foundations of Secure Markets," *Journal of Institutional and Theoretical Economics*, 1993, vol. 149, no. 1, pp. 286–320.

4 For an analogous argument, see D. North's discussion of the Northwest Ordinance in *Institutions, Institutional Change and Economic Performance*, Cambridge: Cambridge University Press, 1990, pp. 97–9.

5 W. Riker, *Federalism: Origin, Operation, Significance*, Boston: Little, Brown and Co., 1964, p. 11.

6 Riker's theory is also explicit in portraying federalism as the result of a "bargain" between central and regional actors.

7 The classic references on reputation build on analyses of the "chain store game," in which a national monopolist must confront challenges from regional competitors. See R. Selten, "The Chain Store Paradox," *Theory and Decision*, 1978, vol. 9, pp. 127–59; as well as the subsequent discussions in D. Kreps and R. Wilson, "Reputations and Imperfect Information," *Journal of Economic Theory*, August 1982, vol. 27, pp. 253–79; and P. Milgrom and J. Roberts, "Predation and Entry Deterrence," *Journal of Economic Theory*, August 1982, vol. 27, pp. 280–312.

8 J. Litvack, "Regional Demands and Fiscal Federalism," in C. Wallich (ed.), *Russia and the Challenge of Fiscal Federalism*, Washington, DC: World Bank, 1994. For further details on the Chinese model, see R. Agarwala, "China: Reforming Intergovernmental Fiscal Relations," *World Bank Discussion Paper 178*, 1992.

9 The Chinese leadership, for instance, has manipulated tax and investment policy to reward provincial leaders for their continuing loyalty to the regime in general and economic reform programs in particular. These fiscal policies are renegotiated annually. Susan Shirk has called this strategy "playing to the provinces" (S. Shirk, *The Political Logic of Economic Reform in China*, Berkeley, CA: University of California Press, 1993).

10 D. J. Elazar, "International and Comparative Federalism," *PS: Political Science and Politics*, 1993, vol. 24, no. 2, pp. 190–5. The practice of negotiating special privileged deals with sub-national units was perpetuated by the post-Franco Spanish regime, which ultimately granted powers beyond those provided for in the constitution to the Basques and Catalans, and, later, Galicians and Andalusians.

11 For a general analysis of collective action see, of course, M. Olson, *The Logic of Collective Action*, Cambridge, MA: Harvard University Press, 1965.

12 Barry Weingast analyzes this "transgression game" in some detail in "The Political Foundations of Democracy and the Rule of Law," unpublished manuscript, February 1993.

13 The review of events presented in this section does not aim to be a comprehensive account of the 1990–5 period. For more detailed overviews of events up to the passage of the December 1993 constitution, see D. Slider, "Federalism, Discord and Accommodation: Intergovernmental Affairs in Post-Soviet Russia," in J. Hahn and T. Friedgut (eds), *Local Politics in Post-Soviet Russia*, Armonk, NY: M.E. Sharpe, 1994, pp. 239–69; E. Teague, "Center–Periphery Relations in the Russian Federation," in R. Szporluk (ed.), *National Identity and Ethnicity in the New States of Eurasia*, Armonk, NY: M.E. Sharpe, 1994, pp. 21–57; K. Stoner-Weiss, "Local Heroes: Political Exchange and Governmental Performance in Provincial Russia," Ph.D. dissertation, Department of Government, Harvard University, 1994, especially Chapter 2.

14 Stoner-Weiss, "Local Heroes," p. 72.

15 TASS, 7 August 1990, cited in Teague, "Center–Periphery Relations," p. 30. Yeltsin initially directed the comment to oil-rich Tatarstan, whose sovereignty declaration did not acknowledge its membership in the Russian Federation. Yeltsin's remark was repeated, and more widely cited, in an interview with *Komsomol'skaia Pravda*, 14 March 1991.

16 These property rights were to be constrained in practice by federal-level legislation; thus the real devolution of power in the area of resource revenues appears to have been ambiguous at best. See C. McClure, "The Sharing of Taxes on Natural Resources and

the Future of the Russian Federation," in C. Wallich (ed.), *Russia and the Challenge of Fiscal Federalism,* World Bank, 1994, pp. 181–217.

17 O. Glezer, *Moscow News,* no. 7, 1992, cited in Teague, "Center–Periphery Relations," p. 32.

18 For more background on the relabeling of territories effected by the treaties, see V. Tolz, "Thorny Road toward Federalism in Russia," *RFE/RL Research Report,* 3 December 1993, vol. 2, no. 48, pp. 1–8; and R. Sakwa, *Russian Politics and Society,* London, Routledge, 1993, pp. 111–30. Actually, only 20 republics were recognized in the March treaties, but Chechen–Ingushetia later split into two separate republics.

19 *Rossiiskaia Gazeta,* 19 May 1993, p. 2. These figures do not include returns from the Aga Buriat okrug.

20 Tolz, "Thorny Road Toward Federalism in Russia," pp. 4–5.

21 E. Teague, "Russia's Difficult Road Toward Elections," *RFE/RL Research Report,* 15 October 1993, vol. 2, no. 41, pp. 3–4.

22 Provincial responses to the October dissolution of parliament are reviewed in E. Teague, "North-South Divide: Yeltsin and Russia's Provincial Leaders," *RFE/RL Research Report,* 26 November 1993, vol. 2, no. 47, pp. 7–23.

23 *Izvestiia,* 22 December 1993, p. 1

24 This list of treaties is current as of 1 May 1996.

25 Leonid Smirniagin (member of Boris Yeltsin's Presidential Council), interview with author, Moscow, November 1994. Not surprisingly, Smirniagin claimed this massive shift was the result of deliberate federal policy to "empower" the regions.

26 Variation among the regions was, not surprisingly, vast. See D. Slider, "Privatization in Russia's Regions," *Post-Soviet Affairs,* 1994, vol. 10, no. 4, pp. 367–96.

27 Several of Yeltsin's advisors warned him against seeking a "treaty," noting that the terminology suggested provinces had the option to not sign.

28 Slider, "Federalism, Discord," p. 247.

29 R. Bahl, "Revenues and Revenue Assignment: Intergovernmental Fiscal Relations in the Russian Federation," in C. Wallich (ed.), *Russia and the Challenge of Fiscal Federalism,* Washington, DC: World Bank, 1994, pp. 129–80.

30 See, for instance, P. LeHouerou, "Decentralization and Fiscal Disparities Among Regions of the Russian Federation," Internal Discussion Paper (IDP-138), The World Bank, January 1994.

31 Beginning in 1995, the Ministry of Finance began determining subsidy transfers to regional and republican budgets according to a uniform "formula" for determining need. Significant exceptions to this policy persisted, however, especially during electoral campaigns. This formula did not apply to the regional distribution of strictly federal budgetary expenditures.

32 O. Dmitrieva, "Political Games Around the Budget," *Moskovskie Novosti,* 1993, no. 28, pp. 8–9.

33 L. Smirniagin, "The Federation: Processes from Below," *Rossiiskie Vesti,* 26 June 1993, p. 2, FBIS-USR-93-090, pp. 17–19.

34 L. Smirniagin, "Political Federalism versus Economic Federalism," *Segodniia,* 25 June 1993, p. 2, FBIS-USR-93-089, pp. 54–7

35 Dmitrieva, "Political Games Around the Budget."

36 Ibid.

37 "On Measures for the Observance of Legislation of the Russian Federation on Budgetary Arrangements," 27 October 1993, FBIS-SOV-93-207. The decree was apparently drafted by Boris Fedorov during the previous month's "tax war," but Yeltsin presumably feared alienating regional leaders on the eve of his decisive showdown. See Fedorov's comments in *Rossiiskaia Gazeta,* 17 September 1993, p. 1.

38 The treaty-signing strategy is apparently the brainchild of Sergei Shakhrai, former Deputy Prime Minister for Regional Policy. Several policy makers in Moscow described his role to me as "decisive" during interviews in July 1995 and January 1996. Shakhrai now heads the commission charged with coordinating the negotiation of bilateral agreements between the federal center and federation subjects, see *Rossiiskaia Gazeta*, 19 March 1996.

39 See, for instance, M. Hechter, "Nationalism as Group Solidarity," *Ethnic and Racial Studies*, October 1987, vol. 10, no. 4, pp. 415–20; or R. Bates, "Modernization, Ethnic Competition, and the Rationality of Politics in Contemporary Africa," in D. Rothchild and V. Olorunsola (eds), *State Versus Ethnic Claims: African Policy Dilemmas*, Boulder, CO: Westview, 1983, pp. 152–71.

40 Chuvashia received a special treaty on the last day of the 1996 Presidential campaign. Unfortunately for Boris Yeltsin, however, it did not help him carry the republic in the June 16 voting.

41 Stoner-Weiss, "Local Heroes," pp. 76–8. See also Teague, "Center–Periphery Relations," pp. 30–2.

42 Cited by Teague, "Center–Periphery Relations," p. 31.

43 V. Pogorelii, "Debates on Constitution Intensify Split Among Regions," *Kommersant-Daily*, 19 May 1993, p. 11, FBIS-SOV-93-096, p. 49.

44 A. Tikhonov, *Trud*, 5 May 1994. Presidential hopeful Grigorii Yavlinskii endorsed a similar proposal during a visit to the United States.

45 *Segodniia*, 12 August 1994, p. 10, FBIS-USR-94-095, p. 57.

46 For a sampling of reactions, see, "Regions' Heads Feel Threatened by Chechen War," *Current Digest of the Soviet Press*, 1995, vol. 47, no. 3.

47 Nikolai Petrov, "The Regions are Not Keeping Silent," *Nezavisimaia Gazeta*, 20 January 1995, p. 3.

48 The meeting of the "Cheboksary Seven" (Cheboksary is the capital of Chuvashia) was reported in *Segodniia*, 6 January 1995. For an analysis of the Council of Heads of the Republics proposal, see *Nezavisimaia Gazeta*, 12 January 1995.

49 The decree in question, "On the Protection of Servicemen," issued on 11 January 1995, did not mention Chechnya directly, but rather addressed the use of the army in domestic conflicts. The president of Chuvashia, Nikolai Fedorov, is a former Russian Minister of Justice.

50 See, for instance, *The Wall Street Journal*, 20 January 1995, p. A8.

51 OMRI Daily Digest, 29 March 1995.

52 J. Hughes, "Regionalism in Siberia: The Rise and Fall of the Siberian Agreement," *Europe–Asia Studies*, 1994, vol. 46, no. 7, pp. 1133–61

53 S. Ryabov, "The Urals Community: Five Plus Three," *Pravda*, 3 January 1992, p. 3.

54 "Divide the Country into Provinces," *Rossiiskaia Gazeta*, 19 May 1993, p. 1.

55 B. Kalmantaiev, "Who Needs a Ural Republic and Why," *Rossiiskie Vesti*, 20 May 1993, p. 2. In January 1996, Orenburg was further rewarded with its own bilateral treaty with the center. The treaty was announced by Chernomyrdin in December 1995, on the eve of the Duma elections—and of Orenburg's gubernatorial elections.

56 *Rossiiskie Vesti*, 3 July 1993, p. 1.

57 *Rossiiskaia Gazeta*, 6 July 1993, p. 2.

58 Ibid.

59 Ibid.

60 ITAR-TASS, 6 July 1993.

61 *Nezavisimaia Gazeta*, 7 July 1993, p. 3.

62 *Izvestiia*, 15 July 1993, p. 4.

63 *Izvestiia*, 17 September 1993, p. 2.

64 *Oblastnaia Gazeta*, Yekaterinburg, 14 March 1996, translated in FBIS-SOV-96-093-S, pp. 57–63.
65 Ibid.
66 The constitution was published in *Vash Vybor*, 1993, no. 5.
67 This, at least, was the interpretation offered by *Kommersant-Daily* on 4 November 1993.
68 *Rossiiskie Vesti*, 5 November 1993.
69 The importance of clear guidelines for upgrading should be apparent from Figure 4.2. If the center dealt with regional upgrades on an *ad hoc* basis, it would have found itself immediately confronting a spiral of escalating demands, as on arrow "A."
70 As an example of this, Moscow had been replying to calls for further bilateral negotiations with a request to impose a moratorium on such deals until a "Law on Delineation of Jurisdictions Between the Federal and Regional Levels" can be passed. Recently, however, it acknowledged the momentum of the treaty-signing process by forming a Presidential commission for the drafting of such treaties. The long-promised "Law on Delineation of Jurisdictions . . . "—essentially a plea to trade bilateral bargaining for multi-lateral bargaining—was passed by the Duma in 1997 but blocked by the Federation Council.

5

ETHNO-LINGUISTIC AND RELIGIOUS PLURALISM AND DEMOCRATIC CONSTRUCTION IN UKRAINE

José Casanova

Given the widespread skepticism one finds among "experts" concerning the very viability of Ukraine as an independent nation-state, the dire warnings about the dangers of Ukrainian nationalism, and the interjected references to Bosnia and nuclear disaster when discussing the Crimea question, to pose the question of the chances of democratic consolidation in Ukraine would seem a provocative, almost futile exercise.[1] My aim in this chapter, nonetheless, is to inject some cautious optimism into the discussion and argue that there are compelling signs indicating that a democratic political order is being established in post-Soviet Ukraine.

Of the three often discussed possible futures of the post-Soviet space—competitive ethno-nationalism, the re-establishment of empire, and the creation of a liberal, democratic zone—it is the path of an independent, civic-territorial, democratic state which Ukraine appears to be following.[2] Such a path is being pursued more than halfheartedly by the ruling political elites in Ukraine. Both the external geopolitical environment and internal structural conditions are favorable to such an outcome.[3] The results of public opinion polls indicate, moreover, that this is the only outcome which can find the support of a majority of the Ukrainian population. The aim of this paper is to examine these favorable internal structural conditions in Ukraine and specifically to present the complex ethno-linguistic and religious pluralism in Ukraine as cross-cutting cleavages conducive to the integration of a democratic order in Ukraine rather than to conflictive polarization and disintegration.

The other two options, ethno-nationalism and/or reintegration into Russia, appear much less viable. Alexander Motyl has constructed a compelling structural argument as to why the logic of a nationalizing state in Ukraine should face the neo-imperialist logic of revolutionary elites in Russia, thus irremediably fueling competitive ethno-nationalism both within Ukraine and between Ukraine and Russia.[4] The empirical evidence so far, however, does not point in such a direction. It may be true that ultimately the course of developments in Ukraine will be determined structurally by the course of developments in Russia. However, internal structural conditions within Ukraine are unlikely to fuel, much less start the spiraling logic of confrontation.

The Ukrainian transition

One should not minimize the difficulties and obstacles ahead. It is often asserted that the further east one goes the more insoluble appear the dilemmas of the transitions facing post-communist societies. However, besides the double transition from an authoritarian to a democratic regime and from a command to a market economy, Ukraine is faced with the additional double transition of basic post-colonial nation building and post-imperial state making.[5]

Yet, although the projects of state making and nation building are still very much unfinished, the foundations established in the last six years appear sound, and the basic direction taken seems to be one conducive to the eventual consolidation of a democratic state. This is not the place to reconstruct in detail the milestones of the Ukrainian transformation. But it is necessary to keep in mind some of the most characteristic and determinant factors of the ongoing process.[6]

Geopolitically, the current attempt at establishing an independent Ukrainian state has not occurred in the midst of a world war conflagration, as was the case of the two previous failed attempts in this century, but on the crest of the "third wave" of democratization and the 1989 "refolutions" of East and Central Europe, which without major changes in international borders (other than those of a reunified Germany) have radically altered the European geopolitical balance. The immediate recognition of Ukraine's sovereignty and independence by its most relevant neighbors (Russia and Poland) as well as by the Western powers (U.S., Canada, and the European Union) and the smooth integration of Ukraine into the world system of states and the most relevant international agencies and economic organizations testifies to the relative success of the process.

The independence of Ukraine from the Soviet Union was not the hard-fought outcome of a national liberation struggle against imperial rule (as nationalist theories would have anticipated) but rather the result of a decisive yet near effortless seizing of a gift from historical *fortuna*, following the failed coup of August 1991 in Moscow. The process took place without resistance or violence. The practically uncontested transfer of control over the Soviet army and police forces (including the KGB and other special security forces) to a newly established Ukrainian Ministry of Defense are telling indicators of the smoothness of the process. Like the historically novel pattern of transitions from authoritarian to democratic regimes through legal-constitutional procedures and consensual political negotiations—a model that was first implemented in Spain and was later reproduced in various ways in Eastern Europe, Latin America, East Asia and South Africa—the independence of Ukraine and other Soviet republics from the Soviet Union took place basically through constitutional channels. The process entailed a radical break in sovereignty, with a corresponding transfer of sovereign power from Moscow to Kyiv, but no revolutionary break in legality. It was, as Leonid Kravchuk pointed out, the "anti-constitutional" character of the failed Moscow coup of August 1991 that facilitated and precipitated the constitutional dissolution of the Soviet Union.[7]

Internally, the consolidation of Ukrainian state sovereignty has also taken place relatively smoothly and practically without contestation (with the exception of Crimea). The declaration of Ukraine's independence was passed without significant resistance by the Supreme Soviet of the Ukrainian SSR on 24 August 1991 and was ratified overwhelmingly by the citizens of Ukraine in republican referendum on 1 December of the same year. The absolute majority for independence—91 percent throughout Ukraine, over 80 percent in the Russified eastern industrial oblasts, and 54 percent in Crimea itself—gave the aura of democratic legitimacy to an intra-elite agreement that now became the basic national consensus within which the struggles for power, the negotiations of the basic rules of the game, and the policy compromises could be regulated and contained.

The tacit coalition between the reformed ex-communists in power and the national-democratic opposition (with its origins in the Rukh nationalist movement) in support of state sovereignty and national independence began to emerge already after the March 1990 elections to Ukraine's Supreme Soviet. This coalition became the fundamental factor in Ukrainian politics during the Kravchuk administration, has been strengthened during the Kuchma administration with the passage of the new constitution and the initiation of economic reforms, and is likely to continue for the foreseeable future.

Most significantly, an anti-democratic and anti-reform nationalist–communist (brown–red) coalition of the kind one finds in Russia is unthinkable in Ukraine. The anti-democratic nationalist forces are numerically insignificant and rabidly anti-Soviet, while the anti-nationalist and anti-reform nostalgically pro-Soviet forces, notwithstanding their numerical strength in Parliament, are politically in disarray and unable to formulate a viable alternative, at least as long as the pro-reform pro-democratic forces are in power in Russia. Thus, Ukraine is unlikely to follow the Belarus pattern.

Indeed, despite generalized apathy and the relative weakness of the actively pro-democratic and pro-reform forces, and despite fundamental differences concerning the model of nation building and economic reform that Ukraine should pursue, public opinion polls from independence to the present show that there is a basic passive national consensus for an independent democratic Ukraine. In this respect, Ukraine seems almost destined to continue, slowly but steadily, the process of state formation and democratic consolidation as if by inertia, aided by favorable external geopolitical and internal structural conditions, and facing so far no major organized internal or external opposition.

Internally, within Ukraine at least, there is little empirical evidence and diminishing plausibility for any of the three scenarios which could possibly alter the existing inertia and undermine the democratizing trends: increasing ethnic Ukrainian–Russian polarization and conflict, ending in civil war, partition and/or reunion with Russia; growing politicization and intervention of the armed forces in Ukrainian domestic and foreign politics, possibly ending in outright military dictatorship; or the emergence of populist authoritarian presidentialism. Neither the behavioral or discursive propensities and dispositions of the political elites, nor existing patterns of political mobilization and collective action, nor the results of public opinion surveys seem to offer empirical support for the likelihood of any of these scenarios.

While simultaneously reassuring and uninspiring, this image of democratizing inertia can only serve at best to counter those arguments which assume that the greatest threats to political stability are likely to result from excessive democratization, that is, from internal cleavages, hyper-mobilization, the overload of social and political demands, and the ensuing crisis of governability or paralysis of centralized, unified command. Indeed, one could argue that in the long run the potentially more serious threats to Ukraine's independence and political stability are likely to derive from democratic deficits, that is, from the absence of citizen mobilization of any kind, from the weakness of the party system and other mediating institutions of representation and participation, and from the growing crisis of legitimacy which could ensue from such a situation. In the short run, however, the combination of favorable external geopolitical and internal structural conditions is sufficient to maintain the democratizing reformist inertia.

The dissolution of Rukh and the decision by its leaders not to become an opposition party after Kravchuk's victory in the December 1991 presidential elections, the demobilization of civil society, the slow institutionalization of a political society restricted to elites with a very weak party base, the deadlocks and self-restraints in intra-elite power struggles, the apathy, lack of voice and loss of confidence in the political elites on the part of the citizenry, combined with patient stoicism, fundamental system loyalty, and surprising civility, all are interrelated pieces of the Ukrainian political puzzle. One must be surely concerned about the absence of a genuine party system in Ukraine and the demobilization of civil society from the public sphere. However, this can also be viewed as the price to be paid for a successful process of political and administrative elite formation in post-imperial Ukraine, without which the tasks of state making and nation building could not have any chance of success. Nor could any serious economic reform be entertained before these other processes had already been set on the right track.[8]

The basic issues in the tug-of-war between central and regional administrative elites, between president and parliament, and between the reform and anti-reform factions within parliament were not much different in Ukraine than in Russia. The deadlock and the impossibility of adopting or carrying through any meaningful reform measures were also similar in both places. Yet the relative civility with which Ukrainian elites carried on their disputes and power struggles in comparison to the greater incivility of the Russian process points to some fundamental differences in the emergence of intra-elite trust, of basic elite consensus, and even of a democratic elite culture.

Alexander Motyl has argued perceptively that government deadlock in Ukraine actually facilitated the process of learning the rules of the democratic political game, with both sides coming to recognize the indispensability of each other to the very act of playing the game:

> The inertia of the political process created an elite *esprit de corps*, a perhaps unconsciously and unwillfully developed tolerance, and a sense of moderation that facilitate the formation of a genuine Ukrainian elite. The parliamentary and presidential elections of 1994, and the smooth transfer of power from Kravchuk to Kuchma, testified to the growth of real institutions within the Ukrainian state.[9]

The final compromise achieved to pass the new constitution in July 1996 after much wrangling and brinkmanship confirmed the same pattern and will serve to solidify the acceptance of the basic rules of the political game.[10]

Moreover, the same public opinion surveys which register a profound lack of confidence in the political class and in all political institutions also indicate clearly that the majority of the population do not want to change the rules of the game. Indeed, the political portrait which emerges from public opinion surveys is that of a completely atomized electorate, with a profound mistrust of politicians, parties, and all political institutions, including parliament and the central and local administrations, yet one also bound by constitutionalism, rule of law and belief in the basic soundness of the democratic system. One finds a realistic and sober assessment of the weak institutionalization of democracy so far achieved in Ukraine, together with basic confidence in its progressive institutionalization in the future.[11]

Above all one finds a very strong reluctance to become mobilized for any cause, due to a combination of political apathy and low civic consciousness. According to the May 1995 survey only 10.8 percent of respondents were "very interested" in politics, while 29.3 percent were "totally uninterested," and the rest, 59.9 percent, "somewhat interested." The level of political and civic participation is extremely low. Less than 1 percent of the population are members of a political party, while 84 percent of respondents said that they were "not a member of any civic or political organization." Yet, 74.5 percent of respondents affirmed that they had taken part in the 1995 parliamentary elections.[12] In a February 1996 survey of "economic culture," when asked: "What is better, to endure hardship or to protest in the street running the risk of breaching peace and quiet," the responses were "necessary to preserve order, peace and accord at any cost" (47.5 percent), "necessary to actively protest against deteriorating conditions" (31.7 percent), and "difficult to answer" (20.8 percent).[13] In this respect, Ukraine appears to be almost a paradigmatic model of a Schumpeterian elitist democracy, in which the citizens exercise their right to choose and recall their rulers through open elections, but remain passive and let their rulers manage public affairs between elections even when they have no trust in their ability to do so effectively.

State making and citizenship in Ukraine

Probably the single most important conditioning factor in the relative success of the process of state making so far was the initial decision to define the new independent state not as an ethnic nation-state but as a territorial and legal entity in which all power derives from "the people of Ukraine."[14] The category "the people of Ukraine" included all inhabitants of Ukraine irrespective of nationality, ethnicity, language, religious confession, or any other ascriptive marker. In other words, the *polis*, that is, the political community of the Ukrainian state, was being explicitly differentiated from the Ukrainian *demos*, that is, from the ethnic imagined community of the historical Ukrainian nation. The two ambiguously overlapping identities of the Ukrainian *narod* (people) as "the people of Ukraine" and as "the Ukrainian nation" were now open to individual and collective reflexive dissociations, contestations and rearrangements.

The conscious adoption of a policy of inclusive state making in Ukraine was as much a carryover of Soviet constitutional discourse and practices by a Ukrainian nomenklatura turned nationalist overnight, as it was a reflexive contribution of the national democratic opposition. From its inception, Rukh had incorporated explicitly such an inclusive policy in its platform.

Given Ukraine's geopolitical conditions, if the project of Ukrainian independence was to have any realistic chance of success, Ukraine could ill afford either to alienate its large Russian minority (21 percent of the population) or to provoke any kind of inter-ethnic Russian–Ukrainian conflict. Both the fact that a majority of ethnic Russians in Ukraine voted for Ukraine's independence in the December 1991 referendum and the absence of major incidents of inter-ethnic conflict in Ukraine in the last five years, leaving aside here the more complex issue of Crimea, are evidence of the success of the policy. Similarly, the absence of major incidents of anti-Semitism in Ukraine today, despite a long and tragic history of Jewish–Ukrainian conflicts, is not a mere fortunate coincidence, but it is the result of a process of reflexive collective learning from the negative experiences of the past on the part of Ukrainian nationalist elites and of the principled adoption on the part of the Ukrainian state of the appropriate policies.

Surveys of privately expressed public opinion in Ukraine still register rates of latent anti-Semitism almost as high as those in Russia.[15] The fundamental difference is the conscious decision on the part of all prominent political elites in Ukraine not to "play the ethnic card" and to banish from Ukrainian public discourse anti-Semitic and other xenophobic expressions. There is, no doubt, also an extreme nationalist right in Ukraine that advocates "Ukraine for Ukrainians only." But it is no more radical, and it is numerically and electorally less significant than the extreme nationalist right in most Western European democracies with supposedly normally working civil societies.[16] According to the April 1995 survey, only 1.5 percent of respondents support the radical nationalists. Even more significantly, "nationalists" are at the top of the ranking of negative trust. A combined 76 percent of respondents indicate that they either "completely distrust" (60.3

percent) or "distrust more than trust" (15.7 percent) the nationalists. Next in the ranking of negative trust come "political parties" (68 percent), "the Communist Party" (62 percent), parliament (61 percent), and "the militia" (61 percent).[17]

Public opinion surveys from independence to the present also show that there is a basic national consensus shared by the overwhelming majority of the population in nationalist western Ukraine as much as in Russified eastern Ukraine around the principle of "equality before the law" and the project of a state bound by the rule of law to protect the universal, individual, equal rights of all its citizens irrespective of their ethnic origin or allegiance.[18]

It is concerning issues of nation building, the economic system, and geopolitical orientations that public opinion surveys show drastic differences between the nationalist, pro-western and pro-capitalist western Ukraine and the more Russified, pro-Soviet and pro-socialist eastern Ukraine.

Nation building

The question of whether Ukraine has already succumbed to the temptation of the "nationalizing state" is not easily answerable in so far as the very category of a nationalizing state is and must perforce be ambiguous and imprecise.[19] My own answer would be that the Ukrainian state can be characterized as a "nationalizing" one only in the most minimal sense. In any case the Ukrainian state, if it is to survive as a state, cannot avoid the task of nation building in the sense of constructing some kind of Ukrainian political community. The empirically and normatively relevant question of course is which type of community or which type of political integration.

Here Juan Linz's systematic conceptualization of the categories of *polis* and *demos* and the extent of their congruence, as well as the conceptual differentiation between "nation-states" and "state–nations" seems more useful for an analysis of nation building in Ukraine than the lately fashionable category of the "national-izing state."[20] Ukraine is not and cannot become a nation–state in the strict sense of the term of absolute congruence of its *polis* (community of citizens) and its *demos* (national community). Paradoxically, it was fortunate for Ukrainian nationalism that, unlike in the Baltic Republics, the liberation of Ukraine took place almost without the help of a national liberation movement and that the construction of the Ukrainian state proceeded almost without nationalist intervention. Rukh certainly played an important indirect conditioning role, but not a directly active one in the process of independence or state making. As a result, the process in Ukraine could take the form of what Linz has called state–nation rather than nation-state formation.[21]

But what complicates the dilemmas of nation building in Ukraine is the fact that the very criteria of national inclusion and exclusion are not, and under modern democratic conditions are unlikely ever to become, unambiguous. Ethnicity, language, and religion have been historically and continue to be today the three main symbolic bricks customarily used either singly or in various combinations for the construction of national identities, that is, of collective memories of the common past, of collective symbolic representations of the common present, and of collective shared projects of the future. Even in those ever rarer cases in which the three markers happen to coincide, so that the criteria of national inclusion may seem unambiguous, the contents of the collective representations of that identity are likely to be open to various contested interpretations and to diverse individual appropriations and reconstructions. When, as it happens in Ukraine, ethnicity, language and religion do not coincide but rather overlap in different directions, national identity becomes more ambiguous and the task of nation building much more complex.

Ethno-linguistic pluralism

In Ukraine, the category of ethnicity is relatively unproblematic only in so far as the Soviet system ascribed to each of its "citizen-subjects" one single ethnic identity.[22] Thus, according to the 1989 census, the population of Ukraine was made up of over 37 million Ukrainians (approximately 75 percent of the population), over 11 million Russians (21 percent), half a million Jews, and some additional significant numbers of neighboring nationalities: Belarusians (440,000), Moldovans (324,500), Bulgarians (234,000), Poles (219,000), Hungarians (163,000), Rumanians (135,000), and so on.[23]

The dilemmas of Ukraine's nation building would be relatively straightforward, though politically more dangerous due to the greater risk of Ukrainian–Russian polarization, if the main problem would be simply how to accommodate, that is, include or exclude the large Russian minority into the Ukrainian *demos*. The inherent risk derives from the fact that the Russians in Ukraine are a relatively privileged "imperial minority" which can respond to the real or perceived threat of Ukrainization with the counterthreat of secession.[24] Yet what really complicates matters for the task of Ukrainian nation building is that ethnic Ukrainians are linguistically split between Ukrainophones and Russophones in such a way that there are three clearly distinct "ethno-linguistic groups" in Ukraine, though of course even those boundaries are rather porous and labile: Ukrainophone Ukrainians (40 percent), Russophone Ukrainians (33–4 percent), and Russophone Russians (20–1 percent). The fourth possible ethno-linguistic combination, Ukrainophone Russians, is numerically insignificant (1–2 percent).[25] Table 5.1 shows the distribution of ethnic and linguistic groups across different regions of the country.

Paradoxically, Russophone Ukrainians hold the key to the politics of nation building in Ukraine, being free to privilege either the ethnic or the linguistic component of their identity and thus to form majority coalitions with their fellow Ukrainians on certain issues or majority coalitions with their Russophone fellows on other issues. Their national identity being more a matter of choice than is the case with the other two groups, their identity will also tend to be more ambiguous and labile. In so far as they do not renounce their equivocal identity by assimilating

Table 5.1 Ethno-linguistic portrait of Ukraine (percentages)

Native language	National	Lviv	Kyiv	Donetsk	Simferopil
Ukrainian	59.5	76.0	58.0	19.4	9.3
Russian	37.9	22.8	41.7	79.6	82.2
Other	2.7	0.5	2.3	1.7	8.5

Language spoken at home	National	Lviv	Kyiv	Donetsk	Simferopil
Only Ukrainian	31.9	63.2	16.1	1.5	0.5
Only Russian	32.8	17.3	38.7	78.6	84.3
Both	34.5	19.5	45.2	19.4	12.4
Other	0.9	0.0	0.0	0.5	2.8

National self-identification	Nation
Ukrainian	69.8
Russian	23.9
Other	6.2

To which population group do you feel most closely aligned?	National	Lviv	Kyiv	Donetsk	Simferopil
Ukrainian	48.3	75.4	64.9	29.6	12.2
CIS	6.7	3.8	8.2	9.2	9.0
Former Soviet	20.5	8.5	11.9	32.8	33.5
Russian	2.0	0.5	0.2	2.0	3.5
Regional	14.5	8.0	8.0	20.4	38.3
European	2.3	3.0	4.7	2.7	1.3
Don't know	5.7	0.8	2.1	3.2	2.3

Source: May 1995 National and Four Cities Survey, Democratic Initiatives Centre, Kyiv, 1995.
Note: Rounding error and a few discrepancies in the tables from which these figures were taken mean that not all columns add up to 100.0 percent. The differences are too small to affect the overall results.

into any of the other two groups, they can also help to build the bridges of trust between the otherwise polarized groups.

In this respect, Russophone Ukrainians hold the key to the emergence of a genuinely pluralistic, and not just plural, civil society in Ukraine, a society that not only accepts diversity as the perhaps unfortunate but inevitable fact of the imperial legacy, but actually accepts cultural diversity and flexible individual identities as values in themselves.[26] Being in the middle, they serve as a structural guarantee of the survival of Ukraine's independence. They can literally hold Ukraine together in a way in which neither of the other two poles can. Without them, both temptations, the nationalizing one on the part of aggrieved Ukrainian nationalists and the colonial one on the part of alarmed Russian *pieds noirs*, and the concomitant danger of Russian–Ukrainian communal violence which could easily spill over into an international confrontation between Russia and Ukraine, would be much greater. In this respect, Russophone Ukrainians can simultaneously protect Ukrainian nationalism from its natural impulse to attempt to form a more homogeneous national community and free the Russian imperial minority from its impulse to secede and thus to provoke a Russian–Ukranian conflagration that would most likely end in a reincorporation of Ukraine into a Russian empire.[27]

Religious pluralism in Ukraine

The ideal type of a highly pluralistic, open and free linguistic market is certainly conceivable, but the sociological reality principle tells one that it can hardly be practicable. A multicultural society could plausibly have hundreds of languages as the viable means of communication in as many private lifeworlds. But if that society is to be a civil one, and if its *polis* is to be a democratic one, it will require that a very reduced number of languages serve as public ones, functioning as open *linguae francae* that guarantee universal equal access to the public sphere to all the members.

The model of a free and highly pluralistic, indeed, almost boundless religious market is, by contrast, conceivable and viable. In fact, the American religious market comes close to an actualization of the ideal type. The argument presented in the following section is that, of all European societies, Ukraine is the one most likely to approximate the American model. Indeed, Ukraine has already gone through the first incipient stages of religious denominationalism to an extent unusual in Europe. This augurs very well for the success of civil society in Ukraine.

The dual clause of the First Amendment to the Constitution of the United States of America, guaranteeing "free exercise of religion" and "no establishment thereof" serves as the constitutional regulative principle of the American religious market. The American constitutional formula challenged the notion taken for granted and shared at the time by religionists and secularists alike that the state or the political community of citizens needed a religion, ecclesiastical or civil, as the base of its normative integration and that, moreover, it was the business of the sovereign to regulate the religious sphere. The First Amendment raised not only a "wall of separation" between church and state, but actually established a principle of differentiation between the political community of citizens and any and all religious communities. Eventually, all religions in America, churches as well as sects, irrespective of their origins, doctrinal claims and ecclesiastical identities, would turn into denominations, formally equal under the constitution and competing in a relatively free, pluralistic, and voluntaristic religious market. As the organizational form and principle of such a religious system, denominationalism constitutes the great American religious invention.[28]

After the independence of the American colonies, the establishment of any particular church at the federal national level was probably precluded by the territorial distribution and the relative equal strength of three colonial churches at the time of independence: Congregational, Presbyterian, and Anglican. However, either multiple establishment or the establishment of a generalized Christian (i.e.,

Protestant) religion could have been likely outcomes, had it not been for the active coalition of Jefferson, Madison, and dissenting Baptists in Virginia.

In Europe, by contrast, we find two different patterns of separation. Some states, notably England and the Scandinavian Lutheran countries, also attained a high level of toleration of sectarian religions but would nevertheless maintain one religion as the established official church. In other countries, France being the paradigmatic model, the disestablishment of religion from the state became an issue of heated political contestation, and when it took place, it did so usually under secularist premises of suspicion, if not open hostility, toward religion. Here, the state not only failed to protect the free exercise of religion in society, but actually developed a secularist republican ideology which functioned as a civil religion in competition with ecclesiastical religion.

Everywhere in Europe, moreover, the model has remained either that of one single national church which claims to be coextensive with the nation or that of two (usually Catholic and Protestant) competing but territorially based national churches along with an indefinite number of religious minorities which have assumed the structural position of sects *vis-à-vis* the officially established church or churches. Eventually, the process of secularization in Europe has entailed not only the constitutional separation of church and state, but also the privatization of religion and the dramatic decline of religious beliefs and practices, particularly among those churches which have maintained some kind of formal or informal quasi-establishment. The particular historical arrangements tend to oscillate between three patterns: that of the formal establishment of the Church of England, that of the formal disestablishment of the Catholic Church in France—which maintains, nonetheless, an informal status as the national church—and that of formal constitutional separation along with informal multi-church establishment of Germany or corporatist-consociational arrangements such as pillarization in Holland.[29]

It is not necessary to emphasize in this context that a proper resolution of the problem of religious freedom and religious pluralism is crucial for the development of civil society, both in its historical emergence in early modern Europe and today. The drive toward politico-religious unification continues to be today, as the experience in Bosnia shows, the main obstacle to the institutionalization of civil society. What is important about the situation in Ukraine today is not only that such a drive is very weak but, more importantly, that the structural conditions in Ukraine do not permit it to gain more strength.

One can observe today in Ukraine the rather striking phenomenon of the emergence of four Eastern rite churches, all competing with one another, all claiming to be the legitimate heir of the Kievan Rus Church, and therefore claiming also to be the legitimate church of the entire Ukrainian territory. These churches are the Ukrainian Orthodox Church–Moscow Patriarchate (UOC–MP), the Ukrainian Orthodox Church–Kyiv Patriarchate (UOC–KP), the Ukrainian Autocephalous Orthodox Church (UAOC), and the Ukrainian Catholic Church. The first two emerged as the result of a recent schism that split the Russian

Orthodox Church in Ukraine just as it was trying to develop a strategy to counter the legalization and explosive re-emergence of the other two churches.

The existence of the Ukrainian Greek Catholic or Uniate Church, which is Eastern in rite and spiritual doctrines but accepts Roman canonical and administrative jurisdiction, goes back to the 1596 Union of Brest. Under that accord, the Ruthenian church of the Ukrainian lands in the Polish–Lithuanian Commonwealth agreed after much Polish political pressure and Jesuit maneuvers to "reunite" itself with Rome. In nineteenth-century Galicia, under Habsburg rule, there took place the fusion of a revitalized Greek Catholic Church and Galician–Ukrainian nationalism, which has remained the fundamental factor in Western Ukrainian politics until today. In 1945, following the incorporation of Galicia into the Soviet Union, the Uniate Church was forcefully "reunited" with the Russian Orthodox Church. Proscribed and severely persecuted, the UCC maintained its identity underground, and also latently within the Orthodox Church.[30]

The moment *glasnost* reached Ukraine in the fall of 1989, massive mobilizations for the legalization of the proscribed Uniate Church took place throughout Galicia. As the process of legalization promised by the Moscow authorities was too slow in coming, the parishioners took affairs into their own hands and reclaimed forcefully their churches for the UCC. By early 1991 the UCC had regained its predominant position in the three Galician oblasts, having repossessed 1,865 congregations, as compared with 905 parishes belonging to the Ukrainian Autocephalous Orthodox Church and 734 congregations maintaining allegiance to the Ukrainian Orthodox Church–Moscow Patriarchate.[31]

The Ukrainian Autocephalous Orthodox Church (UAOC) was established in Kyiv in 1922, in the aftermath of the Russian Revolution, Civil War, and the failed attempt to establish an independent Ukraine. Because of its populist national (*narodnik*) orientation, and its conciliar, anti-hierarchical ecclesiastical structure, the Soviets at first supported its growth in order to use it in their struggles against the Russian Orthodox Church. The UAOC was able to gain a significant stronghold in Soviet Ukraine, but it was not able to gain recognition from either the Patriarch of Constantinople or other Orthodox Churches. In the 1930s the UAOC was liquidated by Stalin along with every manifestation of Ukrainian nationalism. It survived in the Ukrainian diaspora in the US and Canada, under the leadership of Patriarch Mstyslav, who returned to Kyiv in 1992 and reclaimed the title of Patriarch of Kyiv and All Rus.[32]

The stubborn resistance of Ukrainian Catholics and the re-emergence of the UAOC have frustrated the various attempts of the Moscow Patriarchate to establish an oligopolistic bargain between Rome and Moscow, which would have forced Ukrainian believers to choose between Roman Catholicism and Russian Orthodoxy. As the politics of Ukrainian independence spilled over into the ecclesiastical sphere, an internal schism developed within the Ukrainian Exarchate of the Russian Orthodox Church. In January 1990, trying to counter the nationalist appeal of its two historical competitors, the Russian Orthodox Church in Ukraine was officially renamed the Ukrainian Orthodox Church (UOC). Following the declaration of Ukrainian independence in August 1991 and the breakup of the USSR, there emerged a movement for independence of Ukrainian Orthodoxy from Moscow, which was supported by religious as well as secular Ukrainian elites and revived the age-old rivalry between Orthodox Kyiv and Orthodox Moscow.[33]

As the capital of Kyivan Rus and center of Christianization of the East Slavs, Kyiv occupies a crucial place in the history of Russian Orthodoxy as well as in the foundational myths of the Russian state and nation. Both history and myths, however, are vehemently contested by the counter-histories of Ukrainian Orthodoxy and the counter-foundational myths of modern Ukrainian nationalism. Orthodox Metropolitans, who had been forced by feudal warfare and the Mongol invasions to abandon Kyiv and eventually took up residence in Moscow, continued until the middle of the fifteenth century to use the title "Metropolitan of Kyiv" and to assert their jurisdictional claims over all Rus. From the second half of the fifteenth to the first half of the seventeenth century, the Metropolitanate of Kyiv resumed its traditional independent status, under the jurisdiction of the Patriarch of Constantinople. This was precisely the period when first the legitimating concept of Moscow as the Third Rome and then the Moscow Patriarchate (1589) emerged, but also the period when a separate Kyivan Orthodox tradition was formed.

After the coup of August 1991, following traditional Orthodox cesaro-papist policies as well as the Soviet practice of state control of the Orthodox church, the newly independent Ukrainian government promoted the establishment of a Ukrainian state church. Metropolitan Filaret, who had occupied the Kyivan See since the mid-1960s and had proven a pliable tool of Soviet policies and of the Moscow Patriarchate, was happy to comply with the new government directives. The first ethnic Ukrainian to be appointed to the Kyivan See in more than 150 years, Metropolitan Filaret, who had eagerly persecuted any sign of Ukrainian bourgeois-nationalist deviation within the Orthodox church, found it easy now, like the rest of the Soviet Ukrainian nomenklatura, to adopt a new nationalist ecclesiastical policy.

In March 1992 a bishops' synod of the Russian Orthodox Church conducted a disciplinary trial of Filaret, accusing him of openly maintaining a family. In May 1992 a synod of bishops of the Ukrainian Orthodox Church in Kharkiv removed the controversial Filaret and elected Metropolitan Volodymyr Sabodan as head of the Ukrainian Orthodox Church–Moscow Patriarchate. With the support of the Kravchuk administration, which protested the interference of Moscow in the internal affairs of the "independent and self-governing" Ukrainian Orthodox Church, Filaret was able to establish an autocephalous Kievan Patriarchate of the Orthodox Church in Ukraine. Efforts to unify the UAOC and the UOC–KP ultimately failed, and the schism between the three Orthodox churches in Ukraine has widened.

The situation of incipient religious denominationalism that has emerged in Ukraine is closer to the American than to the European models. The structural conditions are similar to those in the United States after independence. No particular denomination could possibly become the established religion of the new Ukrainian state or, for that matter, the disestablished but quasi-official national religion.

The UCC has reasserted its historical hegemony in much of Galicia, as over 60 percent of the parishes there have reverted to Greek Catholicism. Despite its geographical restriction to Western Ukraine, the UCC, with over 14,000 priests serving a deeply religious population of over 3 million, organized in over 4,000 parishes, is in fact the largest denomination in Ukraine. However, its traditional territorial monopoly over Galicia has been broken as a significant number of priests and parishes chose to remain Orthodox, while transferring their allegiance from the Moscow Patriarchate either to the UAOC or to the UOC–KP.

With the help of government support, Filaret's UOC–KP was able to expand its influence beyond Galicia, establishing itself as the predominant denomination in Kyiv and in all central oblasts as well as in the Western oblasts of Chernivsti, Khmelnytsky, and Volyn, but it lost much of its earlier support in the Lviv region. The official support it received from the Kravchuk administration through the Council of Religious Affairs, moreover, prompted the opposition Communist nomenklatura in the more Russified oblasts of the East and the South to openly support the Ukrainian Orthodox Church–Moscow Patriarchate. These southern and eastern oblasts, where the UOC–MP and the Russian Orthodox Church remain predominant, are also the ones most secularized, with a majority of the population there being unchurched and declaring themselves either atheists or not religious.[34]

There are no fully reliable statistics measuring the religious situation in Ukraine today. Moreover, completely different pictures of denominational support for the various churches emerge whether one uses as a measure organizational criteria such as the number of eparchies, parish churches, and priests that a church controls, or popular support criteria such as the number of people who actually identify with a church. In terms of organizational strength, at the UOC–KP October 1993 synod, Metropolitan Antonii stated that the UOC–KP had under its jurisdiction twenty eparchies, more than 2,000 parishes, and 1,600 priests. The UAOC reported that as of 10 November 1993 it had under its jurisdiction five bishops administering twelve eparchies, 800 parishes, and 300 priests. Organizationally, the UOC–MP remained the largest Orthodox denomination in Ukraine, as it claimed to have under its jurisdiction over 6,000 parishes and over 4,000 priests. Clearly, the UOC–MP has inherited most of the ecclesiastical structure of the Russian Orthodox Church in Ukraine outside of Galicia, and it has been able as well to maintain control of the most important holy places of Orthodoxy in Ukraine.[35]

In terms of popular identification, however, public opinion surveys show the UOC–KP as the largest denomination in Ukraine, despite its smaller ecclesiastical infrastructure.[36] Such surveys, however, measure only popularity and nominal allegiance to the various denominations, but no actual membership or religious practice. In fact, public opinion surveys show that, with the exception of Galicia, the overwhelming majority of the population throughout Ukraine remains unchurched, and its allegiance to the various denominations is nominal at best. Only 13 percent of respondents in the May 1995 survey affirmed having "attended a service (at a church, synagogue, mosque, prayer house, etc.) at least once in the past week."[37]

A few facts stand out as significant (see Table 5.2). Aside from Lviv, where the unchurched comprise only 15 percent of the population, the "not religious" are the largest category, with the extreme of 55 percent in Donetsk. Indeed, in combination with the "don't knows," the unchurched represent the absolute majority in all three cities. The Greek Catholic Church is the largest denomination in Lviv, although surprisingly it only comprises slightly over a third of the population (34.8 percent). All-Galician regional surveys, however, show a much more hegemonic presence of the Greek Catholic Church in rural areas as well as in other urban centers of Galicia, such as Ternopil and Ivano-Frankivsk.[38] It has practically no support outside Galicia and Transcarpathia. The UOC–KP has been able to establish a significant presence throughout Ukraine, being hegemonic in the city of Kyiv with 34.3 percent, while the next two largest denominations, the UOC–MP and the Russian Orthodox Church combined, obtained only 8.4 percent of support. It also shows a remarkably strong presence in the Greek Catholic stronghold of Lviv (27.3 percent) and has even proved to be the most popular denomination in heavily Russified Donetsk (18.9 percent, higher than the 17.7 percent of the UOC–MP and the Russian Orthodox Church combined). The Russian Orthodox Church and its branch, the UOC–MP, are clearly dominant in Crimea (37.8 percent), where a majority of the population are Russian. These churches also have a strong presence in the Russified East and South (17.7 percent), while showing a very weak presence elsewhere in Ukraine.

The complex category of "other" is a catch-all residual category that includes religious confessions and minorities with a long historical presence in Ukraine, such as Jews, Muslims, Roman Catholics, and Protestants, particularly Lutherans and Baptists, as well as different new sects and new religious movements. Significantly, Lviv emerges as the city with the most competitive religious market and with the highest percentage of "other" (10.5 percent). One can assume that "other" refers primarily to three different groups, Roman Catholics, Jews, and rapidly growing new evangelical sects.

In addition to the revival of Protestant sects and churches with historical roots in Ukraine, countless branches of American Evangelical Protestantism are pursuing zealously their own missionary efforts, comfortably ignorant of local language, culture, and religious traditions but eager to bring the Gospel of Jesus Christ to the natives. The re-emergence of Jewish and Muslim (Crimean Tatars) religious identities adds complexity and pluralism to the emerging denominational pattern.[39] Furthermore, Ukraine is also emerging as a flourishing center for new religions, exotic cults and spiritual movements of all kinds, such as Mormons, Roon Virists trying to revive pre-Christian pagan traditions, Hare Krishnas and

Table 5.2 Religious portrait of Ukraine (percentages)

Confessional allegiance	National	Lviv	Kyiv	Donetsk	Simferopil
Not religious	31.3	12.5	41.7	55.0	37.3
UOC–KP	32.4	27.3	34.3	18.9	5.5
UOC–MP	8.9	2.3	4.0	5.5	2.5
Greek Catholic	7.8	34.8	0.2	0.5	0.3
Russian Orthodox	7.4	5.5	4.4	12.2	35.3
Ukrainian Autocephalous	0.8	4.0	1.4	0.0	0.5
Other	3.8	10.5	2.1	3.0	7.1
Difficult to answer	8.0	3.0	12.4	5.0	11.6

Source: May 1995 National and Four Cities Survey, Democratic Initiatives Centre, Kyiv, 1995.
Note: Rounding error and a few discrepancies in the tables from which these figures were taken mean that not all columns add up to 100.0 percent. The differences are too small to affect the overall results.

other Eastern religious movements, or the more bizarre and apocalyptic White Brotherhood which captured the international news in the fall of 1993 when it announced that it would stage in Kyiv the crucifixion and resurrection of its messianic leader, Maria Devi Khristos. In short, Ukraine's independence and the partial institutionalization of religious freedom have created the conditions for the most pluralistic and competitive denominational religious market in all of Eastern Europe.

From the perspective of Christian ecumenism, the Byzantine denominational schisms may be viewed as unfortunate and unfraternal divisions. From the perspective of Ukrainian nationalism, religious pluralism can be viewed as an impediment to the establishment of a single national church which could be used instrumentally in the efforts to build a homogeneous nation under an independent Ukrainian state. Yet the absence of religious unity may turn out to be a blessing in disguise, in so far as it may be conducive to the formation of a culturally pluralistic, religiously tolerant, and democratic Ukraine.

The failure of the Kravchuk administration to establish a Ukrainian national state church must be viewed as a fortuitous development of the greatest significance for the institutionalization of religious freedom and the development of a democratic system in Ukraine. After the 1994 presidential elections, the new administration of Leonid Kuchma put an end to the pro-Filaret policies of the previous administration and has followed a more even-handed policy towards the competing Ukrainian churches. In one of his first decrees, President Kuchma abolished the old Council for Religious Affairs and transferred its functions to the newly created Ministry of Nationalities, Migrations, and Religious Denominations. The new policy of clear separation of church and state and protection of religious freedom is now inscribed in the new Ukrainian Constitution, a development which is likely to consolidate the process of inclusive state making and nation building that, from the very beginning, was consciously adopted by Ukrainian political elites.

Although it goes against the religious and nationalist traditions so ingrained in the region, the wall of separation between church and state, along with the differentiation of the religious and the political community which this creates, is crucial not only for the well-being of all religions, but also for the establishment of democratic states and for a long-term resolution of ethnic, religious, and nationalist conflicts. Churches, at least those which doctrinally are part of transnational religious bodies and maintain universalistic religious claims, may cease viewing themselves as community cults of the nation-state and become voluntary religious communities anchored in civil society rather than in the nation. Such a move would facilitate the organization of democratic states and political society through the individualist principle of citizenship rather than through ascriptive ethnic principles.

The dissociation of the religious and political communities is *per se* no guarantee that serious inter-denominational religious conflicts may not be the order of the day.[40] But once religion is disestablished from the state and differentiated from political society, litigation over ecclesiastical property rights could be resolved in the courts, and religious conflicts could be routinized into the normal institutional competition between religious firms competing on a more or less free and open religious market.

Barring the unlikely unification of the various Ukrainian denominations, Catholic and Orthodox, under a single Ukrainian national church, religious denominationalism in Ukraine could also be beneficial to Ukrainian–Russian relations. Despite the frequent calls by Ukrainian nationalist elites to this effect, the emergence of a single Ukrainian national church confronting the imperial claims of the Moscow Patriarchate in Ukraine could only serve to exacerbate Ukrainian–Russian conflicts and to jeopardize not only democratic politics in Ukraine but even national independence. Denominationalism is in this sense an additional obstacle to the actualization of the structural logic of competing discourses analyzed by Motyl.[41]

Obviously, the process of decolonization taking place in Ukraine carries with it the difficult task of finding negotiated solutions to the problems of allocating equitably all kinds of contested resources, military, financial, and ecclesiastical. But the challenge of allocating the ecclesiastical resources of Ukraine among the various denominations should not in principle be more intractable than the problem of allocating the resources of the Black Sea Fleet between the Ukrainian and Russian navies.

How democratic is Ukraine's democracy?

A cautious optimism concerning Ukraine's democratization is justified, at least in view of the absence of the catastrophic scenarios anticipated by so many analysts and in consideration of the solid foundations already established, the significant milestones already passed, and the avoidance of false starts and major mistakes. The transition, however, is far from being over and the outcome is still uncertain. There are evident democratic deficits in all three areas of the polity.

Despite the passage of a new constitution, Ukraine still lacks a fully institution-alized *Rechtsstaat*. Both the liberal political tradition that would place limits on state power and a legal-constitutional tradition are still very weak. There is no clear distinction of matters of state and matters of law. There is an étatist tradition of legalism, but not of constitutionalism; of rule of legislators by decree, but not of rule of law. Ukraine still lacks a fully institutionalized independent judiciary, autonomous professional lawyers' associations, and professional civil servants and "neutral" administrative cadres. All three are essential for the establishment of the rule of law, the only partially effective antidote against rampant corruption in the state administrative and economic spheres. The result is likely to be kleptocracy rather than technocracy and the unrestrained conversion of political into economic capital by the old nomenklatura and the new political elites.

Despite the relatively smooth functioning of political society, the mediating institutions between state and society are woefully inadequate, and Ukraine lacks a proper party system. Rukh's decision to dissolve itself and tacitly support the Kravchuk administration in its state-making efforts, rather than become an oppo-sition party, had significant consequences. It left the Communist Party, an anti-systemic party, as the only functioning national party, and it freed Kravchuk from the need to organize his own presidentialist party in support of his re-election. The so-called "party of power" is not a party at all, but a complex of interlocking nomenklatura networks that rule the country without transparency or public accountability. The chasm between professional politicians and ordinary citizens appears almost unbridgeable. The trust in professional politicians, parties and political institutions is extremely low. An absolute majority of the population (64 percent combining the "don't knows," "undecided," and "none of the above") show no political tendency or party preference. The four largest political tenden-cies (Communists, Socialists, Social Democrats, and National Democrats) together can only gather the support of 28 percent of respondents, while the rest (8 percent) is fragmented into a plethora of minuscule groupings.

Despite the development of a civic culture of pluralism and inter-ethnic tolerance that recognizes the structural conditions of ethno-linguistic and denomi-national pluralism in Ukraine, the development of civil society in Ukraine is weakest on the mobilizational active dimension of the self-organization of society. Voluntary associationism of any kind—cultural, civic, or political—is practically non-existent. So far, the combination of apathy and low civic consciousness, lack of mobilization and stoic self-restraint has facilitated the process of state formation without major conflicts or cleavages, the routinization of elite competition, and the development of a culture of political compromise. The clear aspiration to a free and open civil society is tempered by a recognition of the fragility and the indeterminacy of the process.

We do not know whether there are limits to the lack of trust in political elites and political institutions or at what point negative trust could turn into anti-systemic, anti-democratic, and anti-national sentiments. Confronted with extreme economic hardship, the Ukrainian population has shown amazing resilience, sober realism, and stoic resignation, but we do not know what are the limits to this resignation in the face of the continuing deterioration of the standard of living. We only know from comparative historical experience that democratic systems with high levels of political legitimation are much more resilient to economic crises than less democratic ones.

Given Ukraine's transitional situation, one could equally view the political glass as being half-full or half-empty. Table 5.3 shows that the country is uncertain about the transformation and is basically torn between political and economic alternatives. In this sense, the data capture perfectly the ambiguity and transitional nature of the process. One could interpret this evidence as a confirmation that the country is suspended in a transition between an old order which has been irremediably destroyed, and a desired new one which appears unreachable. A more sanguine and cautiously optimistic reading of the same evidence derives from the following interrelated facts:

- The ruling political elites have made a clear commitment to democratic and economic reforms and towards the progressive integration of Ukraine into the Western hegemonic economic and political international system. The disaffected anti-reform counter-elites can be obstructionist but are unable to formulate a viable alternative. Moreover, they are basically conservative rather than revolutionary elites, who are already benefiting from the emerging political and economic order.
- Due to the geopolitical significance of Ukraine, the West has no choice but to support and pressure the Ukrainian political elites to continue along the chosen path. Given the weakness of the internal pressure from below, Western international pressure serves as external check and as the single instrument of accountability. As long as the Russian stick appears lighter than the Western carrot, the reorientation of Ukraine towards the Western international system is likely to continue.
- There is a tacit, and perhaps all too passive, but increasingly clearer support by at least a plurality of the Ukrainian population of the reform process combined with a sober realism concerning the long-term hardship and difficulties it entails. Though silent, this majority is likely to prevail as long as the anti-reform minorities are equally silent and unwilling or unable to become mobilized. Moreover, the overwhelming consensus on maintaining the rule of law, social peace, and unity at any cost augurs well for the continuation of the reformist inertia. Even if the competing discourses described by Motyl were to gain increasing volume, in Ukraine they are likely to fall on deaf ears. Given the cross-cutting ethno-linguistic and religious cleavages and the ambiguous ethno-political and national identities described in this paper, there is little room for the kind of internal ethnic conflicts in Ukraine which could fuel inter-state conflict between Ukraine and Russia.

Table 5.3 Assessment of the Ukrainian transformation

Do you agree with the following statements?

	Agree	Disagree	Unsure
Ukraine needs to develop along a path similar to that of Western countries	48.6	29.9	21.5
Our country will never have democracy	24.6	46.2	29.3
We currently have the same form of democracy as in Western countries	4.6	78.4	17.0
A capitalist economy based on free business is the best system for Ukraine	35.3	29.3	35.5

Attitudes toward economic transformations:

We need to speed up market transition	28.3
We need a step-by-step market transition	25.2
We need to return to centralized state conditions	26.3
Difficult to say	20.2

Can economic transformation lead Ukraine out of the current crisis?

Yes, in 2–3 years	9.7
Yes, in 4–10 years	23.8
Yes, but it will require over 10 years	31.2
No, any transformation will not help Ukraine	21.2
Difficult to say	14.3

What is your attitude to the privatization of:

	Rather negative	Rather positive	Hard to say
Land	26.1	52.9	21.0
Large business	44.8	27.0	28.2
Small business	18.3	58.2	23.6

Attitudes toward the development of private entrepreneurship:

Completely approve	28.7
Approve more than disapprove	20.2
Difficult to say	23.3
Disapprove more than approve	14.6
Completely disapprove	13.3

Source: "Economic Culture of the Ukrainian Population," February 1996 national survey, Democratic Initiatives Center, Kyiv.

Notes

1 See, for instance, "Ukraine, The Birth and Possible Death of a Country," *The Economist*, 7 May 1994; E.B. Rumer, "Will Ukraine Return to Russia?," *Foreign Policy*, 1994, no. 96, pp. 129–44; P. Klebnikov, "Tinderbox," *Forbes*, 9 September 1996, pp. 158–64.
2 On the incompleteness of the emergence of any of these three patterns, see Chapter 1.

3 On the favorable international environment, see Chapter 8.

4 See Chapter 2.

5 For pessimistic views of the viability of the double or "triple" transition, see A. Przeworski, *Democracy and the Market, Political and Economic Reforms in Eastern Europe and Latin America*, New York: Cambridge University Press, 1991, and C. Offe, "Capitalism by Democratic Design? Democratic Theory Facing the Triple Transition in East Central Europe," *Social Research*, 1991, vol. 58, p. 872. I have countered these views in J. Casanova, "Las enseñanzas de la transición democrática en España," *Ayer*, 1994, no. 15.

6 See T. Kuzio and A. Wilson, *Ukraine, Perestroika to Independence*, New York: St. Martin's Press, 1994; and B. Krawchenko, "Ukraine, The Politics of Independence," in I. Bremmer and R. Taras (eds), *Nation and Politics in the Soviet Successor States*, Cambridge: Cambridge University Press, 1993, pp. 75–98.

7 G.W. Lapidus, V. Zaslavsky, and P. Goldman (eds), *From Union to Commonwealth. Nationalism and Separatism in the Soviet Republics*, Cambridge: Cambridge University Press, 1992, p. 16.

8 The need to solve first the fundamental political problems of the transition before issues of economic reform can be tackled successfully has been argued persuasively by Juan J. Linz and Alfred Stepan on many occasions, notably in "Political Crafting of Democratic Consolidation or Destruction, European and South American Comparisons," in R.A. Pastor (ed.), *Democracy in the Americas. Stopping the Pendulum*, New York: Holmes & Meier, 1989, pp. 41–61, and *Problems of Democratic Transition and Consolidation. Southern Europe, South America, and Post-Communist Europe.*, Baltimore: The Johns Hopkins University Press, 1996.

9 A.J. Motyl, "Structural Constraints and Starting Points, Postimperial States and Nations in Ukraine and Russia," paper presented at the conference on "Post-Communism and Ethnic Mobilization," Cornell University, 21–23 April 1995, p. 10; and A.J. Motyl, *Dilemmas of Independence. Ukraine after Totalitarianism*, New York: Council on Foreign Relations, 1993.

10 D. Arel, "Elite Formation and Elite Conflict," paper presented at the international conference on "Ukrainian National Security," 8–9 May 1997, at The Woodrow Wilson Center of the Kennan Institute Washington, DC.

11 The Democratic Initiatives Research and Educational Center in Kyiv, jointly with the Institute of Sociology of the National Academy of Sciences of Ukraine, has been periodically carrying out national surveys. The results are published by the Democratic Initiatives Center, in its periodical series, *Politychnyi Portret Ukraine*. I have used primarily the May 1994, May 1995, and February 1996 national surveys, and the May 1995 "Social-Political Portrait of Four Ukrainian Cities." In the latter Lviv, represented nationalist Western Ukraine, Donetsk represented Russified Eastern Ukraine, Kyiv was included as the capital and geographic center of the country, and Simferopil represented Crimea.

12 "Ukrainian Society 1994–1995: Opinions, Assessments and Living Standards of the Ukrainian Population," Democratic Initiatives Center, Kyiv, 1995, pp. 6–9.

13 "Economic Culture of Ukrainian Population," no. 16, Democratic Initiatives Center, Kyiv, 1996. This survey was conducted after the adverse consequences of the economic reforms initiated by the Kuchma administration in the fall of 1995 were already being felt.

14 R. Szporluk, "Reflections on Ukraine After 1994: The Dilemmas of Nationhood," *The Harriman Review*, March–May 1994, vol. 7, nos. 7–9.

15 T. Carnes, "Measuring Anti-Semitism in Russia," paper presented at the Annual Meeting of the Association for the Sociology of Religion, Washington, DC, 19 August 1995.

16 O. Khomchuk, "The Far Right in Russia and Ukraine," *The Harriman Review*, July 1995, pp. 40–4.

17 "Ukrainian Society 1994–1995," pp. 5, 8. Results of the Four Cities Survey (Lviv, Kyiv, Donetsk, and Simferopil) show that even in the supposedly nationalist stronghold of Lviv only 2.3 percent of respondents support the radical nationalists ("Political Portrait of Ukraine" 13, 1995, p. 42).

18 E.I. Golovakha and N.V. Panina, "The Development of a Democratic Political Identity in Contemporary Ukrainian Political Culture," in R.F. Farnen (ed.), *Nationalism, Ethnicity, and Identity. Cross National and Comparative Perspectives*, New Brunswick, NJ: Transaction Publishers, 1994, pp. 403–25; and *A Political Portrait of Ukraine. The Results of Four Polls Conducted during the 1994 Election Campaign in Ukraine*, Kyiv, Democratic Initiatives Research and Educational Center, 1994.

19 It was this question, whether the Ukrainian state or some of its policies can be characterized as "nationalizing" in the sense of the term first used by Rogers Brubaker, that provoked the most lively debates in the Conference on "Peoples, Nations, Identities, the Russian–Ukrainian Encounter," at The Harriman Institute, Columbia University, 21–23 September 1995. For a discussion of the concept see Rogers Brubaker, "National Minorities, Nationalizing States, and External National Homelands in the New Europe," *Daedalus*, 1995, vol. 124, pp. 107–32. On its applicability to Ukraine see D. Arel, "Ukraine, The Temptation of the Nationalizing State," in V. Tismaneanu (ed.), *Political Culture and Civil Society in the Former Soviet Union*, Armonk, NY: Sharpe, 1995, and papers presented at the above-mentioned conference: A. Wilson, "Ukraine as a Nationalising State: Will the 'Russians' Rebel?" and I. Bremmer, "How Russian the Russians? New Minorities in the Post-Soviet Regions."

20 J.J. Linz, "Plurinazionalismo e Democrazia," *Revista Italiana di Scienza Politica*, 1995, vol. 25, pp. 21–50.

21 J.J. Linz, "Staatsbildung, Nationbildung und Demokratie," *Transit*, 1994, vol. 7, pp. 43–62.

22 That the simple and not uncommon fact of mixed marriages brings complexity into the neat scheme should be obvious. That individuals and groups can change their ethnic identity either voluntarily or involuntarily is the most elementary fact of Ukrainian history. That ethnic identities do not need to be exclusionary, and that individuals and groups might have simultaneously or sequentially multiethnic identities, is also obvious. In any case, that ethnicity is not a matter of nature, birth, or blood but rather a matter of culture, nurture, and soul should be perfectly clear, despite the many disastrous attempts of modern nationalist ideologies to hide the fact.

23 V. Evtoukh, "Ethnische Minderheiten der Ukraine, Zwischen Realitaeten und Politik," paper presented at the conference on "Peoples, Nations, Identities," at The Harriman Institute, Columbia University, 21–23 September 1995.

24 Y.I. Shevchuk, "Dual Citizenship in Old and New States," unpublished manuscript, Political Science Department, New School for Social Research, New York.

25 V. Khmelko and D. Arel, "Russian Factor and Territorial Polarization in Ukraine," paper presented at the conference on "Peoples, Nations, Identities," at The Harriman Institute, Columbia University, 21–23 September 1995, p. 7.

26 On the difference between a plural and a pluralistic society, see Linz, "Plurinazionalismo e Democrazia."

27 On Russian–Ukrainian relations, see R. Solchanyk, "Russia, Ukraine, and the Imperial Legacy," *Post-Soviet Affairs*, October–December 1993, vol. 9, no. 4, pp. 337–65; J.-P. Himka, "Ukrainians, Russians, and Alexander Solzhenitsyn," *Cross Currents, A Yearbook of Central European Culture*, 1992, vol. 11, pp. 193–205; and J. Morrison, "Pereslayav and After: The Russian–Ukrainian Relationship," *International Affairs*, 1993, vol. 69, no. 4, pp. 677–703.

28 For a more detailed and systematic elaboration of these issues see José Casanova, *Public Religions in the Modern World*, Chicago: University of Chicago Press, 1994.

29 The most comprehensive comparative-historical analysis of processes of secularization in Europe is to be found in D. Martin, *A General Theory of Secularization*, New York: Harper & Row, 1978.

30 On the Uniate Church and its relation to Ukrainian nationalism from the Union of Brest to the present, see O. Halecky, *From Florence to Brest, 1439–1596*, Rome: Sacrum Poloniac Millennium, 1959; J.-P. Himka, "The Greek Catholic Church and Nation-Building in Galicia, 1772–1918," *Harvard Ukrainian Studies*, December 1984, vol. 8, pp. 426–52; P.R. Magocsi (ed.), *Morality and Religion, The Life and Times of Andrei Sheptyts'kyi*, Edmonton: Canadian Institute of Ukrainian Studies, 1989; V. Markus, "Religion and Nationality, The Uniates of the Ukraine," in B. Bociurkiw and J. Strong (eds), *Religion and Atheism in the USSR and Eastern Europe*, London: Macmillan, 1975, pp. 101–22; V. Markus, "Religion and Nationalism in Ukraine," in P. Ramet (ed.), *Religion and Nationalism in Soviet and East European Politics*, Durham, NC: Duke University Press, 1984; and M. Labunka and L. Rudnytzky (eds), *The Ukrainian Catholic Church 1945–1975*, Philadelphia: St. Sophia Religious Association, 1976.

31 B. Bociurkiw, "The Ukrainian Catholic Church in the USSR Under Gorbachev," *Problems of Communism*, November–December 1990, vol. 39, no. 6, pp. 1–19; B. Bociurkiw, "The Ukrainian Greek Catholic Church in the Contemporary USSR," in *Nationalities Papers*, Special Issue on Religious Consciousness in the Glasnost Era, Spring 1992, vol. 20, no. 1, pp. 16–28.

32 On the Ukrainian Orthodox Church, see I. Wlasovsky, *Outline History of the Ukrainian Orthodox Church*, 2 vols, New York: Ukrainian Orthodox Church of USA, 1974–1979; B. Bociurkiw, "The Ukrainian Autocephalous Orthodox Church, 1920–1930: A Case Study in Religious Modernization," in D. Dunn (ed.), *Religion and Modernization in the Soviet Union*, Boulder, CO: Westview, 1977, pp. 310–47; and B. Bociurkiw, *Ukrainian Churches under Soviet Rule, Two Case Studies*, Cambridge, MA: Harvard Ukrainian Studies Fund, 1984.

33 S. Plokhy, "Kyiv vs. Moscow: The Autocephalous Movement in Independent Ukraine," *The Harriman Review*, Spring 1996, vol. 9, nos. 1–2, pp. 32–7.

34 J. Martyniuk, "Religious Preferences in Five Urban Areas of Ukraine," *RFE/RL Research Report*, 9 April 1993, vol. 2, no. 15; J. Martyniuk, "The State of the Orthodox Church in Ukraine," *RFE/RL Research Report*, 18 February 1994, vol. 3, no. 7, pp. 34–41.

35 Martyniuk, "State of the Orthodox Church," p. 38; Plokhy, "Kyiv vs. Moscow," p. 35.

36 According to a Media and Opinion Research (MOR) national survey in May 1993, 48 percent of respondents identified with the UOC–KP, 6 percent with the UOC–MP, 10 percent with the Russian Orthodox Church, and 6 percent with the Greek Catholic Church, while 1 percent declared themselves Roman Catholic, 1 percent Protestant, Jewish or Muslim, 13 percent identified with other religions, 5 percent declared themselves atheist, and 10 percent did not know with which beliefs to identify (Martyniuk, "State of the Orthodox Church," pp. 38–9).

37 "Ukrainian Society 1994–1995," p. 6.

38 The MOR survey of May 1993 indicated that popular support for the Ukrainian Greek Catholic Church was 50 percent in Lviv oblast, 52 percent in Ivano-Frankivsk oblast, and 87 percent in Ternopil oblast (Martyniuk, "State of the Orthodox Church," p. 40).

39 See J. Rupert, "After Survival, Revival for Ukraine's Jews," *The Washington Post*, 30 March 1995; and R. Della Cava, "Jews and Christians of Russia and Ukraine Speak about Anti-Semitism: Notes from a Travel Journal, May–June 1995," unpublished manuscript, 1995.

40 D. Little, *Ukraine, The Legacy of Intolerance*, Washington, DC: United States Institute of Peace Press, 1991.

41 Motyl, "After Empire."

6

POSSIBILITIES FOR CONFLICT AND CONFLICT RESOLUTION IN POST-SOVIET CENTRAL ASIA*

Rajan Menon and Hendrik Spruyt

Few events have been as unforeseen as the end of the Cold War and the disintegration of the Soviet Union into disparate political units. Some of these former union republics, such as the Baltic states, had a previous tradition of independence. The Central Asian states, by contrast, had no historical legacy of modern statehood; they were imperial artifacts. Their borders are artificial creations, and their policies reflect tribal, clan, or kin affiliations more than affinity with the nation-state.

Late state formation and the particularities of nation building will be powerful influences upon both the internal stability of the Central Asian societies, the economic welfare of their inhabitants, and the patterns of inter-state conflict. This chapter compares the mode of state and nation building in Central Asia and the experience of the West European states that have successfully made the transition from early statehood and heterogeneous populations to more integrated and developed units. In brief, we ask whether the European model offers lessons regarding the likelihood of conflict and the prospects for conflict resolution in Central Asia.

The issues of war and peace in Central Asia have never been decided solely by domestic factors. Once at the crossroads of empires and conquering peoples, the Central Asian states today are still at the geographic nexus of potential upheaval. A rising China to the east, trans-border Islamic affinities, new opportunities for Iran and Turkey to increase their influence, and a declining Russian hegemon make for a volatile mix. In short, international factors are, *a fortiori*, critical to any analysis of the post-Soviet area.

The emphasis in this chapter on domestic factors is not meant to challenge this proposition, but to set right an analytical imbalance. This imbalance exists because while most scholars readily concede that the process of state formation and the nature of resulting states shape the prospects for conflict within a region,[1] the liter-

* We would like to thank the participants in the Columbia University/Carnegie project on the former USSR, in particular, Alexander Motyl, Barnett Rubin, and Jack Snyder.

ature on international relations has traditionally privileged systemic, balance of power factors. As a result, the linkage between systemic and domestic sources of conflict remains under-explored.[2] The analysis offered here, of conflict and conflict resolution in the Russian–Central Asian subsystem, highlights this linkage. We regard the interplay between the dynamics of state formation in the center (Russia) and the periphery (Central Asia) to be as essential a part of the equation as the systemic condition of unequal power between center and periphery.

Neo-realist theories that portray inter-state conflict as essentially a function of power differentials suffer from (at least) two flaws.[3] First, in the quest for parsimony, they end up being mechanistic: state behavior is explained *post hoc* by system-level properties that were not specified before the fact. The salience of variations in state formation and domestic processes is ultimately ignored or given perfunctory acknowledgment. Second, neo-realist theories fail to adequately explain what we call the variance problem: why is it that power imbalances do not, *ipso facto*, give rise to conflict (for example, they seldom appear to precipitate war among democracies)?[4] Why do conflict and intervention assume different forms? Both questions suggest that system-level attributes alone are insufficient for understanding conflict and—by extension—conflict resolution. By stressing the interplay between systemic and domestic conditions, it is possible to establish linkages between conflict and state formation. For example, the mere existence of unipolarity in the Russia–Central Asia subsystem tells us that systemic preconditions for conflict exist—and little more. The issues that make for conflict, the conditions that cause preponderant power to be utilized, and the "style" of conflict will depend on a host of issues (the nature of the ruling elite, the degree of political stability, the principles of state legitimacy, the salience and nature of nationalism) that can be subsumed under the broad rubric of state formation.

To be sure, few neo-realists would deny that domestic variables matter in explaining foreign policy. But in their search for parsimonious explanations, domestic variables are generally relegated to secondary importance. As some realists such as Stephen Walt and Steven David have shown, however, the domestic level of analysis must be given equal weight as the systemic level.[5] In order to operationalize balancing against threat (Walt) and to explain alignment choices (David) an analysis of domestic conditions is essential. This chapter specifies which domestic variables matter and demonstrates how they interact with systemic variables to produce peace or war.

The chapter starts with an evaluation of the peculiarities of state and nation building in Central Asia, using the European experience for comparative insights. It then examines three domestic conditions that might generate strife: the modality of nationalism, the level of institutionalization and social mobilization, and the effects of the post-Soviet economic transition. It concludes with an examination of mechanisms for preventing and resolving conflict, evaluating various alternatives: national policies to promote ethnic harmony, balance of power strategies, regional security mechanisms, and solutions involving extra-regional organizations. Throughout, the analysis assumes a dynamic interaction between domestic and systemic variables.

State formation in Europe and Central Asia

This section highlights the features that were critical to Western state formation and nation building, and contrasts these with developments in Central Asia. There at least three reasons why this is useful.[6] First, it is worth examining whether state formation in Europe and the more recent process of state formation in developing countries, such as those in Central Asia, might evolve through similar dynamics. Jeffrey Herbst has undertaken just such a comparison between Europe and Africa, predicting that state formation in Africa is likely to lead to conflict.[7] Will the ubiquitousness and frequency of conflict that characterized the European process repeat itself in Central Asia? Second, as in early Europe, sovereign, territorial authority in Central Asia is still challenged by alternative systems of rule such as clan membership, religious affiliation, extended kinship structures, and so on. What effect does this have on governmental capacity, and how might it shape the political strategies of ruling elites? Third, given the weakness of both political institutions and democracy in Central Asia, and the degree of ethnic diversity, it behooves us to understand how the Western European states succeeded in integrating their societies and economies in the face of these obstacles.

The Western experience of early state formation

The current Westphalian system of discrete, territorially-defined states first emerged toward the late Middle Ages in Western Europe. Roughly from the eleventh century on, aspiring rulers started to re-assert their long dormant claims to central authority. In order to assert such claims, they had to combat the fragmented powers of local lords, counts, dukes, towns, and bishops. At the same time, kings and princes started to challenge more universalistic forms of rule, such as that of the German emperors and the Roman church, that claimed authority over them. The construction of sovereign, territorial states was thus at once the evolution of political authority upward from the feudal fragments of the neo-Carolingian period and, at the same time, a devolution of power downward from those who still had universal and imperial aspirations to control all of Christian Europe.

How did state formation succeed given the opposition of local centers of power? What forms of government emerged out of this? How did disparate ethnic groups come to identify with, and if necessary die for, the nation-state? Explanations vary considerably as to what ultimately drove the formation of territorial states in Western Europe. One explanation stresses the changes in the nature of warfare from roughly 1400 onward.[8] Among such changes were the shift from relatively small armies, based primarily on the heavy cavalry of the mounted knight, to larger infantry armies using new weapons such as the longbow, pike and, later, artillery and firearms. These new modes of warfare necessitated greater taxation and commensurate larger administration. To use Charles Tilly's phrase, "war made the state, and the state made war."[9] Others tend to stress the renewal of trade, particularly long-distance trade, which led to urbanization and the monetary means to make state building possible. The bargains that kings struck with the aristocracy or the towns enabled kings to acquire the resources to diminish the political power of local lords and at the same time challenge non-territorial forms of rule.[10] The local and cross-cutting nature of feudal jurisdictions made trade and economic transactions very difficult, and hence there were incentives for the mercantile classes to favor a more centralized rule under a king or prince rather than the haphazard jurisdictions of local lords.

We will not try to settle here the debate about whether warfare or the economic transformation of the Late Middle Ages was ultimately the driving force. What is more important is to highlight the critical elements of the Western European state building process. The first element worth emphasizing is that territorial rulers had to forge coalitions with local centers of power. From its very beginning, the transition from feudalism to sovereign, territorial state contained a contractual element. This contractual element has arguably been one of the bases of the emergence of modern democracies. Ironically, as James Given suggests in his comparison of French and English strategies of incorporation, *ad hoc* bargaining with local centers of power tended to lead to more durable central control than outright coercion.[11] Second, the consolidation of internal power logically entailed the differentiation from external systems of rule. To establish a hierarchical and final locus of decision making, the king had to assert his power and authority over competitors: the church, kinship groups, and tribes. In other words, the establishment of sovereign rule entailed a twofold process: the creation of internal hierarchy and its external demarcation by formal borders. Alternative systems of rule, at both the translocal and sub-state level, had to be displaced in a long historical process in which the positive state capacity of modern states negated alternative political loyalties.[12]

Third, because an international system emerged out of relatively small and territorially discrete elements, these early states could not avoid competing and interacting. Military competition and economic mercantilism therefore went hand in hand. Continuous warfare required economic mobilization. Economic mobilization in turn led to the competition over resources and trade routes and thus more war. Thus in the sixteenth and seventeenth centuries there was roughly one major war under way every three years.[13]

In Europe, this Darwinian process of competition gradually ratcheted the capacities of governments upward. From the late Middle Ages on, Europe witnessed not only the emergence of sovereign, territorial rule but also a gradual increase in the capacities of government to affect many spheres of social life. But again, such demands on social groups were at least partially tolerated because of the contractual nature of government. Without suggesting that democracy was ubiquitous, it is fair to say that European governments required at least a measure of quasi-consent from critical social actors.[14]

Elsewhere in the world, by contrast, imperial or theocratic states tended to dominate. They interacted less with one another and thus were not subject to the continuous process of competitive pressures in Europe.[15] While other empires were recognized, they were considered peripheral and inferior and thus preferably avoided. As a consequence, the non-European empires never developed the governmental capacities of the European states. As Michael Mann noted, imperial governance ran wide but not deep.[16] The relatively limited impact that these states had on society coexisted with a more despotic form of rule. Such government was likely to be more despotic because social bargains were less fundamental to governance and because autonomous forms of local government had not emerged to the same degree as in medieval Europe. This inability of empires to mobilize and control their disparate societal groups plagued even modern empires such as Tsarist Russia and even the USSR.[17]

Fourth, early state formation meant that the transition from decentralized and fragmented rule to sovereign, well-integrated governments was gradual and protracted. The earliest states faced an environment where armies and, concomitantly, the revenue necessary to support them, were relatively small. Feudal armies were rarely much larger than ten thousand strong, and quite often smaller. Moreover, while military technology changed, the implications of such change took a long time to work themselves out politically. True, the size of armies started to increase rapidly in the fifteenth and sixteenth centuries, but it was not until the French revolution and its *levée en masse* that warfare would become a national and hence nationalist endeavor. Only in the nineteenth century did competitive pressure force others to adopt the French integration of state and nationalism.[18] In this sense, early state formation required fewer material resources to be devoted to military expenditures, and only over time were greater societal sacrifices necessary.

Fifth, and following from the above, the sovereign, territorial state preceded the full incorporation of its members. That is, there were borders before everyone within those borders considered themselves citizens.[19] When the government expanded its powers it incorporated its members by civic nationalism, by using territorial markers of whom to include.

Finally, early modernization and industrialization allowed some governments to make the transition to modernity with relatively little government intervention. The resources required to obtain a competitive position were sustainable by the private sector. Late modernizers, as in Central Europe, and states that made an even later transition, such as Russia, adopted far more intrusive economic and political structures.

In sum, the process of European state formation was a process of negotiation between roughly symmetrical powers of rulers and feudal periphery. The gradual crystallization into distinct territorial units, none of which managed to dominate the others by itself, and shifts in military technology, precipitated many conflicts. Social mobilization and national integration occurred through civic nationalism. The European states were at the forefront of a great economic transition. Even though economic rationalization took place through mercantilist strategies, the finance and management required for developing capitalist enterprises came largely from the private sector.

Late state formation in Central Asia

The development of independent states in the post-Soviet space diverged considerably from the European historical experience on virtually all dimensions. This poses particular and unique problems for these newer states.

First, sovereign territoriality has been imposed by external agents and events. The Central Asian states were formed by veritable administrative fiat in the Stalinist era.[20] Whereas Lenin saw nationalism as a transient problem but one which, for the time being, needed to be taken seriously, Stalin was far less tolerant. As a result, Moscow-imposed governments that were favorably disposed to the Stalinist system and assigned largely arbitrary borders to the republics and autonomous territories. In Central Asia, as elsewhere in the USSR, state boundaries and ethnic composition thus lacked correspondence. This was part of a deliberate strategy to weaken peripheral resistance.

Second, in the post-Soviet period, sovereign states emerged in Central Asia due to the collapse of the Soviet system rather than as the result of strong independence movements. Unlike the Baltic republics, Moldova, and the states of the Trans-Caucasus, the Central Asian states gained independence thanks to imperial collapse and not the interplay between that collapse and pro-independence nationalist mass movements.

Third, the Central Asian states emerged on the scene as late developers. They are newly-formed political units in an existing global system where sovereign, territorial rule is a prerequisite for recognition by and respect from other states. Moreover, they face other states with well-established bureaucracies and modern national armies. If it is a precondition for late economic developers to have a strong government in order to compete effectively with earlier developers, as Alexander Gerschenkron and others suggest, it is that very precondition, an effective and strong government, that is sorely lacking in Central Asia.[21]

As noted previously, the European states emerged in a three-way contest among fragmented, non-territorial rule, territorial rulers, and universalistic authorities. By contrast, in Central Asia, the principle of sovereign, territorial rule has simply been the product of external dynamics. While states are supposed to adhere to territorial rule and have a final locus of authority, in Central Asia, rival forms of rule such as clan membership, Islam, and ethnic and regional affinities have not been displaced by centralizing, high-capacity states. Nor have these states been the beneficiaries of competition. Where competition with foes allowed for greater unity and stronger government, as in the Second World War, this largely favored the central government in Moscow, thus undercutting the very strength of the republics which have now become independent.

For all these reasons, the governments in Central Asia lack positive state capacity.[22] They have to adhere to territorially-defined rule, and in this respect resemble the European states. However, the ability of Central Asian governments to place demands on their societies, and their legitimacy to do so, are weak at best.

Thus, Central Asia's historical trajectory is the virtual opposite of Europe's.

Imperial domination meant that the union republics did not have to mobilize their societies for frequent conflict. When external enemies had to be confronted, the locus of identification was Moscow. Consequently, the administrative power of the imperial center grew at the expense of the peripheral units during wartime. Moreover, the governments of the union republics were economically caught in a division of labor that was defined by the center.

This inability of local elites to create alliances and provide side-payments to increase their own power made it unattractive for non-titular ethnic groups to orient their allegiance toward the titular nationality. If there was any inducement to downplay ethnic markers or to dissociate from clan and other sub-national loyalties, it was to obtain benefits from the center. Russification, party allegiance, and secularization were part of a strategic exchange with Moscow. The titular groups, who are now the rulers of the independent Central Asian states, did not, however, have much to offer. Hence, the current problem: how can weak states induce sub-national ethnic, clan, and regional groups to recognize the legitimacy of a national state run by the titular nationality?

The interplay of systemic and domestic causes of conflict

Systemic variables

A variety of systemic (balance of power) variables will influence developments in Central Asia. The first and most important condition is the large asymmetry of power between Russia and the Central Asian states, which is not going to diminish in the foreseeable future. The balance of power still overwhelmingly favors Russia, despite its many problems. Consider, for example, the comparison offered in Table 6.1 between Russia and Central Asia using some standard measures of military power. If other measures, such as GNP, population, and industrial output, are used, the picture remains the same: Russia has an overwhelming advantage.[23]

True, the disarray in the Russian military has made intervention in the periphery problematic for Moscow.[24] Yet, as Russia's role in shaping the conflicts in Tajikistan, Moldova, and Georgia shows, in peripheral states characterized by weak regimes, poorly-integrated societies, and minuscule militaries, the extent of Russian leverage remains considerable. Moreover, as the civil wars in Tajikistan and Georgia demonstrate, peripheral ruling elites may be forced to call on the forces of the erstwhile hegemon to maintain territorial integrity against internal and external foes.

The second significant systemic variable is the power transition underway between Russia and China.[25] Should China continue its rapid economic and military growth, the Central Asian states will be forced to balance an incipient threat, thus ensuring continued dependency upon Russia.[26] In the future the changing balance of power may well negate the possibility of Russia serving as an effective counterweight. Should this occur, and be compounded by the ethnic

Table 6.1 Russia and Central Asia: power comparisons

	Tanks	APCs	Artillery	SSMs	Aircraft	Helicopters	1994 Defense budget (million $US)
Russia	19,500	35,000	24,000	600	3,000	2,400	79,000
Kazakstan	1,100	2,200	2,000	0	32	100	450
Kyrgyzstan	240	465	135	0	200	0	57
Tajikistan	200	420	200	0	0	0	115
Turkmenistan	900	1,500	800	12	160	0	153
Uzbekistan	125	700	465	4	100	50	375

Sources: For military hardware: Institute for National Strategic Studies, *Strategic Assessment 1995*, Washington, DC: Institute for National Strategic Studies, 1995, p. 65. For budgets: International Institute for Strategic Studies, *The Military Balance, 1994–1995*, London: International Institute for Strategic Studies, 1995, pp. 111, 156, 162–3.
Note: Abbreviations are: APCs (armored personnel carriers and infantry fighting vehicles); SSMs (tactical surface-to-surface missiles)

Balkanization of Russia, China might become the external hegemon.[27] However, given that China remains predominantly oriented toward Northeast Asia, the more relevant balance of power for the near term is between Russia and the Central Asian states.

Domestic variables

As important as the systemic variables are, conflict is only likely to occur when they interact with certain domestic variables. In other words, Russia's preponderant power is a necessary but not sufficient condition for predicting its relationship with Central Asia. Given the nature of state formation in Central Asia, local governments face three principal domestic challenges. First, how do they create a national identity? Do they use a civic or ethnic strategy? Second, how do they create robust political institutions? Third, how do they engage in economic reform and modernization?

Ethnic nationalism

In the literature on nationalism, it has become a commonplace to distinguish between the "ethnic" and the "civic" variants. In ethnic nationalism cultural traits that cannot be acquired serve as the criteria for community membership. (One cannot, for example, "become" a Kazak in a historical-cultural sense by an act of volition or an administrative procedure.) Civic nationalism, by contrast, confers citizenship and belonging based on attributes that can be acquired regardless of original ethnic affiliation.[28] By definition, ethnic nationalism is exclusive and civic nationalism inclusive.

While inter-state and intra-state conflict are most likely if ethnic nationalism is mobilized by state elites as a device to create solidarity and legitimacy, there is, of course, no inherent reason why they should do so. Indeed, in Central Asia, ruling elites have shied away from embracing ethnic nationalism for a variety of reasons, and we do not assume that the triumph of ethnic nationalism is inevitable. Central Asia's leaders are well aware of the danger of alienating Russia, which remains watchful over the fate of ethnic Russians in the so-called "near abroad." Moreover, Central Asia's leaders do not want to accelerate the already substantial exodus of ethnic Russians, whose technical skills are essential to local economies. They are also mindful of the danger of promoting tensions between the titular nationality and other ethnic groups. Finally, as former Soviet-era leaders, they have been socialized to look askance at ethnic nationalism.

Yet these inhibiting conditions do not rule out the rise of ethnic nationalism.[29] Ruling elites may be driven to construct and mobilize ethnic modalities of nationalism when economic crises and concomitant political instabilities make them vulnerable to challenges from counter-elites who use the politics of clan, region, and religion as symbols to recruit followers. Under such conditions, state elites may embrace ethnic nationalism both to bolster their legitimacy and to delegitimize the opposition as divisive. But the construction and mobilization of ethnic nationalism (as the experience of the former Yugoslavia shows all too well) entails delineating a negative reference society or an "out group."[30] In multiethnic societies, this is a recipe for turmoil.

Ethnic nationalism may emerge for another reason. The turnover in ruling elites may bring to power individuals who are much more willing to use nationalism for purposes of displacing the existing Soviet-era ruling elites and, later, for state legitimation. And, given Central Asia's demographic structure, which is marked by a population that is both very young and increasing rapidly, there is bound to be considerable scope for elite turnover.[31]

Ethnic nationalism underscores the differences between "us" and "them," and defines political power and community membership in ways that privilege the "in group." It follows that the greater the degree of ethnic diversity within a state, the greater the danger that ethnic nationalism will create instability and conflict. It also follows that the conflictual consequences of ethnic nationalism will be particularly acute where the disjuncture between state and national boundaries creates diasporas and the potential for irredentism. The data in Table 6.2 should be studied with these two stipulations in mind. Particularly worth noting are the ethnic diversity of Kazakstan, Kyrgyzstan, and Tajikistan, the existence of a diaspora of 10 million Russians in Central Asia (of which 6 million are in Kazakstan alone), and the potential for irredentist conflicts between Russia and Kazakstan, Uzbekistan and Tajikistan, and Uzbekistan and Kyrgyzstan. In the Russian–Central Asian subsystem, the rise of ethnic nationalism could result in a volatile mix between systemic conditions (with the power imbalance favoring Russia) and domestic conditions (with conflict and instability generated by ethnic nationalism).

Table 6.2 Central Asia: ethnic composition of states, 1989 (percentages)

	Russians	Kazaks	Kyrgyz	Tajiks	Turkmen	Uzbeks	Total (1,000s)
Kazakstan	38	39	(negl.)	(negl.)	(negl.)	2	16,464
Kyrgyzstan	22	(negl.)	52	(negl.)	—	13	4,258
Tajikistan	7	(negl.)	1	62	(negl.)	24	5,093
Turkmenistan	9	2	—	(negl.)	71	9	3,552
Uzbekistan	8	4	(negl.)	5	(negl.)	71	19,810

Source: Central Asia Monitor, 1992, vol. 1, no. 3, pp. 39–40.
Notes:
a) negl. (neglegible) means under 1 percent;—means none reported.
b) Figures are for 1991–2.
c) Percentages denote given nationality as a share of total population.

Social mobilization and political institutionalization

Political institutionalization here means the legitimacy (degree of support) and capacity (ability to extract resources, maintain stability, and cope with opposition—whether by repression, co-optation, or offering opportunities for participation) possessed by states. Social mobilization is defined as the increased aspirations and activism of citizens who organize to make demands on the state as a result of dissatisfaction and exposure to (internal and external) political, cultural, economic, and religious forces. The weaker political institutionalization is in relation to social mobilization, the greater are the chances that the state will be overburdened and susceptible to instability.[32] Under conditions of weak political institutionalization and significant social mobilization, ruling elites will either be robbed of their capacity to rule, or they will react with repression to prevent instability. Inherent in either response is the prospect for greater domestic instability.

In turn, this condition creates an incentive for powerful neighboring states to intervene, whether in the guise of protecting their ethnic kin, or safeguarding security interests deemed vital. A chain reaction might result. The best example of this is the Tajik civil war.[33] In Tajikistan, an imbalance between institutionalization and social mobilization (a weak regime led by communist-era holdovers facing an assorted opposition featuring democrats, Islamists, and regional and nationalist elites) led to a breakdown of state authority. This sparked intervention by Russia and Uzbekistan, who acted to defend their interests: Russia feared that turbulence in its southern perimeter would have a domino effect, while Uzbekistan's authoritarian ruler, Islam Karimov, was similarly worried that the spectacle of a Tajik regime being overpowered by mobilized citizens could spark instability at home— a fear compounded by the presence within Uzbekistan of 934,000 Tajiks.

The challenge of social mobilization can be dealt with in at least three ways. First, ruling elites might resort to those strategies that marked the European process. Simply put, they might highlight differences and controversies with other republics, and perhaps even resort to war to justify efforts to increase state capacities and as a means to channel social mobilization outward. Rulers have tended to maintain that challenges to the existing regime, if not to the state itself, require increased powers of surveillance and a stronger military. While they have not always highlighted conflicts with other states in the region, they have tended to dramatize challenges by non-state actors and non-regional states. For example, the Tajik government has emphasized the threat posed by Islamic elements in the opposition (and the support extended to them by Afghan Islamists) both to bolster its authority and to gain support from other governments (principally Russia and Uzbekistan) who fear similar dangers.[34]

Second, state elites can seek to co-opt social mobilization. Such a strategy would use civic organizations, a free press, elections, and parliaments (all mechanisms for extending political participation) to tame social mobilization by diverting it from the streets into political institutions. The calculation would be that dissatisfaction would be manifested through institutions, resulting in within-system bargaining and resolution. This strategy could be combined with patronage directed at disaffected elites so that mass disaffection is rendered leaderless. This approach has been followed in Russia, Kazakstan, and Kyrgyzstan so far, although we avoid the term "democratic" to categorize this strategy.[35]

Third, regimes can deal with social mobilization by closing off opportunities for political participation, or even resorting to outright repression. This approach has been adopted in Tajikistan.[36] It is also evident in Turkmenistan and Uzbekistan, where the opposition (*Agzybirlik* in the former, and *Birlik*, *Erk*, and the Islamic Renaissance Party in the latter) has been subjected to harassment, intimidation, and bans—with little evidence of popular opposition. In Turkmenistan a one-party system exists (the former communist party structure of the Turkmen Soviet Socialist Republic has essentially been reincarnated as the Democratic Party, the only registered party in the country) with true power belonging to the president, Saparmurad Niazov, whose portraits, statues, and sayings are everywhere.[37] In Uzbekistan, the cult of Islam Karimov is far less pervasive (but still apparent), but he runs the country by balancing regional and tribal interests via the National Democratic Party and by concentrating power in his hands. While the *Watan Tariqiati* party contested the December 1994 elections and poses as an effective opposition (and is so depicted by the regime), it is, in fact, a docile organization created with the approval of Karimov in a move to defuse Western criticisms of Uzbekistan's human rights record.[38]

This response to social mobilization may work indefinitely, particularly if citizens remain passive, an economic crisis does not occur, and the ruling group avoids internecine conflict. But the danger—as illustrated by the ongoing civil war in Tajikistan—is that festering problems (economic deterioration, a political opposition that feels disenfranchised) can culminate in instability and undermine this strategy. Worse still, to the extent that state formation creates systems that allow for little or no within-system participation, instability can produce extra-systemic, revolutionary movements. Such revolutionary agendas and strategies are apt to be radical precisely because they have not been "tamed" by the bargaining and wheeling and dealing inherent in systemic participation. In states that face social mobilization, but lack mechanisms for within-system participation, such radical movements are most apt to become potent under two circumstances: when economic crises and political stability have weakened the legitimacy and capacity of the state, making it more vulnerable; and when a void has been created by the departure (by death or overthrow) of a dominant leader such as Karimov in Uzbekistan or Niazov in Turkmenistan.

The political fallout of economic reform

The most likely context for the rise of ethnic nationalism and social mobilization that overwhelms the state is a failed post-Soviet economic transition. For Central Asian states, this transition involves the transformation of Soviet-era economies— based on state-owned industries, heavy subsidies from Moscow, and the usurpation by the state of the market's role in allocating resources and determining prices— into systems defined by markets and private property.

There are many reasons why the old system cannot be maintained indefinitely in Central Asia. First, its counterpart in the center (Russia) is being dismantled, and subsidies, guaranteed markets, and cheap inputs can no longer be taken for granted. Second, acquiring aid from international agencies (the IMF and the World Bank) and attracting foreign investment will require reforms that expand the role of markets and private property.[39] Third, Central Asian states will be operating in a global environment in which it is assumed that the model of state ownership and regulation has proven a failure: the changes afoot in China, the former Soviet Union, Eastern Europe, Vietnam, Brazil, and India testify to this. Economic efficiency requires a transition to market systems. Consequently, main- tenance of the status quo would make Central Asia not just an anomaly but a poor partner for trade and foreign investment. True, the degree to which ruling elites in Central Asia are convinced by this logic varies: Kyrgyzstan and Kazakstan have made significant strides towards economic reform, Uzbekistan is a late starter and a cautious and reluctant convert, while Turkmenistan and Tajikistan have made few changes. Nevertheless, it is reasonable to assume that, with due allowance for variations within the region and a trajectory marked by backsliding, an inexorable process of economic reform is underway.

While economists have insisted (correctly) that market reforms are essential for long-term efficiency in the post-Soviet states, they have paid less attention to the implications of their advice for short-term stability.[40] Yet policies adopted in the name of long-run efficiency can create short-term instability: dismantling ineffi- cient state enterprises can increase unemployment at a time when budgetary conditions preclude an increase in social welfare programs to cushion the blow; removing the subsidies on staples in order to curb budget deficits can cause prices to soar; market reforms can increase the opportunities for the well connected and powerful, while pushing those without such attributes to the margins of economic life.

The creation of private enterprises in the long term could expand the supply of goods and employment opportunities. However, for nascent states marked by weak institutionalization and legitimacy that depend heavily on the longevity of an all-powerful leader (a description that applies in varying degrees to all Central Asian states), it is precisely the political short run that is the most dangerous. If they encounter a wayward post-Soviet economic transition marked by rising inequality and unemployment, counter-elites could emerge, using mobilizational strategies based on ethnic nationalism and Islam. The use of repression against such challenges could increase the danger of political instability, while efforts by ruling elites to steal the thunder of the opposition could push regimes in the direction of ethnic nationalism. Economic dislocations can also create struggles over relative gains and promote ethnic tensions. This was exemplified in Central Asia by the 1989 clash between Uzbeks and Meshketian Turks in the Ferghana Valley and the 1990 conflict between Uzbeks and Kyrgyz in Kyrgyzstan's Osh province. Economic reforms that restructure industries in which the non-titular ethnic groups are statistically over-represented can increase ethnic conflict. Thus defense industries in northern Kyrgyzstan and heavy and defense industries in northern Kazakstan employ a disproportionate number of ethnic Russians, and economic reforms in these regions could, in the short-run, entail an efficiency versus stability tradeoff.

To the extent that fragile state structures are unable to withstand the short-run externalities (whether resulting from willful economic reform or unforeseen consequence of post-Soviet economic deterioration) generated by economic dislocations, the prospect for upheaval (marked by ethnic nationalism and heightened social mobilization) within states increases. It is at this point that the systemic condition (the power imbalance between center and periphery) becomes relevant. The reason is that instability within its strategic perimeter could induce elites within the center to intervene in the name of national security or the protection of endangered ethnic kin.

In the unipolar Russia–Central Asia subsystem, three domestic-level variables (type of nationalism, the strength of political institutions, and the success or failure of economic reform) will interact with the preponderant power of the traditional hegemonic power (Russia) to promote conflict. There is, of course, no automaticity involved here: instability in the periphery does not, for example, guarantee Russian intervention. That depends as well on the nature of state formation and domestic politics in Russia. Intervention using military force is least likely when a democratic regime exists in Russia and the power of ultra-nationalist groups is weak. The prospects for intervention are increased when logrolling by ultra-nationalist groups deploying imperial myths puts state elites on the defensive; democrats inside and outside the government become divided and some tack to the right for political survival; and state legitimacy is low due to severe economic problems.

Authoritarian-nationalist elites are more likely to resort to intervention for a variety of reasons. They have traditionally been less concerned with Western disapproval and, indeed, have viewed what the West can offer as leverage (aid and investment), not as assets to be sought but as forces of dependence and subversion to be kept at bay. Their power base is constituted by nationalist forces and national security bureaucracies (the intelligence services and the armed forces), for whom a secure frontier is a first-order objective. And their legitimacy derives heavily from a promise to assert Russian interests in the periphery.

To sum up, scenarios for conflict in Central Asia take Russian preponderance, the key systemic variable, as a given. Consequently, it is the inter-relationship between stability in the periphery (itself a function of the type of nationalism, the robustness of political institutions, and the success or failure of economic reform) and the nature of the regime in the center.

Conflict resolution and conflict prevention

Mitigating internal causes of conflict

Measures to reduce the possibility for ethnic strife are most relevant for those Central Asian states in which a significant percentage of the population is constituted by non-titular nationalities.[41] The three most diverse republics are Kazakstan, Kyrgyzstan, and Tajikistan. Kazakstan had 6.2 million Russians who made up 38 percent of the population in 1989, although the emigration of Russians, the immigration of Kazaks (from Russia, Chinese Xinjiang, and Mongolia), and the higher rate of population growth of the Kazaks is reducing the proportion of Russians. Kazakstan's Russian population is concentrated in northern provinces near Russia.[42] Kyrgyzstan's Russian population (916,558) constitutes 21.5 percent of the total, while the 550,000 Uzbeks account for 13 percent. In Tajikistan, the number of Russians, which stood at 338,481 in 1989, has been reduced drastically by emigration propelled by the ravages of civil war, but the Uzbek population is large both in absolute terms (1.2 million) and as a proportion of the total population of the country (24 percent). By contrast, Turkmenistan, where the titular nationality accounts for 71 percent of the population, and Uzbekistan, where Uzbeks make up an identical percentage of the total population, are far more homogeneous.

A number of measures could be considered to reduce the likelihood of ethnic conflict in the three relatively non-homogeneous Central Asia states, but each has significant tradeoffs. One approach is consociational politics along the lines suggested by Arend Lijphart.[43] This would allocate key political posts at both the central and local levels on a proportionality principle that mirrors the ethnic segmentation of the country. For central positions, aggregate proportions could be used as the criteria for allocation, while at the local level, the ethnic composition of a given region could be the standard. The objective would be to quell fears of domination by the titular nationality by giving other ethnic groups access to institutions that determine the allocation of resources and control the direction of policy so as to create a state in which all members feel represented and enfranchised.

This strategy has disadvantages. Consociationalism worked well in the Netherlands, where authority was fragmented, "pillarized" in Lijphart's terms, among various religious denominations. Ethnic conflict has been avoided through a system of compromise among powerful elites and the equal allotment of political representation and governmental revenue. Consociationalists have thus suggested that a similar strategy might work in such heavily divided and contentious societies as Northern Ireland, Lebanon, and South Africa. However, the latter cases suggest to others that where consociationalism has worked, the prevailing institutional arrangements have been the effect rather than the cause of stability. In a more general sense, it is not clear which particular institutional designs are likely to yield desirable outcomes.

Consociational strategies may also reinforce, indeed institutionalize, the tendency to see politics as an arena for ethnic strife and actually retard the salience of other markers of identity and loyalty (region, class) that could emerge as cross-cutting cleavages and undermine the potentially explosive marker of ethnicity. Ethnic strife may not take an extra-systemic/conflictual form, but may become permanently imbedded in systemic politics such that public policy decisions concerning priorities, goals, and resource allocation are driven by ethnic discord and competition over relative gains. The net effect may be to retard the development of a civic nationalism in which the ethnic origin of political elites is seen as secondary to the larger objectives of national welfare and efficiency. Finally, given that certain ethnic groups (Russians in Kazakstan and Kyrgyzstan, for example) dominate key sectors such as industry and defense in Central Asia, the move to implement proportional representation along ethnic lines may actually exacerbate ethnic conflict. Nevertheless, a long-term, gradual consociational strategy may increase the sense of belonging.

The consociational approach could be supplemented by other measures: the acceptance of the principle of dual citizenship (Turkmenistan and Russia reached agreement on this in December 1993);[44] political autonomy for regions inhabited principally by a non-titular nationality; the recognition of Russian as having co-equal status with the language of the titular nationality (President Askar Akaev of Kyrgyzstan supports this policy); and the creation and preservation of an intellectual and cultural infrastructure (newspapers, radio stations, televisions channels, schools and universities) that represents the culture and utilizes the language of non-titular nationalities.[45] These measures would be designed to reduce the prospects for ethnic conflict by increasing the likelihood that all members of the political community, irrespective of ethnic affiliation, feel that the state reflects their aspirations.[46]

Here again, however, there are tradeoffs. Such measures of ethnic conciliation in general reinforce ethnic segmentation. Moreover, with the states of Central Asia only recently having become independent, expectations for empowerment on the part of the titular nationalities run high, and there is a widespread belief that local cultures and languages should be protected against erosion. Governments that are seen as appeasing the Russian minority and the Russian government may face a nationalist backlash, particularly if economic crises create opportunities for harnessing titular nationalism as a means to mobilize support against governments. More specifically, Central Asian governments may look askance at the concept of dual citizenship, fearing that it would be a justification for Russia to insert itself into ethnic disputes in other countries as a champion of the local Russian population.

Yet on balance, such steps are likely to reduce the sense of alienation and non-belonging. Ethnic segmentation is an existential fact in Kazakstan, Kyrgyzstan, and Tajikistan. The real issue is whether it will be manifested peacefully within institutions or in a disruptive, and potentially violent, extra-systemic manner. As for the danger of legitimating interference by hegemons on behalf of their ethnic kin, the likelihood of this happening will have much more to do with the variables of relative national power and internal ethnic discord than with legal and administrative principles.

A final approach to reducing internal ethnic conflict (and, by extension, inter-state war resulting from it) involves managing economic restructuring in a way that minimizes strife among nationalities. As we have argued, the move toward markets and private property can increase instability in general by aggravating inequality and increasing misery via inflation, unemployment, and reduced social welfare benefits. However, in societies marked by significant ethnic segmentation, these externalities are particularly apt to create ethnic mobilization and protest if the burdens of change are perceived as falling disproportionately on a non-titular ethnic group. Thus, restructuring should proceed with an awareness of the sectoral distribution of ethnic groups within the economy. Sectors that employ large numbers of major non-titular nationalities should be made to move toward marketization and privatization only once the state has plans in place for compensation, retraining, and social welfare programs. Both bilateral and multilateral aid donors should encourage and support programs that seek to mitigate the ethnic fallout of economic reform.

International financial institutions (the IMF and World Bank) can reduce the problems posed by the externalities of economic reform. External support will ease the difficult transition to the market by enabling the state to compensate those segments in society (such as ethnic groups that are over-represented in declining industries) that are likely to bear disproportionate burdens. This will lessen the prospects for ethnic strife and radical social mobilization—the very factors that could contribute to inter-state conflict.[47]

Mitigating systemic causes of conflict

Recently, international organizations have received considerable attention as mechanisms for conflict resolution and prevention.[48] While international organizations can contribute to mitigating conflict, given the vast preponderance of Russian power, we remain skeptical about the great salutary effects sometimes ascribed to them; but there is no reason why solutions to conflict through international organizations should not be tried. A multi-layered approach involving bilateral, regional and global organizations is the most appropriate strategy.

This approach is desirable for a number of reasons. First, some issues, such as accords on borders, are best negotiated bilaterally by the concerned parties. Second, purely narrow regional solutions may work primarily to the advantage of would-be hegemons (Russia and Uzbekistan). Third, inasmuch as some solutions (the creation of conflict resolution centers staffed by trained personnel) presuppose funding, the involvement of non-regional actors increases the potential resource base. Fourth, the judicious involvement of extra-regional actors may offset the lack of leverage that weaker regional states suffer in bargaining.

Since Russia favors the Commonwealth of Independent States (CIS) as a vehicle for security co-operation between the former Soviet republics, the CIS could serve as the foundation of a regional collective security system. The 1992 Tashkent agreement on collective security, the agreement for the joint defense of the CIS borders, and the creation of a common air defense system suggest *prima facie* that such a co-operative approach to security is evolving.[49] So does the co-operation between Russia, Kazakstan, Kyrgyzstan, and Uzbekistan on defending the Tajikistan–Afghanistan border. Except for Turkmenistan, which has stayed clear of participating in the security structures of the CIS, the other Central Asian states favor multilateral security co-operation.

But there are drawbacks to this strategy. If one assumes that the major threats to Central Asian states are internal upheaval (as exemplified by the Tajik civil war) or acts of a non-CIS state such as Iran, Afghanistan, or China, the pursuit of collective security via the CIS has merit. In particular, it is a solution to the combination of political and military weakness that characterizes the Central Asian states. The joint defense of Tajikistan's borders has already been cited as an example that demonstrates how multilateralism can offset national weakness. Another example is the reliance of Kazakstan, Kyrgyzstan, and Tajikistan on Russian personnel to patrol their borders with China.

If, however, one assumes that Russia itself could become the principal security threat to Central Asia—and the historical record and geopolitical circumstances provide ample reason to make this a valid assumption—then the CIS is of limited utility. Contrary to the reasoning of Kazakstan's president, Nursultan Nazarbaev, the CIS will not restrain Russia by entangling it in the coils of consensual, multilateral decision-making. What is far more likely is that the CIS will be a Russian-dominated organization that serves as an instrument of Moscow's policy.[50] Indeed, Russia's enthusiasm for enlarging the CIS (which it did successfully by forcing Georgia and Azerbaijan to join the organization by using its leverage over the civil wars in both countries), and having it receive the imprimatur of the UN for exclusive peacekeeping rights within its domain, show that this is precisely the role Moscow envisages for the CIS. Thus the joint defense of borders and air space, agreed upon by all members of the CIS except Ukraine and Turkmenistan, are of little value if the origin of the threat to Central Asia is from the old imperial center.

Furthermore, there are really no viable means to balance Russia's potential threat to Central Asia. The United States has no vital security interests in Central

Asia and is not about to extend a security guarantee to the region—especially amidst pressures to reduce the budget and to maintain commitments to vital areas such as East Asia, the Persian Gulf, and Europe.[51] Nor is it likely that the European Community or NATO will assume this role: the latter organization's Partnership for Peace initiative encompasses Central Asia; but it is a consultative mechanism, not a prelude to alliance. Neighboring states such as Iran, Turkey, and China have neither the means nor the inclination to offset Russian power. And, despite the confidence of some scholars that the OSCE (Organization for Security and Cooperation in Europe, as the CSCE has been renamed) can emerge as a viable collective security organization, this is most unlikely for a host of reasons.[52]

First, the OSCE operates on the basis of consensus, thus in effect giving Russia a veto on what the organization can do in the realm of Central Asian security. Second, the OSCE has no military enforcement power; nor is it likely to acquire it. Third, divisions among the organization's members can severely constrain its activities. As an example, the OSCE did not monitor the November 1994 Tajik presidential elections or the February 1995 parliamentary elections as originally planned because of a lack of agreement between the European Union (EU) and the United States. The EU, unlike the United States, felt that it would do little good to observe an election that, given the announced ground rules, was going to be unfair. Fourth, there is little evidence that the OSCE will overcome the problems (the lack of consensus among the major powers who are members, the lack of enforcement power, the resilient stubbornness of sovereign states unwilling to yield too much power to supranational entities) that have traditionally hamstrung collective security enterprises. It is even more unlikely that the OSCE will be able to carry out some of the grandiose tasks—such as countering ultra-nationalism and promoting democracy—envisaged by scholars such as Charles and Clifford Kupchan.[53]

Another aspect of conflict management involves arms control and confidence-building measures (CBMs). Here, the proposals generated during the Conventional Forces in Europe (CFE) negotiations between NATO and the Warsaw Pact and the CSCE process have potential applicability to the Russian–Central Asian subsystem as part of a broader process covering Eurasia.[54] The CIS, the OSCE, and the Partnership for Peace could serve as fora for exchanging ideas among foreign policy officials, military officers, and strategic analysts to formulate arms control and CBM proposals which, while perhaps initially modest, create trust through institutionalized dialogue. This would lay the foundation for more ambitious follow-on initiatives. Discussions could center on promoting regular contacts among foreign policy and defense officials from Russia and Central Asia that lead to jointly devised proposals covering advance warning for troop movements, no-weapons zones along borders, the development of defense-dominant military doctrines and force structures, the formulation of arms control agendas, and procedures for rapid communication and consultation in the event of crises.

The principal problem with such CBMs is that Russia's doctrine and force structure cannot be adjusted solely with Central Asia in mind, given the country's wider security problems. Additionally, should an external threat to the Central Asian states emerge, Russia will require some offensive capabilities if it is to be a useful source of security.[55] Emphasizing defense-dominant military doctrines and force structures might, however, be a feasible and effective way to promote peace among the Central Asian states.

A third aspect of conflict management is dealing with war once it has broken out. Assuming a willingness on the part of the combatants to stop fighting, peace-keeping can be utilized to separate opposing troops, reinforce ceasefires, and create a climate conducive to negotiations. Potentially, such non-regional organizations as NATO, the OSCE, and the UN can play a useful role, although there are several obstacles to their involvement.

Consider first the potential role of the UN. Russia has lobbied for the idea that Russian forces be authorized under Chapter Eight of the UN Charter to assume peacekeeping responsibilities in the near abroad. Moscow would have the UN subcontract peacekeeping missions to Russia under the auspices of the CIS. Yet this would merely lend UN legitimacy to the Russian hegemony, of which many states are eager to be rid. In general, peacekeeping and the more activist approach of peace enforcement have been a source of contention within the UN.[56] Such operations have vastly overstretched the resources of the UN, and the countries embroiled in conflict have often seen UN operations as other than impartial. Indeed, some experts have questioned whether peace enforcement should even be among the missions of the UN.[57] Yet delegating peacekeeping and peace-enforcement tasks to regional organizations that are the instruments of regional hegemons is not an effective solution to the problem posed by an exhausted, over-committed UN.

Russia has also been unenthusiastic about a peacekeeping role for organizations other than the CIS.[58] Moscow would object less to a peacekeeping role for the UN or perhaps OSCE, but it would vehemently oppose any introduction of NATO troops to the area. OSCE and UN activities can be influenced by a Russian veto, and neither organization is perceived as hostile. Both OSCE and the UN would have to operate within parameters demarcated by Russia; and the stronger the Russian stake or role in a given conflict, the narrower these parameters will be.

Notes

1 One specific way in which it can do so is by creating an environment conducive to nationalist conflicts. See R. Brubaker, "Nationhood and the National Question in the Soviet Union and Post-Soviet Eurasia: An Institutionalist Account," *Theory and Society*, 1994, vol. 23, pp. 47–78, for the argument that nationalism in the post-Soviet states has a ready-made institutional context given that these states arose from the fifteen ethnically constituted union republics of the USSR. To extend Brubaker's argument, it is reasonable to wonder whether nationalist conflicts are a likely byproduct, especially given the need for legitimating strategies on the part of ruling elites and the mismatch between state and national borders that characterizes the post-Soviet space.

2 For important recent exceptions, see J. Snyder, *The Myths of Empire*, Ithaca, NY: Cornell University Press, 1991; and C. Kupchan, *The Vulnerability of Empire*, Ithaca, NY: Cornell University Press, 1994.

3 See R. Menon and J.R. Oneal, "Explaining Imperialism: The State of the Art as Reflected in Three Theories," *Polity*, Winter 1986, vol. 19, no. 2, pp. 169–93.

4 Admittedly, this widely-held belief must be provisional, as democracies have constituted but a small percentage of states in the international system in this century until quite recently. The literature on the absence of conflict among democracies is vast. A recent study that takes stock of the literature and systematically tests the central proposition is B.M. Russett, *Grasping the Democratic Peace*, Princeton, NJ: Princeton University Press, 1993. For the argument that democracies are likely to be more pacific see M. Doyle, "Liberalism and World Politics," *American Political Science Review*, December 1986, vol. 80, no. 4, pp. 1151–69. For a discussion of the merits of this argument see the articles by C. Layne, D. Spiro, and J. Owen in *International Security*, Fall 1994, vol. 19, no. 2.

5 S. Walt, *The Origins of Alliances*, Ithaca, NY: Cornell University Press, 1987; S. David, "Explaining Third World Realignment," *World Politics*, January 1991, vol. 43, no. 2, pp. 233–56.

6 Others have similarly suggested the values of such a comparison. See D. Laitin, "The National Uprisings in the Soviet Union," *World Politics*, October 1991, vol. 44, no. 1, pp. 139–77. Karen Dawisha and Bruce Parrott suggest that "for closer analogies one must turn to the era of European state-building during the sixteenth and seventeenth centuries" (K. Dawisha and B. Parrott, *Russia and the New States of Eurasia*, New York: Cambridge University Press, 1994, p. 2.)

7 J. Herbst, "War and the State in Africa," *International Security*, Spring 1990, vol. 14, no. 4, pp. 117–39. See also J. Herbst, "The Creation and Maintenance of National Boundaries in Africa," *International Organization*, Autumn 1989, vol. 43, no. 4, pp. 673–92.

8 E. Ames and R. Rapp, "The Birth and Death of Taxes: A Hypothesis," *Journal of Economic History*, March 1977, vol. 37, no. 1, pp. 161–78; W. McNeil, *The Pursuit of Power*, Chicago: University of Chicago Press, 1982; C. Tilly (ed.), *The Formation of National States in Western Europe*, Princeton, NJ: Princeton University Press, 1975.

9 C. Tilly, "War Making and State Making as Organized Crime," in P. Evans, D. Rueschemeyer and T. Skocpol (eds), *Bringing the State Back In*, Cambridge: Cambridge University Press, 1985, pp. 169–91.

10 For arguments that pay more attention to the economic side of the bargain see P. Anderson, *Lineages of the Absolutist State*, London: Verso, 1974; R.J. Holton, *Cities, Capitalism and Civilization*, London: Allen & Unwin, 1986; H. Spruyt, *The Sovereign State and Its Competitors*, Princeton, NJ: Princeton University Press, 1994.

11 J. Given, *State and Society in Medieval Europe*, Ithaca, NY: Cornell University Press, 1990. D. Laitin ("National Uprisings") notes the relevance of this comparative case for drawing inferences for the post-Soviet case.

12 J. Migdal, *Strong Societies and Weak States*, Princeton, NJ: Princeton University Press, 1988, discusses how the imposition of statehood on less developed societies means that governments are constantly challenged by alternative logics of political organization. In Central Asia one can see how such alternative logics—kinship structures, organized crime—have permeated the state.

13 See G. Parker, *The Military Revolution*, New York: Cambridge University Press, 1988, pp. 1, 155, fn. 2.

14 This is the argument of M. Levi, *Of Rule and Revenue*, Berkeley, CA: University of California Press, 1988.

15 For a discussion of the reasons behind the different historical trajectories and their effects, see J. Baechler, J. Hall, and M. Mann (eds), *Europe and the Rise of Capitalism*,

London: Blackwell, 1988. See also P. Kennedy, *The Rise and Decline of the Great Powers*, New York: Vintage, 1987, Chapter 1.

16 For that argument see M. Mann, *The Sources of Social Power*, vol. 1, Cambridge: Cambridge University Press, 1986; and J. Hall, *Powers and Liberties*, Berkeley, CA: University of California Press, 1985. Thus, external challenge and internal decay can lead to swift demise—perhaps a relevant perspective on the demise of the USSR.

17 A. Motyl, "From Imperial Decay to Imperial Collapse: The Fall of the Soviet Empire in Comparative Perspective," in R. Rudolph and D. Good (eds), *Nationalism and Empire*, New York: St. Martin's Press, 1992.

18 B. Posen, "Nationalism, the Mass Army, and Military Power," *International Security*, Fall 1993, vol. 18, no. 2, pp. 80–124.

19 This distinction should not be taken too far. The emergence of sovereign rule to some extent precipitated nationalism. For example, the king's claim to be sovereign and independent from the church in secular matters corresponded with the shift from Latin to the vernacular as the language of administration. But what we mean to emphasize is that state and nation, in the modern sense, were initially distinct categories of reference.

20 See R. Pipes, *The Formation of the Soviet Union*, Cambridge, MA: Harvard University Press, 1954; G. Wheeler, *The Modern History of Soviet Central Asia*, Westport, CT: Greenwood Press, 1975; H. Carrère-d'Encausse, *The Great Challenge*, New York: Holmes & Meier, 1992.

21 A. Gerschenkron, *Economic Backwardness in Historical Perspective*, Cambridge, MA: Harvard University Press, 1962.

22 Robert Jackson has discussed this for newly developing states in general in *Quasi-States: Sovereignty, International Relations and the Third World*, New York: Cambridge University Press, 1990.

23 R. Menon, "In the Shadow of the Bear, Security in Post-Soviet Central Asia," *International Security*, Summer 1995, vol. 20, no. 1, p. 151.

24 On Russia's military weaknesses, see S.M. Meyer, "Yeltsin's Military Bluff, Mr. Doubtfire," *The New Republic*, 14 March 1994, pp. 11–12. For a critique of the view that the Russian military is eager to wield political power, see B.D. Taylor, "Russian Civil–Military Relations after the October Uprising," *Survival*, Spring, 1994, vol. 36, no. 1, pp. 3–29. The war in Chechnya provides a graphic illustration of the problems plaguing the Russian military. Overall, the readiness of some military units might have declined markedly. Some 70 percent of the divisions might be at as low as 50 percent of authorized strength (*The Military Balance*, 1994–1995, p. 109).

25 For discussions of the potential dangers of China's growth and high level of defense expenditures, see A. Friedberg, "Ripe for Rivalry, Prospects for Peace in a Multipolar Asia"; R. Betts, "Wealth, Power and Instability"; and D. Ball, "Arms and Affluence," all in *International Security*, Winter 1993/94, vol. 18, no. 3.

26 S. Walt, *The Origins of Alliances*, Ithaca, NY: Cornell University Press, 1987, suggests that powers balance against threat. Only when their behavior would not affect the balance in any meaningful way do they tend to bandwagon.

27 The most likely context for an interventionist Chinese strategy in Central Asia is the rise of ethnic nationalism in this predominantly Turkic-Muslim region, leading Beijing to fear that this could spread among the Turkic-Muslim Uighurs of Xinjiang.

28 L. Greenfield, *Nationalism: Five Roads to Modernity*, Cambridge: Cambridge University Press, 1992, and R. Brubaker, *Citizenship and Nationhood in France and Germany*, Cambridge, MA: Harvard University Press, 1992, are two recent studies that incorporate this distinction.

29 See, for example, the discussion of Kazak attempts to restructure northern municipal governments run by Russians in I. Bremmer, "Nazarbaev and the North: State-

Building and Ethnic Relations in Kazakstan," *Ethnic and Racial Studies*, October 1994, vol. 17, no. 4, pp. 619–35.

30 On the concept of negative reference society, see R. Bendix, *Kings or People*, Berkeley, CA: University of California Press, 1978.

31 Seventy percent of the region's population is under 40 years of age, and the average number of net births per thousand for Kyrgyzstan, Tajikistan, and Turkmenistan far exceeds the average for the other former Soviet republics. A. Rashid, *The Resurgence of Central Asia: Islam or Nationalism?*, London: Zed Books, 1994, p. 57; *The First Book of Demographics for the Former Soviet Union*, Shady Side, MD: New World Demographics, 1992.

32 S. Huntington, *Political Order in Changing Societies*, New Haven, CT: Yale University Press, 1968.

33 Details in B. Brown, "Tajikistan, The Conservatives Triumph," *RFE/RL Research Report*, February 12, 1993, vol. 2, no. 7, pp. 9–12; O. Roy, "The Civil War in Tajikistan: Causes and Implications," occasional paper, United States Institute of Peace, February 1993; B.R. Rubin, "The Fragmentation of Tajikistan," *Survival*, Winter 1993–1994, vol. 35, no. 4, pp. 71–91; S. Tadjbakhsh, "The Bloody Path of Change: The Case of Post-Soviet Tajikistan," *Harriman Institute Forum*, July, 1993, vol. 6, pp. 1–10.

34 This would exemplify Steven David's contention that alliance choices are driven by domestic factors as well; see David, "Explaining Third World Alignment."

35 We eschew the term "democratic" for two reasons. First, there is the general uncertainty about the post-Soviet transition in all of the former Soviet states. Second, specific developments recommend caution even in the case of the more open states. For example, in Kazakstan, President Nursultan Nazarbaev held a national referendum in April 1995 to settle the issue of whether he should serve as president until 2000, thus bypassing the elections that had been scheduled for 1996. Nazarbaev claimed an overwhelming victory. A similar referendum was held in March 1995 in neighboring Uzbekistan. Given the country's restrictive political system, it was hardly surprising that 99 percent of the voters were said to have favored extension of Islam Karimov's term as president until 2000. Nazarbaev also dissolved parliament in 1995 and proceeded to rule by decree. As for Tajikistan, Turkmenistan, and Uzbekistan, they are in effect one-party states. In Russia, the violent confrontation between Yeltsin and the parliament in late 1993, which led to the dissolution of the latter and the tendency of Yeltsin to rule by decree makes the uncritical application of the label "democratic" problematic.

36 The opposition could not participate in the 1994 elections, and the *ancien régime* was thus perpetuated.

37 In the December 1994 elections to the *Mejlis*, the national parliament, the candidates, virtually all of whom belonged to the Democratic Party, faced no opposition.

38 Interview with the leaders of the *Watan Tariqiati* party, Tashkent, December 1994.

39 Paradoxically, late economic modernization has usually been accompanied by considerable government intervention. So the Central Asian governments are to some extent in a bind. On the one hand, they must show international lending agencies that they reject the types of government intervention that typified centrally planned economies. On the other hand, they are likely to be tempted and inspired by the model offered by East Asia's newly-industrializing countries, which have relied extensively on economic strategies based on state intervention.

40 The classic statement of the challenges posed by markets for political stability remains K. Polanyi, *The Great Transformation*, New York: Farrar & Reinhart, 1994 [first edition 1944]. A more recent inquiry into the political implications of economic reform is A. Przeworski, *Democracy and the Market*, Cambridge: Cambridge University Press, 1991.

41 The following discussion of the ethnic composition of the Central Asian states is based on the data in *Central Asia Monitor*, 1992, vol. 1, no. 3, pp. 39–40. See also the data in M.

Mandelbaum (ed.), *Central Asia and the World*, New York: Council on Foreign Relations, 1994, p. 7.

42 Qostany, North Kazakstan, Qaraghandy, East Kazakstan, Pavlodar, and Aqmola contain 61 percent of Russians in the country. The ethnic composition of Kazakstan's northern provinces is calculated from the data in P.S. Gillette, "Ethnic Balance and Imbalance in Kazakstan's Regions," *Central Asia Monitor*, 1993, vol. 2, no. 3, table 2, p. 21.

43 See A. Lijphart, *Democracy in Plural Societies*, New Haven, CT: Yale University Press, 1977; A. Lijphart, *Democracies: Patterns of Majoritarian and Consensus Government in Twenty-One Countries*, New Haven, CT: Yale University Press, 1984; and A. Lijphart, "Democratic Political Systems: Types, Cases, Causes and Consequences," *Journal of Theoretical Politics*, 1989, vol. 1, no. 1, pp. 33–48.

44 ITAR-TASS in English, 1624 GMT, December 23, 1994, in *FBIS-SOV*, December 27, 1993, pp. 78–9.

45 Kyrgyzstan's establishment of a Slavonic University, was, for example, a clear attempt to allay the fears of the local Russian population and to stem the emigration of skilled Russians needed to the country's economic future.

46 A point made by Istvan Hont about European state stability is, in this respect, applicable to Central Asia as well. He observes, "Whether the large 'nation-states' of Europe can preserve their territorial integrity . . . depends on whether their populations accept them as their own 'state' or whether they see it as in their interest to secure a 'state' more authentically of their own." I. Hont, "The Permanent Crisis of a Divided Mankind: 'Contemporary Crisis of the Nation State' in Historical Perspective," *Political Studies*, 1994, vol. 42, p. 231.

47 The IMF's support for Kyrgyzstan's policies should be seen in this regard. In addition to Kyrgyzstan, Russia itself and the Ukraine have obtained considerable IMF support. Recent standby agreements should give Russia about $6.4 billion and Ukraine $1.5 billion. See *The Economist*, March 11, 1995, p. 50; March 18, 1995, p. 51.

48 For a range of discussions on this topic, see M. Esman and S. Telhami (eds), *International Organizations and Ethnic Conflict*, Ithaca, NY: Cornell University Press, 1995.

49 For a discussion of some of the Russian efforts to invigorate the CIS for some of these security tasks see "Russia and the Near Abroad," in *The Economist*, February 18, 1995, pp. 51–2.

50 See A. Sheehy, "The CIS: A Shaky Edifice," *RFE/RL Research Report*, January 1993, vol. 2, no. 1, pp. 37–40; J. Adams, "CIS: The Interparliamentary Assembly and Khasbulatov," *RFE/RL Research Report*, June 1993, vol. 2, no. 26, pp. 19–23; S. Foye, "End of CIS Command Heralds New Russian Defense Policy?" *RFE/RL Research Report*, July 1993, vol. 2, no. 27, pp. 45–9; S. Crow, "Russia Promotes the CIS as an International Organization," *RFE/RL Research Report*, March 1994, vol. 3, no. 11, pp. 33–8.

51 True, the United States has initiated some limited forms of security co-operation in Central Asian. It provided $170 million to facilitate the removal of Kazakstan's strategic nuclear weapons to Russia and for defense conversion. Washington has also given Kazakstan six boats for patrolling the Caspian Sea and has helped train the crews. But these instances of security co-operation are not precursors to an American policy of balancing Russian power for the benefit of the states of the former Soviet Union.

52 For an optimistic assessment of the potential of OSCE to become a robust collective security system, see C.A. Kupchan and C.A. Kupchan, "Concerts, Collective Security, and the Future of Europe," *International Security*, Summer 1991, vol. 16, no. 1, pp. 114–61. For a critique, see R. Betts, "Systems for Peace or Causes of War," *International Security*, Summer 1992, vol. 17, no. 1, pp. 5–43. See also K. Huber, "The CSCE and Ethnic Conflict in the East," *RFE/RL Research Report*, July 1993, vol. 2, no. 31, pp. 30–6;

E. Fuller, "The Karabakh Mediation Process: Grachev versus the CSCE?" *RFE/RL Research Report,* June 1994, vol. 3, no. 23, pp. 13–17.

53 Kupchan and Kupchan, "Concerts," pp. 157–60.

54 See R. Blackwill and F.S. Larrabee (eds), *Conventional Arms Control and East-West Security*, Durham, NC: Duke University Press, 1989, on the CSCE process of arms control and CBMs involving NATO and the Warsaw Pact.

55 See Scott Sagan's argument that defense-oriented systems are double edged. True, they diminish the propensity of aggressive foreign policies, but on the other hand defense oriented powers cannot come to the aid of allies. S. Sagan, "1914 Revisited: Allies, Offense, and Instability," *International Security*, Fall 1986, vol. 11, no. 2, pp. 151–75.

56 Boutros Boutros Ghali, *Agenda for Peace*, New York: United Nations Publications, 1992, gives the optimistic view of the UN's abilities.

57 For discussions of some of the reasons for the UN's problems see S. Touval, "Why the U.N. Fails," *Foreign Affairs*, September 1994, vol. 73, no. 5, pp. 44–57; J. Ruggie, "Peacekeeping and U.S. Interests," *The Washington Quarterly*, Autumn 1994, vol. 17, no. 4, pp. 175–84.

58 The 134 UN observers in Georgia play a minor role compared to Russian troops that are separating Georgian and Abkhaz fighters; the same can be said for the minuscule United Nations Military Observers Group in Tajikistan.

7

RUSSIAN HEGEMONY AND STATE BREAKDOWN IN THE PERIPHERY

Causes and consequences of the civil war in Tajikistan*

Barnett R. Rubin

Tajikistan was the least fit of all Soviet Republics for independent statehood. The poorest and most externally dependent of all Soviet republics, it has become the "independent" state where Russian officials and military forces exercise the greatest direct power. The inability of its state apparatus to integrate the population of the republic's arbitrarily demarcated territory into a common society with reciprocal rights and responsibilities precluded the immediate success of any civic nationalist project and prepared the ground for external intervention.

Culturally distinct, more purely "Iranian" subgroups, whose mountain origin underlay both their relative ethnic homogeneity and their lack of access to the assets of the Soviet state and economy, took advantage of the weakening of the state to seek a radical break with the imperial heritage. That heritage included integration into a political and economic space dominated overall by Russia and regionally by Uzbekistan, while Russian speakers (11 percent) and Uzbeks (23 percent) together constituted over a third of Tajikistan's population.[1] Islam (with a populist, anti-imperial tinge), Tajik/Persian nationalism (often colored by fear of Central Asia's Turkic majority), and democracy (expressing the resentment of portions of the intelligentsia excluded from power) all functioned, albeit to unequal effect, as mobilizing symbols of this break. International allies in the Islamic world provided modest amounts of aid; to the lasting disappointment of the democrats, the "democratic" world did not. Nonetheless, the main cleavage

* I would like to thank Steve Solnick, Jack Snyder, Daria Fane, Peter Sinnott, and Shahrbanou Tadjbakhsh for constructive comments. Peter Sinnott also provided indispensable advice and research assistance about Soviet censuses. Participants in a seminar at the Institute of Political and International Studies, Tehran, January 1996, offered helpful comments on a draft. Some of the research for this paper took place on visits to Tajikistan and the neighboring countries sponsored by Human Rights Watch/Helsinki and the Open Society Institute. I would like to thank these institutions while noting that they bear no responsibility for any conclusions herein.

was among Tajiks, as that group was defined by the Soviet state, rather than among ethnic groups or nationalities.

Those threatened by the break, who owed their livelihood or power to the former imperial connection, or whose identities were simply threatened by this movement, mobilized against it; they too ultimately received international support, and they prevailed. The process of military mobilization, and the substitution of direct coercion or despotic power for the more pervasive infrastructural power of the Soviet state, led in turn to a shift in power among the coalition that supported the maintenance of the old links.[2] Those who held the guns, rather than those who controlled the factories and party personnel committees, came out on top.

The disoriented Russian state of 1991–2 played little role in provoking these outbreaks, except indirectly, through its strategy of breaking up the Union. Members of Russian military units stationed in Tajikistan were largely left on their own without clear political direction. Some initially assisted the restorationist forces out of their personal interests, not as part of Russian foreign policy. When Russia finally intervened in favor of the victors of the civil war, and most especially against guerrillas based in Afghanistan, building clearly demarcated nation-states of Russia and Tajikistan who would relate to each other on the basis of sovereign equality was no longer possible, if it ever had been.

This outcome resulted not only from Tajikistan's internal weakness, but also from its geopolitical position. It had a 1,500 km border with Afghanistan, where the USSR had fought its last war. The USSR withdrew its last troops only in February 1989 and continued aid to the government it had installed through the end of 1991. Afghanistan, especially the northern areas bordering the former USSR, contains more Tajiks than Tajikistan. In April 1992, not long after Tajikistan gained independence as a result of the Soviet breakup, a military force led by Afghan Tajik Islamic mujahidin took control of Afghanistan's capital, Kabul.

In May 1992, fighting broke out between opposing forces in Dushanbe, capital of Tajikistan. President Nabiev, former First Secretary of the Republic's Communist Party, agreed to a coalition government with the opposition, but this merely made the government itself a locus of fighting. Fed by the weapons hemor-rhaged by both the disintegrating Soviet Army and the hyperarmed patronage networks of stateless Afghanistan, the war spread across the south of Tajikistan and back into the capital itself. In September a coup by irregular opposition units forced Nabiev from the capital, leading to a counter-offensive by restorationist forces spearheaded by a para-military organization, the Popular Front, led by a career criminal, Sangak Safarov.[3] A precarious stability returned only in December when these forces, now supported by Russia and Uzbekistan, pushed the fighters of the "Islamic-democratic" opposition and tens of thousands of refugees across the freezing Amu Darya into Afghanistan. Russian border forces patrolled the frontier, a Russian-dominated self-defined "peacekeeping" force of the Commonwealth of Independent States controlled key roads and economic installations, and the emergent, chaotic civil society of the previous year's "Tajik spring" was suppressed.[4]

The militias engaged in massive reprisals, destroying houses, indeed whole villages, and summarily executing men thought to sympathize with the opposition. Curiously, the evidence of sympathy for the opposition was not possession of a membership card in a political organization or indeed any record of political activity, but an indication on Soviet internal passports of birth in certain regions of the country. The number of dead, 20,000 to 50,000 in a republic where the 1989 census counted 5.1 million inhabitants, exceeded the total in any other post-Soviet conflict except perhaps Chechnya. About 300,000 ethnic Russians (the 1989 census had counted 388,000) emigrated, never to return, and over half a million Tajiks and Uzbeks were displaced or fled as refugees.

In 1997, even after the signature on June 27 of a general peace accord in Moscow between the Government of Tajikistan and the United Tajik Opposition (UTO), over 25,000 Russian troops remain in Tajikistan as part of an operation at least nominally commanded by the Commonwealth of Independent States. About 8,000 belong to the 201st Motorized Rifle Division of the Russian Ministry of Defense, which guards key roads and installations. The rest belong to the Border Security Forces answering to the office of the Russian Presidency. Both the border and peace-keeping forces include largely nominal contributions from the other Central Asian states, except Turkmenistan. These forces are monitored by the United Nations Mission of Observers in Tajikistan (UNMOT). While the troops have not been recognized as peacekeepers by the UN, despite repeated Russian requests, the peace agreement accords them a role in monitoring disarmament. They identify their mission as a "peacemaking force" (*mirotvorcheskoe silo*) of the CIS.

At time of writing, it remains to be seen if the peace accord will be successfully implemented. It was concluded under a deadline imposed by the advance of the militant Taliban movement into northern Afghanistan. That movement's capture of Kabul in September 1996 seemed to convince the Russian security establishment that the risk of leaving the Tajik opposition in Afghanistan now outweighed the risk of reintegrating it into the Tajik state.

Regardless of the effect of the peace accord, the political outcome includes:

- A weak state apparatus dependent on Russian troops, Russian subsidies, and Russian financial support. While no comprehensive statistics are available, reports claim that Russian subsidies pay for 50–70 percent of the republic's state budget, a higher proportion than was accounted for by officially recorded federal devolution from Moscow during the Soviet period. The Russian ruble was the only legal tender in Tajikistan until May 1995, and the Tajikistan ruble that succeeded it is dependent on backing from the Russian Central Bank, which had previously received control over Tajikistan's gold reserves and other assets.[5]
- An authoritarian regime maintaining social control through armed force backed by Russia and the distribution of profits and rents from various murky activities ("mafias," in the local argot) to its supporters; the drug trade plays a particularly important role.

- A political elite recruited more and more exclusively from the parallel power networks (nomenklatura-mafia) of one region of the country (Kulab), which supplied the muscle to the local Communist party elites during the civil war but had been excluded from the heights of power during Soviet rule. While the peace agreement calls for sharing power, sharing the loot of power will prove more difficult.
- The absence of any project of civic nationalism, liberalism, or democracy. The peace agreement calls for new elections including the opposition and will test whether democracy is possible under such conditions.
- The marginalization of an emergent project of ethno-nationalism, similar to the "Popular Fronts" that emerged in many republics during late perestroika.[6] In the context of Tajikistan, ethno-nationalism took the form of a hybrid "Islamic-democratic" movement; at time of writing, it remains to be seen if the peace agreement marks the reentry of this movement into the political scene of Tajikistan.
- The integration of Tajikistan into the post-Soviet space as a dependent buffer state, whose main function is to serve as a garrison against the threats of militant Islam and the smuggling of arms and drugs, even though some of the authorities and the Russian troops are themselves involved in the drug trade.

This case suggests how in a period of post-imperial transition where new states are poorly institutionalized and both geographical and social boundaries are much less demarcated than in the classic model of a system of nation-states, political conflict within one state can spread through other levels of the system. The disintegration of Tajikistan led to military deployments by Russia and Uzbekistan, who are competing over defining the area as their sphere of influence. Tensions with neighboring states have risen.

Analysis of the origins of the domestic conflict in Tajikistan shows how the conflictual choices made by the political actors were largely determined by the generalized insecurity into which the collapse of Soviet institutions threw so much of the population. System-wide structural variables interacting with specific local conditions provide the best explanation for the local disturbance. Stable long-term resolution thus requires construction of institutions, not simply exhorting, threatening, bribing, or training people to make better choices.

Explanations of conflict and state breakdown

Different analysts have emphasized different factors in explaining why Tajikistan proved so unstable. Analyses of the conflict and its outcome attempt to explain two different though linked phenomena, usually without distinguishing them: why Tajikistan broke down into civil war and how—along what lines of cleavage—it broke down. The failure to distinguish these two questions may result from the assumption that the state broke down because of the intensity of conflict among the social groups that fought each other. Ideological movements, ethnic groups, or regional coalitions opposed each other so virulently that breakdown was inevitable once Soviet repression was removed. This is equivalent to the common explanation of post-Soviet (or post-Yugoslav) ethnic conflicts—once the weight of repression was removed, frozen conflicts re-emerged. Hence, in this view, *how* Tajikistan broke down explains *why* Tajikistan broke down. Such an explanation attributes causality to either social forces or autonomous, ideological conflicts.

A state-centered approach, however, suggests that processes of state formation and breakdown act both to structure forms of collective action and account for the presence or absence of conflict. Furthermore, the characteristics (autonomy and capacity) of state structures shape and limit the possible types of political regime, including institutions of conflict management and national identity.

The presentation in this chapter proceeds dialectically, presenting hypotheses that are rejected as global explanations but subsequently incorporated into other explanations. Some require further development, which will be attempted here. The chapter begins by extracting from existing accounts explanations of why Tajikistan fell into civil war and proceed to explanations of how the civil war was structured. Finally, it links these factors in a state-centered explanation which, it will be argued, is most comprehensive. The dynamic of the conflict is best explained by the way Tajikistan's formation as a peripheral national republic transformed existing social networks into a distinctive Soviet–Central Asian pattern that formed new links with the region-wide political system following the breakup of the USSR. This system exhibited some characteristics of an international system but also featured extensive transnational linkages and juridical states with varying degrees of empirical statehood. Hence, state and non-state actors interacted to form a complex system that is not fully a set of sovereign states, a reconstituted empire, or an institutionalized regional bloc, but that exhibits some characteristics of all three.

Social and economic tensions

A variety of indicators of social and political distress show why Tajikistan was likely to collapse when forced to become an independent state, but other Central Asian states, notably Kyrgyzstan, had similar if less extreme profiles of external dependence, economic involution, and internal fragmentation. These states, however, have not exploded—yet. It makes more sense to argue that other factors—notably Tajikistan's geographical and ethnic proximity to Afghanistan and its consequent role in the international security system—provided the shocks that made the potential explosion actual.[7] Nonetheless, while these social factors cannot be the causes of the conflict, they affected its structure and intensity.

Tajikistan in many respects had a typical colonial economy. Two principal areas of the country, the Ferghana Valley in the northern district (oblast) of Leninabad (Khujand) and the Vakhsh–Kafarnihon–Panj valleys in the south (crossing several administrative divisions, but mainly in Kurgan Tiube oblast) became part of the Central Asia cotton bowl.[8] In the late 1980s Tajikistan, with less than 2 percent of the Union's population, produced about 11 percent of its long-staple cotton.[9] The Ferghana valley received the bulk of the republic's industrial investment, largely in the production of cotton textiles, but there was also significant industry in the Hissar Valley near Dushanbe, including the USSR's largest aluminum factory.

This pattern of development led to social consequences one might characterize as the "Central Asian syndrome."[10] Most important for the analysis here, it left the indigenous population less subject to the typical institutions of Soviet social control than the populations of the imperial core. At the same time that Soviet social control was more tenuous, those elements that did function were more dependent than elsewhere on direct subsidies from the center rather than on a self-sufficient local Soviet economy.

Tajikistan's experience in this regard resembled that of Uzbekistan, Turkmenistan, and southern Kazakstan. It remained a largely agrarian society (compared to other Soviet republics, not to other colonial or post-colonial states), and the titular nationality, together with the other indigenous Central Asian ethnic groups, was far more rural than the Russian and other European settlers, who dominated the capital and, to a lesser extent, other cities. In 1959 Dushanbe had been only 13 percent Tajik.[11] The expansion of local higher education and the recruitment of a new Tajik intelligentsia increased the indigenous representation in the capital and its bureaucracies, but by 1989, though the republic as a whole was 62 percent Tajik, Tajiks were still a minority (38 percent) in the capital. Slavs (Russians, Ukrainians, and Belorussians) constituted 37 percent of Dushanbe's population, while non-Central Asian Soviet nationalities as a whole constituted 48 percent. Half of Tajikistan's Slavic population lived in Dushanbe, compared with 7 percent of the Tajik population.[12]

In the rural areas the population was subject to different incentives and controls than most of the Soviet population. Nothing signaled this more clearly than the continued prevalence of large families, a measure in which Central Asia differed radically from other parts of the USSR. Tajikistan had the highest birth rate of all Soviet republics.[13] While there is a tendency among Russian and Western observers to attribute this to "Oriental" values, it resulted more from the persistence under the cover of the collective farm of small peasant production. Soviet researchers produced convincing evidence that, despite collectivization, a substantial part, and perhaps a large majority, of the rural population's income came from private plots or other forms of quasi-legal or illegal petty commodity production and private exchange.[14] As elsewhere, this social structure produced overpopulation, disguised rural unemployment, and hence pressure on the land.

The increased competition for resources led to conflicts among different groups, mainly between different kolkhozes and their village-like subdivisions (generally known as *qishlaqs* in Central Asia), which in turn tended to have uniform ethnic populations.[15] Hence these conflicts could take on the appearance of ethnic conflict. The practices of Soviet-style monoculture, involving massive application of pesticides and chemical fertilizers, resulted in various forms of ecological devastation and declining health of the population.

The unemployment of the rural population was exacerbated by the pattern of industrialization in Central Asia. The Central Asian republics received industrial investments but their societies were not industrialized. Rather, these republics served as locations for industrial enclaves largely staffed by European settlers transferred by the Union Ministries that controlled the industries.[16] This was particularly true of heavy and military industry (as opposed to textiles, which were important in Tajikistan). The predominance of Russian speakers and exclusive use of the Russian language in the industrial sector were also parts of the enclave pattern of development.

Thus far, all of these factors applied to Central Asia as a whole, though Tajikistan may provide the most extreme cases. One phenomenon that attained far greater proportion in Tajikistan than elsewhere in Central Asia, however, was the forced transfer of populations for economic purposes. Transfer of populations for both economic and political reasons was, of course, a central component of the Soviet mode of development, and the vast steppes of Kazakstan were one of Stalin's main dumping grounds. Tajikistan, however, seems to have been unique in the scale of relocation within a Union republic.

As in other republics, there was massive migration into the capital, Dushanbe, which was renamed Stalinabad (Khujand was renamed Leninabad). More than half of the growth of this city came from immigration from the European part of the USSR, while the other half came from Tajiks moving in from various regions, but especially the central areas of Hissar and Garm, starting in the 1960s.

In addition, however, starting in the 1920s, hundreds of thousands of mountain Tajiks were moved en masse from their resource-poor homelands to newly irrigated areas on the plains. Most of these people came from the Garm region (including the old *bekliks* of Qarategin and Darwaz), Gorno-Badakhshan (in the Pamir mountains) and Maschah sub-district in the upper Zarafshan valley. Many were also moved from Kulab. The characteristics of these areas will be described below, as part of a discussion about the bases for Tajik nationalism. These populations were mostly moved into Kurgan Tiube, a barren, arid area mainly populated by nomads, many of whom had fled to Afghanistan during the suppression of the *basmachi* revolt. Massive irrigation projects transformed this area's lowlands into a densely populated, intensely cultivated plain of cotton fields.

Census data, while not explicitly counting the resettled, gives an idea of the size of the transfers and their ethnic consequences. The 1926 census of the Tajikistan Autonomous Republic of Uzbekistan counted a population of 33,678 in Kurgan Tiube (see Table 7.1). Of this population, 57 percent were classified as Uzbeks, 16 percent as Tajiks (plus 8 percent as Central Asian Arabs, classified as Tajiks in subsequent censuses), 12 percent Turkmen, and 4 percent Kazaks. The area had a large nomadic population, including not only the Kazaks and Turkmen, but another Turkic group called Laqai (classified with the Uzbeks), the Arabs, and a distinctly Tajik descent group called Ghazi Maliks.[17] By the 1989 census, however, Kurgan Tiube's population had increased to 1,044,920, having grown at an average yearly rate of 5.5 percent, compared to the total republic's average growth rate of 2.5 percent, which included both natural increase and net immigration.[18] The population of Kurgan Tiube was by then about 59 percent Tajik and 32 percent Uzbek. Some Uzbeks had settled in the area after irrigation, but the main effect of the population transfers was to settle Tajiks from Garm and Kulab in Kurgan Tiube, where they now predominated. The populations of both Kulab and the central raions (Garm and Hissar) grew at only about two-thirds of the rate of the rest of the republic, a sign of net emigration (Table 7.1). As elsewhere in such settlements, conflicts emerged in Kurgan Tiube over access to water, land, and government services.[19]

Weakness of Tajik nationalism

Other explanations focus on the weakness of Tajik nationalism as a cohesive force.[20] Unlike the Baltic states, Tajikistan and the other Central Asian states had no pre-Soviet state identity. More than other Central Asian states, Tajikistan lacked a cohesive intelligentsia with a common conception of a Tajik nation. Hence there were few leaders or symbols to provide a focal point for ethnic nationalism, even among the 62 percent of the population who were classified as ethnic Tajiks. The weakness of the state, as described below, precluded the building of civic nationalism.

The corollary of the weakness of Tajik nationalism is the relative strength of more local identities, resulting in the predominance of "regionalism" or "localism" (*mahalgarai* in Tajik, *mestnichestvo* in Russian). Thus the hypothesis that attributes the breakdown of the independent Tajik nation-state to the weakness or ambiguity of its nationalist legitimacy corresponds to the depiction of regionalism as an independent variable explaining the lines of cleavage in the conflict.

Analyses of this orientation attribute the weakness of Tajik nationalism to social characteristics of Tajiks, the history of the Tajik intelligentsia (conceived as the potential creator and agent of nationalism), and the mode of formation of the national republic of Tajikistan. While all identities in pre-Soviet Central Asia were weakly territorialized, the Tajiks were the least territorial. If nationalism is the political belief that ethnic and territorial boundaries should coincide, the Tajiks were uniquely unsuited for it.[21] For Tajiks even more than for other Central Asians, the difficulty was not that borders were drawn incorrectly, but that no borders could have been "correct" in a nationalist sense. In the early nineteenth century, Montstuart Elphinstone, British envoy to the Afghan court, observed:

> The Taujiks are not united into one body, like most other nations, or confined to one country, but are scattered unconnected through a great part of Asia. They are mixed with the Uzbeks through the greater part of their dominions, in the same manner as with the Afghauns [i.e. Pashtuns] .... [T]hey possess independent governments in the mountainous countries of Kurrategeen [Qarategin], Durwauz [Darwaz], Wakheeha [Wakhiha], and Budukhshaun [Badakhshan]. Except in these

Table 7.1 Composition of population of Tajikistan, 1926–89: ethnic and social changes

Region:	1926					1989					
	Tajik (%)	Main Turkic (%) K=Kyrgyz otherwise Uzbek	Slavic (%)	Total	Urban (%)	Tajik (%)	Main Turkic (%) K=Kyrgyz otherwise Uzbek	Slavic (%)	Total	Urban (%)	Yearly population growth rate (%), 1926–89
Tajikistan SSR	71.2	24.7	1.0	1,033,711	10.4	62.3	23.5	8.6	5,092,803	33.0	2.5
Tajikistan ASSR	74.6	21.2	0.8	827,083	4.9						
Khujent	57.7	38.7	1.6	206,628	32.4						
Ura Tiube	61.6	37.8	0.0	82,085	2.0						
Penjkent	74.4	20.7	0.0	52,189	6.9						
Leninabad	61.2	35.7	1.0	340,902	25.1	56.9	31.3	7.0	1,554,145	33.6	2.4
Garm	94.9	4.8 (K)	0.0	174,231	0.3						
Hissar[a]	65.5	33.1	1.5	196,328	4.4						
Central raions[b]	79.2	17.7	0.0	364,952	1.0	69.0	21.2	4.6	1,112,084	16.2	1.8
Dushanbe	34.1	6.2	41.3	5,607	100.0	38.3	10.6	37.0	592,233	100.0	7.4
Kulab	77.5	19.9	0.3	230,975	1.8	84.8	12.7	1.5	619,066	25.2	1.6
Kurgan Tiube	24.3[c]	56.5	2.3	33,678	2.5	59.0	31.9	3.8	1,044,920	17.4	5.5
Gorno-Badakhshan	86.8	9.3 (K)	0.8	26,761	3.2	89.5	6.7 (K)	2.7	160,887	24.9	2.7[d]

Sources: Tsentral'noe Statisticheskoe Upravlenie SSSR: Otdel Perepisi, *Vsesoyuznaya perepis' naseleniia 1926 goda*, vol 15, *Uzbekistan* (Moscow: Izdanie Ts.S.U. Soyuza SSR, 1928), pp. 49–52, 152 4; Statisticheski Komitet Sodruzhestva Nezavisimykh Gosudartsv, *Itogi Vsesoyuznoi perepisi naseleniia 1989 goda*, vol. 7, *Natsional'nyi sostav naseleniia SSSR* (Minneapolis: East View Publications, 1993), part 2, pp. 592–632.

Note: Administrative boundaries shifted between 1926 and 1989. I have added together 1926 units in several cases in order to construct a retrospective analysis of the territories that formed administrative units in 1989, as follows:

1926 units added together (equivalent 1989 units):
Tajikistan ASSR and Khojent (Tajikistan SSR)
Khojent, Ura Tiube, and Penjkent (Leninabad (Khujand))
Garm and Hissar, excluding or including Dushanbe as noted (central raions)

In addition, one raion (Kalaikhum, in the Darwaz region) was moved from Garm to Gorno-Badakhshan. I have found no way to compensate for this.

Average yearly growth rates of population were continuous time logarithmic growth rates calculated as:

$$[log (1989 \ population) - log (1926 \ population)] / (1989-1926)$$

[a] Including Dushanbe.
[b] Excluding Dushanbe.
[c] 15.8 percent listed as Tajiks; 8.5 percent listed as Arabs. The Arabs were listed as Tajiks in subsequent censuses.
[d] Would probably be lower, showing net emigration, except for the transfer of Kalaikhum mentioned above.

strong countries, and in a few sequestered places which will be mentioned hereafter, they are never found formed into separate societies, but mixed with the ruling nation of the country they inhabit . . . .[22]

Not coincidentally, these mountainous regions, at the southern and eastern boundaries of Turkic expansion, were precisely those that formed the last and most determined bases of the anti-Soviet basmachi fighters in the 1920s, that supported the opposition in 1992, and whose natives were the objects of reprisals after the Kulabi victory.[23] As Table 7.1 shows, their populations were also the most "Tajik."

The meaning of the term "Tajik" and the origin of the people so denominated is somewhat controversial. In Soviet juridical usage, it denoted all indigenous Central Asians classified (or self-identified) as speakers of Iranian languages. The Tajik language itself (a Soviet creation) is a variant of Persian written in modified Cyrillic rather than modified Arabic characters. The term "Tajik" in pre-Soviet Central Asia generally referred to Persian-speaking urbanites or peasants, excluding nomadic or tribal populations. It generally did not include the mountain populations who spoke various Iranian dialects, including the family of Eastern Iranian languages known as Pamiri which are spoken in Gorno-Badakhshan.[24] All of the latter groups, however, were included in the Soviet passport definition of "Tajik."

The poor fit between nationalism and Tajik identity was not solely the result of idiosyncratic uniqueness of Tajiks. Ethnic identity in pre-Soviet Central Asia resembled the non-territorial pattern described by Gellner as typical of the premodern empire.[25] Town and country (and in Central Asia, the settled and the nomadic) had different linguistic profiles, and multilingualism was common. Different languages had different functions. The Timurid empire of the fifteenth century, for instance, had two councils that advised the ruler: the Divan of the Amirs, where political and military matters were discussed in Turki, and Divan-i Tajikan (or Sart Divani), where finance and administration were discussed in Persian.[26] In much of the urban and lowland areas now included within Uzbekistan and Tajikistan, speakers of the two languages were thoroughly mixed (with Turki predominant in most areas, Persian in others), bilingualism was common, and intermarriage was normal. The Uzbek-ruled states of Bukhara, Khiva, and Kokand all made extensive use of the Persian language, and leading literary figures often wrote in both Persian and Turki.

Those groups speaking Persian in Central Asia, however, lived in two distinct ecological zones and in two distinct types of societies. Most, as described by Elphinstone, lived among Uzbeks and other ethnic groups in mixed urban and rural lowland settlements. A smaller number lived in those mountain areas listed by Elphinstone as the only places where Tajiks were independent. According to the 1926 Soviet census, those areas (Garm and Badakhshan) were 90–95 percent "Tajik" in the Soviet passport definition and included virtually no Uzbeks (Table 7.1). The other main ethnic group was the Kyrgyz, a nomadic mountain-Turkic group. These mountain areas had never been firmly ruled by Turkic dynasties and were the seat of memories of resistance to Turkic invaders. Indeed, tribes of the eastern Pamirs had appealed for a Russian presence in the area in 1895 to protect them from the Amir of Bukhara.

These peoples differed among themselves, however. The highland Persian speakers of Qarategin and Darwaz spoke a variant of Persian (Tajik) and were Sunni Muslims like the lowland Tajiks and Uzbeks, while the Pamiris spoke various Eastern Iranian languages and had adhered to Isma'ilism, a dissident form of Shi'ism. Isma'ilis place greater emphasis on mysticism, reverence for spiritual leaders, and certain customs than on Islamic law and the range of practices considered pious by Sunnis and orthodox Shi'a.

Hence the linguistically Iranian elements of the Central Asian population presented a challenge to Soviet nationality policy. In some early statements, Stalin even omitted Tajiks from lists of nationalities in Central Asia and seems to have included them with Uzbeks. In the national delimitation of Central Asia of 1924, the districts (vilayets) of Eastern Bukhara with predominantly Persian- or Iranian-speaking populations (together with the sparsely inhabited contiguous vilayet of Kurgan Tiube) were amalgamated into a Tajikistan Autonomous Republic within the Soviet Socialist Republic of Uzbekistan.[27]

In 1929, Moscow decided to make Tajikistan a Union Republic for reasons that seem related to foreign policy. Stalin wanted a Persian-speaking Republic as a means of influencing the large area of Persian cultural influence from Iran to India. The decision was made soon after the overthrow of the reformist, anti-imperialist King Amanullah in Afghanistan and his replacement by a British-backed conservative, Nadir Shah.[28] Ostensibly in order to meet the requirement that Union Republics have a population of at least one million, the Soviet government moved the district of Khujand in the Ferghana valley from Uzbekistan to Tajikistan.[29] Khujand had been part of the Kokand Khanate, not the Emirate of Bukhara, and had been under direct Russian rule since 1860. It was consequently more developed than the other areas of Tajikistan, which, as indirectly ruled *bekliks* of Eastern Bukhara, had been backwaters within a backwater.

Khujand in 1926 was 32 percent urban, comparable to all of Tajikistan in 1989. The 1926 Soviet census showed that Khujand's population was about 58 percent Tajik and 38 percent Uzbek, but in keeping with a common Central Asian pattern, the urban areas were 86 percent Tajik, while the rural areas had an Uzbek majority (53 percent). Separating Khujand from the contiguous areas of the Ferghana Valley with which it was fully integrated, solely on the basis of statistical categories created in Moscow, was a deeply unpopular decision. Khujand maintained its links to Uzbekistan, which emerged in the 1992 war. The vilayets of Ura Tiube and Penjkent were combined with the okrug of Khujand to form the Leninabad oblast, and the city of Khujand was also renamed Leninabad.[30]

The accession to Tajikistan of Khujand gave the republic its largest city (population 37,480 in 1926) and an urban intelligentsia. The second, third, and fourth largest cities were also in the new oblast of Leninabad.[31] The capital of Tajikistan, Dushanbe, was hardly a city. The name means "Monday," when the market was open, implying, as Olivier Roy has noted, that it might be closed on Tuesday. In 1926 the population of Dushanbe was 5,607, of whom 38 percent were Russian (the largest ethnic group) and 80 percent were male, presumably mostly soldiers and police. Dushanbe was a tiny garrison town.

Hence Tajikistan's capital had no indigenous intelligentsia. The centers of Persian culture in Central Asia were cities in the midst of Turkic-speaking rural and nomadic populations, notably Bukhara and Samarqand, as well as Khujand and the other cities of the Ferghana Valley. When the Soviet leaders divided Central Asia into national republics, all of these areas originally became part of Uzbekistan. Virtually all literary and cultural references referring to bonds between the Tajiks and places refer to Bukhara and Samarqand, not to any places that ended up in Tajikistan. Hence the Soviet Republic of Tajikistan lacked an indigenous intelligentsia to elaborate a nationalism linking the people to the land and each other. The territory itself was a meaningless agglomeration of regions, chosen on the basis of categories and rules invented in Moscow and influenced by Soviet foreign policy concerns. There was little legitimation available for a Tajik nationalism and no consensus on the meaning of such a state.

Of course, during the years since the creation of the Republic of Tajikistan, and especially with the expansion of local schooling in the Tajik language after the Second World War, a local intelligentsia had been created, trained in both Soviet-style Tajik "national history" and the moribund doctrine of "internationalism." In addition, the policy of indigenization (*korenizatsia*) had created Tajik elites in all sectors in the Republic, though Russian speakers continued to play important roles especially in technical fields related to Union Ministries. However artificial its origins, the Soviet ethno-federal institutions had laid the groundwork for the creation of a Tajik national identity.[32] The new intelligentsia, however, was of such recent origin that its regional roots remained fresh, giving different segments varying views of Tajik identity.

Weakness of state institutions

A third perspective emphasizes the fiscal and military requirements of state building and social control.[33] Civil peace is not the direct result of social peace; it results from a state apparatus and economy capable of supplying sufficient incentives and sanctions to manage social tensions. Only a strong state can promote civic nationalism by integrating citizens into its institutions and protecting their autonomous activity in civil society.

In the late Soviet system, especially in the core areas, social control was exercised with relatively little overt violence. The population was incorporated into institutions (mainly schools and workplaces) where it was subject to pervasive surveillance. In addition, people received extremely secure if modest compensation along with housing, medical care, and other benefits. In return, the state demanded public obedience and compliance, and the rather rare violations of these could be punished with long prison terms. It was the apparent and even excessive stability and security of this system that led its detractors to call it the "period of stagnation." The success of this model of social control depended on the stable functioning of the administrative-command economy, the monopoly of power by the party, and the latter's ability to coordinate the apparatuses of production, surveillance, and repression.

The means of social control in empires or large states, of course, differ from one region to another. Hence the basis for the exercise of state power was somewhat different in Central Asia, a periphery of the empire, than in the core. The Soviet Union's federal system included not only national republics but a mechanism for redistributing resources among them to subsidize enterprises, implement social guarantees, and thus maintain social integration and social control. Wealthier republics contributed taxes and enterprise surpluses to the center, which redistributed them as subsidies to the budgets of poorer republics. Peripheral republics produced or processed raw materials which were used as inputs to industrial units located elsewhere in the Union while importing fuel, fertilizer, some food items, and consumer goods. Some industrial units were located on the periphery, but these depended on raw materials and other inputs from the center, as well as on purchases of output by the center.

The Central Asian republics were the main recipients of budget and trade subsidies, and Tajikistan depended on them more than any (see Table 7.2). By the end of the Soviet period, nearly half (47 percent) of Tajikistan's budget was paid for by federal subsidies. Tajikistan also depended on the income from the sale of its cotton harvest to enterprises largely located in Russia. The cotton harvest in turn depended on subsidized supplies of fertilizer and fuel. Nonetheless, these exports always fell short, and Tajikistan had the largest deficit in the Union on interrepublican trade. Credits from the center covered this deficit. Central Asian republics in general, and Tajikistan more than the others, thus exhibited some of the characteristics of rentier states, namely a reliance on redistribution rather than extraction with a consequent use of patterns of patronage in political mobilization.[34] At the same time the local economy, specializing in primary products, was the poorest in the USSR and the least able to support a stable pattern of patronage without subsidies. Loss of the subsidies predictably placed the various patronage networks in conflict over the reduced resources.

Tajikistan was both the poorest and the most externally dependent of all the Soviet Republics. The dissolution of the Union gave the largest shock to this Republic, which could least afford it. The Tajik Republic lost nearly half of its budget and much of its supplies of food and energy. By the time that the civil war began in May 1992, the mechanisms of social control were well on the way to breaking down. Factories were not functioning. Many of the participants in the mass demonstrations in Dushanbe that began in March (or resumed from the previous fall) had not received any salaries for five months or more. Many of those who came from the countryside to join them were not receiving the usual cash and supplies from their state and collective farms.[35]

Similarly, the Soviet military and police forces in the republic were not struc-

Table 7.2 Indices of poverty and external dependence, Soviet republics

Republic	Per capita gross domestic product (current rubles, 1990)	Transfers from union budget as % of total government revenue (1991)	Inter-republic (IR) trade deficit (or surplus) as % of IR trade at world prices (1990)
Baltics			
Estonia	5,039	0.0	22.7
Latvia	4,542	0.0	10.6
Lithuania	3,561	0.0	26.6
Slavic / Other Europe			
Belarus	3,902	16.3	3.6
Moldova	2,920	0.0	29.3
Russia	4,224	n.a.	(20.9)
Ukraine	3,177	5.9	2.7
Trans-Caucasus			
Armenia	2,915	17.1	22.7
Azerbaijan	2,056	0.0	(2.9)
Georgia	2,731	0.0	22.1
Central Asia			
Kazakhstan	2,706	23.1	26.5
Kyrgyzstan	1,893	35.6	19.7
Tajikistan	1,341	46.6	30.5
Turkmenistan	2,002	21.7	(5.4)
Uzbekistan	1,579	42.9	22.9

Source: World Bank, *Statistical Handbook: States of the Former USSR*, Washington, DC: 1992.

tured to handle internal disturbances. As we shall see below, the regional origin of cadres was crucial in determining their loyalties, and the Soviet security forces in Tajikistan were there to guard the Afghan border and balance the power of the party apparatus in the interest of Moscow, not to maintain control of an independent Tajikistan.

When the Soviet military broke up, it was unclear to whom the various forces reported or according to what doctrine they should act. There were few Tajik military officers and no Tajik armed forces. The Soviet 201st Motorized Rifle Division in Dushanbe was under the command of a Garmi Tajik who initially kept the unit out of the clashes. Most of the division's conscripts were from Tajikistan, but it was neither integrated into the new Tajikistan state as a national army nor placed under a clear command from Moscow.[36] Most of its officer corps were Russians from the former Turkestan Military district of the USSR, which became the Ministry of Defense of Uzbekistan. The local KGB and Interior Ministry had a strong Pamiri contingent, largely recruited by former CPSU General Secretary and KGB chief Yuri Andropov as a counterweight to the Leninabadi clique in the party apparatus.

Hence, when Tajikistan became independent, it lost both of its principal means of social control: wages and benefits given to the population in return for their obedient participation in state institutions, and cohesive security forces under a unified command. Tajikistan had the most extreme scores on variables which affected all Central Asian republics to a greater or lesser extent.[37]

Competing ideologies

Both actors and observers have offered a variety of analyses of the nature of the cleavages around which the conflict took place. These are now examined in turn, while bearing in mind Stéphane Dudoignon's warning that "one segmentation may conceal another."[38] These explanations are not totally distinct from hypotheses about why Tajikistan disintegrated into civil war, and links are drawn between them wherever relevant. They are also not mutually exclusive; indeed the key is to understand the links among them.

The most evident explanation, the one which appeared most accurate at the beginning, is that the war was based on a political conflict of ideologies. In Tajikistan as in the rest of the Soviet Union, the introduction of a certain degree of ideological and cultural pluralism during the early period of *glasnost* (1987–90) led to the proliferation of new organizations.[39] In the non-Russian republics, the local national intelligentsia launched cultural revival movements or even movements for greater national autonomy. Most of these movements had nationalist wings that more or less openly advocated complete independence. In Tajikistan, the largest such movement was Rastokhez (Rebirth), a movement that advocated strengthening the ties of Tajiks to their Iranian heritage by, for instance, making Persian in Arabic script rather than Soviet-created Tajik the national language. It also promoted nationalist historiography, which had developed in the Tajikistan Academy of Sciences as part of the creation of the Tajik "nationality." Some members saw Tajikistan as part of a Greater Iran than would include the "lost" cities of Bukhara and Samarqand. Such views naturally alarmed Uzbekistan. Pamiris also launched a cultural revival movement called La'li Badakhshan (Ruby of Badakhshan).

As elsewhere during the same period, the party leadership adopted some of the platform of the cultural revivalists in order to acquire a nationalist legitimacy. The Tajik Supreme Soviet enacted a law in 1989 making Tajik the state language and providing for a gradual transition from Tajik in the Cyrillic script to Persian in the Perso-Arabic script. Implementation was slow to begin with and was halted by the war. The current government is not implementing the law, though it has not repealed it.

Together with the nationalist revival went a religious revival. Here the central figure was the head of official Soviet Islam in Tajikistan, Supreme Qazi Hajji Akbar Turajonzoda. Turajonzoda advocated increased Islamic education and measures such as declaring Islamic festivals public holidays. He signed agreements with several international Islamic groups to build new mosques and *madrasas* (Islamic schools). He was elected to the Supreme Soviet of Tajikistan and emphasized that he did not advocate an Islamic state but better observance of Islam by Muslims.[40] Other leaders, including the large network of "unofficial" mullahs also emerged, and numerous new unofficial mosques were built or at least "declared" for the first time, as they were throughout Central Asia. These activities brought to Tajikistan various groups of foreign Muslims, including Iranians involved with the cultural changes and Pakistanis and Arabs involved with the religious ones. (The Shi'a Iranians had little to do with the revival of Sunni Islam in Tajikistan.)

In 1990 the CPSU renounced the monopoly of political power, and new political parties also began to spring up, including the all-Soviet Islamic Renaissance Party (IRP) and the Democratic Party of Tajikistan (DPT). The latter, inspired and even directly aided by the Baltic popular fronts, was allowed to register; an independent IRP was registered only in late 1991. Some members of Rastokhez supported the DPT, while others remained closer to the government. The IRP largely recruited Garmi youth through a network of unofficial mullahs. In addition, Davlat Khudanazarov, a Pamiri who was President of the Soviet-wide Union of Cinematographers and a member of the Central Committee of the CPSU, was elected to the Supreme Soviet of the USSR as a reform candidate from Dushanbe. He gained prominence as an ally of Andrei Sakharov in Moscow.

The continuing monopoly of power by the Tajikistan CP elite, despite the change in the law, together with the introduction of direct presidential elections, helped to produce a bipolar political system. Demonstrations called by the DPT and others against Party conservatives who supported the August 1991 coup in Moscow led to direct presidential elections in November. A coalition including the DPT and the (still unregistered) IRP supported Khudanazarov. While he won 30 percent of the vote, the winner was the nomenklatura candidate, Rahman Nabiev, a resurrected First Secretary (hence a Leninabadi) from the Brezhnev period. These two coalitions later took shape in rival demonstrations in Dushanbe (in Freedom and Martyrs' Squares) where the civil war began to incubate in the spring of 1992.

Regionalism and clan

Without denying that ideological differences played some role, one must note that such an explanation ignores certain obvious phenomena. As mentioned above, the victorious militias chose men to kill not by indications of their ideology but by indications of the region where they were born. Indeed, the further one gets from the capital's intelligentsia, the further one gets from the ideological explanation. A local Uzbek from southern Tajikistan, when asked why so many houses were destroyed answered simply, "When the Kulabis came, they destroyed all the houses of the Garmi Tajiks."[41] He did not mention democracy, Islamic fundamentalism, or communism.

The principal alternative explanation of the structure of the conflict, then, was "regionalism." Tajik national identity is weak; more important is membership in regional "clans." The Garmis (a term that includes natives of the areas of

Qarategin, Wakhiha, and Darwaz) and Pamiris (natives of Gorno-Badakhshan) supported the opposition. So did members of the intelligentsia from Penjkent, especially Maschah. The Khujandi (Leninabadi) clan, which had dominated the communist nomenklatura, led the government, while the Kulabi and Hissari clans (the latter heavily Uzbek) provided the armed forces that won the war.[42] These regions correspond to political units (*bekliks*) from the pre-Soviet period. Soviet developments seem to have transformed rather than eroded such ties.

Arguments linking regionalism to "clan ties," however, generally fail to define "clan" or specify the origin of regional loyalties, which undoubtedly exist and played a key role in mobilization for the civil war. The reductionist version of this theory is the equivalent of the primordialist theory of ethnic conflict. This theory argues that culturally transmitted identities can become politicized, leading to ethnic conflict. Identities are thus pre-political independent variables. Few scholarly writers propose a pure version of the primordialist view, but it seems influential among both Russian and Western officials with a somewhat Orientalist bent.[43]

This view draws on the arguments summarized above about the weakness of the Tajik identity. Tajiks are loyal not so much to their ill-defined nationality as to clans that developed out of the geography of the mountain and desert lands of Central Asia. The ideologies adopted and propagated in the civil war were means of legitimating mobilization (and foreign support) in defense of clan interests. With the removal of the stabilizing imperial hand, clan relations reverted to anarchy, where each clan sought the maximum influence and power (or perhaps security) using whatever means it could.[44] History can be mobilized to show the strength of clan ties and conflicts. Kulab and Qarategin were rival *bekliks* (areas ruled by *beks*, often referred to by the Russian term *bekstvo*) in eastern Bukhara. Their pre-Soviet history included periods of both conflict and co-operation, the latter usually in order to balance the power of Bukhara.[45]

While contemporary clans are largely formed as strategies to capture assets, their formation is not arbitrary. There are indeed long-standing cultural differences between the regions that supported the opposition and those that supported the old order. Opposition supporters came from the mountainous areas which Elphinstone identified as more purely Tajik nearly two centuries ago. These areas were more traditionalist, less Turkicized, and consequently more susceptible to Tajik ethno-nationalism, pro-Iranian sentiments, and political Islam. Foreign aid can also in part be explained by clan ties: the Afghan president, Burhanuddin Rabbani, comes from the Afghan part of Badakhshan, directly across the Panj river from the opposition strongholds of Darwaz and Gorno-Badakhshan, while the Khujandi clan from the Turkicized Ferghana Valley had long-standing ties to Uzbekistan.

The origin and structure of these clans, however, is not specified in this version of the hypothesis of regionalism. In what way, if any, are these Tajik clans (or their Uzbek equivalents) different from solidarity among apparatchiks who served in similar administrative units in other parts of the Soviet system? Brezhnev, for instance, notoriously surrounded himself with the Dnepropetrovsk "mafia" from earlier in his career. Sometimes Central Asian "clans" are also called "mafias." Of course the American Mafia is divided into "families," which seem rather like clans, except that they have stricter rules. The American mafia families even have kinship-based names—Colombo, Bonnano—whereas the Central Asian and Soviet clans and mafias generally take the names of places—or more precisely, of Soviet administrative divisions, rather than the kinship-based names one might expect for clans.

Here one must distinguish between a clan or mafia attached to a unit of administration as a phenomenon within the Party or state apparatus, which appeared throughout the USSR, and its use for purposes of patronage and mass mobilization within a territory or political unit, which appears to be stronger in Central Asia. Many analysts point to the collectivization and continuing rural residence of the Central Asian nationalities as a cause of the politicization of regional identities. All employed Soviet citizens belonged to a work unit; those in the rural areas belonged to geographically defined work units (kolkhoz or sovkhoz) nested within others (raion, oblast). Each of these units had leaders who controlled the distribution of benefits paid for by Soviet subsidies allocated by the republican administration. Hence, the territorial identities were also patronage networks competing for resources. These identities, especially of the resettled people, based themselves on larger regions rather than on the micro-identities of traditional clan (*avlod*, etc.) that had prevailed in the regions of origin themselves.[46] In the imperial core, where a greater part of the population belonged to non-territorialized industrial or bureaucratic work units belonging to all-Soviet ministries, the pattern of identity and political mobilization was consequently different.

This explanation, however, does not yet take into account the perspective of the actors. While most Tajiks agree that regionalism played a role in the conflict, they reject assigning it a primary causal role and insist they were fighting for something other than narrow regional interests. They do not see themselves as sociological automatons whose ideas, for which many were ready to—and did—die, are irrelevant to the true reasons for their actions.

Some who admit the importance of regionalism advance a version of the "instrumentalist" theory of ethnic conflict. Opposition figures, for instance, claim that when the Communist nomenklatura felt it was losing the political battle against the democrats, it manipulated regional ties to build a base for itself. The situation of acute penury into which Tajikistan fell as a result of the Soviet collapse accentuated competition for all resources and thus made identities organized around the administrative units through which resources were allocated to the rural population more acute.

This explanation brings us closer to the truth. But one still must explain why people were susceptible to such manipulation. Such an explanation is offered by the "situational" approach to identity conflict. In situations of insecurity, such as those created by the collapse of an imperial hegemon, people fall back on whatever forms of solidarity are available culturally or politically. Because of the structures of territorial patronage through which Soviet power as exercised in Tajikistan these forms of solidarity were primarily those of the regional "clans." These groupings had different political orientations because the territorial structure of state formation and economic development in Tajikistan provided them with different life chances and experiences. In Jack Snyder's terms, the detritus of empire was distributed unevenly over various territories and the patronage groups linked to them. This explanation of how Tajikistan broke down thus follows from the state formation theory of why Tajikistan broke down.[47]

With this argument, we return to Dudoignon's warning that "one segmentation can conceal another." According to Dudoignon, the fundamental social cleavages in the conflict were those involving different relationships to the assets of the dissolving Soviet state. His account is consistent with those such as Solnick who see struggles over assets in a context of uncertain property rights as key to post-Soviet conflicts.[48] The key categories for Dudoignon are Marxist or Weberian: they are defined by the relations of different social groups to the means of production, exchange, domination and surveillance. He thus refers to various levels of the party apparatus, the economic and state technocrats, the political police, the cultural-literary intelligentsia, directors and members of collective farms, industrial workers, and mafias, in the restricted sense of groups of people engaged in clearly criminal activity such as narcotics smuggling.

These are the categories Dudoignon regards as fundamental. They are articulated, however, with others. The social cleavages are related to ideological ones in obvious ways, in so far as different groups saw their interest lying with or against the dissolution of the empire and other measures associated with the conflict over the nature of independent Tajikistan. Finally, each of the social categories had a particular regional pattern of recruitment. The regional ties of patronage became the mechanism of mobilization for the war that expressed the more fundamental cleavages defined by the relation of social actors to the assets of the disintegrating state.

A more complete account would then link the pattern of elite recruitment to the structures created by the formation of Tajikistan as a peripheral national republic of the USSR. Territorial identities remained key to patterns of redistribution precisely because Tajikistan was created as a strategic periphery of the Soviet empire, subject to a form of disguised indirect rule with relatively weak penetration and surveillance by the central state. Hence, various forms of parallel power networks and resistance undermined the center's goals, as much among the center's primary agents as among the subalterns. These parallel power networks were solidified through the Central Asian practice of using kinship as the idiom of solidarity, giving rise to the appearance of clans. These clans were parallel power networks of rent-seeking, weakly-supervised officials in a hierarchical system. Rather than a survival of a traditional past, they were a typical product of the interaction of Soviet (or imperial or colonial) institutions with a local society that simultaneously joined and resisted them.

An excursus upon "clan"

Clarifying the concept of "clan" is necessary before proceeding to present such an explanation in greater detail. The regional clans of Tajikistan are as different from the tribal clans of Afghanistan as the Colombo crime family is from the Brady Bunch, but in both cases there are enough similarities to explain if not quite justify the use of the common term (with apologies to the Bradys—or perhaps to the Colombos).

"Clan" denotes a unit of social action whose solidarity is based on kinship or a kinship-like form of solidarity. Kinship, however, is not identical to biological relationship: it is as much a social construct as is ethnicity. Some groups in Central Asia and neighboring regions are organized on the basis of patrilineal descent into subgroups (clans) that bear a kinship-based name. For instance, clans and tribes among Pashtuns in Afghanistan often bear the name of a putative common ancestor. Kyrgyz, Kazaks, and Turkmen similarly have hordes or clans that are defined by descent. Where descent-based clans are settled in a certain area, the locality may take on the name of that tribe or clan, as is common in the Pashtun areas of Afghanistan.

In these cases it appears that kinship generated the group, which in turn gave its name to a place. This may be deceptive, as groups seemingly based on kinship often turn out to have a more complex and mixed history in which other groups joined with them, individuals were adopted and so on, by means of creating new genealogies. Such procedures are quite common in societies where kinship is the idiom of political and social solidarity; they are commonly used in India to consecrate the changes in status of various castes.[49]

Uzbeks and Tajiks have no such clans or tribes in the strict sense.[50] They do however, have lineages of various sorts, known as *qawm, taifa,* or *avlod.* These units are strictly local.[51] They are not part of any larger tribal structure like the Afghan *ulus* or Kazak hordes. In Uzbekistan and Tajikistan, the organization of kolkhozes and their subdivisions seems to have perpetuated and strengthened these identities. Brigades or *uchastoks* seem to correspond to *avlod.* Scholars disagree as to whether this was an intentional Soviet policy—maintaining control in the periphery through encapsulation rather than destruction of existing groups—or the unintended consequence of incomplete penetration of society by the state. The result remains the same: Central Asian kinship links strengthened the ties among members of Soviet administrative units and between the members and leaders of such units. Such ties promoted solidarity in the face of pressures from above or outside (rulers or competitors). They were key to the leaders of these units who used their positions to construct parallel power networks by redistributing benefits to clients in a patronage system. Such patronage using the assets of the Soviet state and economy "tied the knot" of the Soviet Central Asian clans.[52]

However, these local clans are not knitted into any wider networks by "traditional" kinship. The "Leninabadi" clan is not a higher level of organization of the smaller clans of Leninabad, in the way that the Durrani Pashtuns are the higher level of organization of the eight Durrani tribes of southern Afghanistan. It is a group of party–state apparatchiks united not by pre-existing kinship but by the distribution of patronage. Resources for patronage came not from property of a patrilineage but control of those assets of the Soviet state and economy under the jurisdiction of the nomenklatura of the Central Committee of the Communist Party of Tajikistan and the oblast of Leninabad.

"Clans" of this sort—like mafia "families"—can be created from groups of people not originally related by kinship. Just as patrilineage defines who is in existing groups (those in the direct male line) so it can create new groups through repeated marriage within a group, however randomly chosen. Richard and Nancy Tapper studied an Iranian tribe, the Shahsevan, created from unrelated people by the Shah of Iran. Olivier Roy has shown how the members of the Politburo of the Parcham faction of the People's Democratic Party of Afghanistan turned themselves into a close-knit solidarity group by arranging marriages among their families.[53] The party nomenklatura of Leninabad similarly arranged marriages within the group: the son of Abdumalik Abdullajonov, the wealthy "businessman" who became Prime Minister of Tajikistan after the civil war, married his son to the daughter of Hamidov, chairman of the Khujand oblast executive committee. Abdullajonov is a passport Tajik and Hamidov a passport Uzbek, but both are mainly comfortable in the Russified milieu of the ex-party elites; Tajik–Uzbek differences are of little importance in Khujand, at least among the elite. When the newly dominant Kulabis defeated Abdullajonov for president in November 1994 and won Hamidov over to their side, their children divorced, but this was for political reasons, not ethnic ones. Loss of control of the state fractured clan and kinship relations.

The clans that went to war in Tajikistan, then, were solidarity groups or parallel power networks organized around the administrative and economic assets of the Soviet state. A powerful regional leadership could use its mafia-like solidarity to hide information from superiors and pursue its own interests through its control of Soviet resources. Poliakov and his collaborators have documented how the networks of the parallel economy, which actually dominated Central Asia, were solidified by arranged marriages and other "traditional" practices.[54] Collective illegal action is always endangered by defection (hence the original prisoners' dilemma), and various forms of exchange and threats to increase solidarity are always needed. "Clan" connotes the use of the idiom of kinship to cement solidarity within the parallel economy and patronage networks of Central Asia; intermarriage creates common interest in the patrimony. "Mafia" connotes the use of violent sanctions within those same networks. The Uzbekistan cotton mafia revealed by the scandal of the 1980s was only the largest and most famous example of this phenomenon. Throughout the history of the Communist Party of Tajikistan, the center periodically excoriated the cadres for familism, nepotism, and corruption; it also found that "thieves" were recruited to the party, at least in Kulab.[55] Poliakov indignantly observes that the most respected social leaders in Leninabad (the area he studied) were illegal businessmen linked to the local party cadres. For decades, Moscow continually shifted personnel without managing to change this pattern. The new policy of "stability of cadres" during the Brezhnev years allowed it to flourish unmolested.

Articulation of regional clans with the state

The key to understanding the origin and structure of the civil war in Tajikistan, then, is the way that the formation of the Soviet Republic of Tajikistan structured the recruitment of different elites and counter-elites along regional lines. There is still no statistical study of regional composition of elites, but some general facts are agreed upon. Some elites had a more or less uniform regional character, while others were split. Links of patronage and solidarity based on regionalism made possible the mobilization of supporters and fighters by elites engaged in what started as an ideological and social struggle in the capital. The loss of social control heightened the stakes and made people available for mobilization.

The most serious obstacle to establishing Soviet power in Tajikistan for decades was the lack of cadres. This lack of personnel led the Soviet center to rule the area, whether by design or default, through a small cadre of poorly-supervised local agents. Eastern Bukhara was the most backward part of that isolated state and had hardly any native educated class. In the absence of any indigenous educated class (other than some *ulama*), neither the Jadids nor Young Bukharans had penetrated the areas that became the Tajikistan ASSR. These areas served as a base for the armed resistance of the Amir of Bukhara and later for the campaigns of Enver Pasha and Ibrahim Beg (a native of Kurgan Tiube). The population of the Tajikistan Autonomous Republic was less than 5 percent urban in 1926, and this by criteria that included the town of Garm (population 604) as an urban locality. This tiny urban population was about 40 percent Russian.

After 1924, the Tajikistan Communist Party was at first a branch of the Uzbekistan party. The intelligentsia that laid the foundations of the Soviet Tajik national identity mostly consisted of émigrés from Bukhara and Samarkand. When Tajikistan became a Union Republic with the addition of Khujand in 1929, it also gained an indigenous intelligentsia. Though Khujand had been only the seventh largest city in Uzbekistan, it became by far the largest city in Tajikistan (Table 7.1).[56] It had decades of Russian administration (hence modern education) behind it and was also home to enough *madrasas* to produce a class of traditional literati, some of whom were attracted to the progressive ideas of the Jadids. The intelligentsia of Khujand gradually took over the Tajikistan party after 1929. The 1930s were a period of Russification under a Russian First Secretary, who purged nearly all the Eastern Bukharan cadres for "bourgeois nationalism" and other flaws.[57] In 1940 he was succeeded by Abdul Ghaffur Ghaffurov, a Leninabadi, and thereafter every First Secretary of the CP of Tajikistan was a native of Leninabad, not just of the expanded Leninabad district, but of the former *okrug* of Khujand. Leninabadis dominated both the party nomenklatura and the economic management of the republic. They even had their own links to Moscow, independent of their former rulers in Tashkent and the local Russian officials. While these links are poorly understood (at least by this author), it is certainly significant that when Ghaffurov was dismissed by Khrushchev in 1956, he was appointed head of the Institute of Oriental Studies of the Soviet Academy of Sciences rather than disappearing into obscurity or being arrested.

Thus the first clan of Tajikistan was the Leninabadi clan, and the organs around which it was organized were the nomenklatura of the Central Committees of the Tajikistan CP and the Leninabad *oblast*. Rakowska-Harmstone describes the mode through which it exercised power:

> Leaders of local power clusters at all levels (starting with kolkhozes and kishlaks and ending in the Party's Central Committee) based their selection, distribution, and transfer of personnel on traditional, familial, friendly relations and cultural obligations, and on the need to secure followers.[58]

The importance of control over administration for the formation of power networks may be a reason for the changes in administrative structure and clan relations that have succeeded each other over time. The expanded Leninabad oblast was a constant as the power base of the leading clan of the republic. For some time, however, the Republic of Tajikistan abolished all oblast level administrative units of southern Tajikistan.[59] Southern Tajikistan was administered as raions directly answering to the republican administration. Hence no southern Tajiks controlled institutions for collective action larger than a raion. Such a structure kept them fragmented and prevented common action to challenge the Leninabadis. Naturally, where the state provides a legal framework for an autonomous civil society, control over administration is not the only means of collective action, as the development of political mobilization under Gorbachev's glasnost showed, but the dominant apparat clans of Central Asia did not permit any such civil society to develop. The fragmenting of potential opposition through administrative measures that promote micro-segmentation is a familiar one in the area; it was also used by the royal government of Afghanistan, which recognized local clans (*qawm*) rather than larger tribes as the administration's interlocutors.[60]

Later, perhaps corresponding to the rise in power of Kulabis as junior partners of the Leninabadis, the oblasts of Kulab and Kurgan Tiube were reinstated, while the regions of Garm and Hissar remained raions directly subject to the republic. Finally, after the civil war, the core of which was the battle between Kulabis and Garmis in Kurgan Tiube, the two southern oblasts were consolidated into the united oblast of Khatlon, under full Kulabi domination.

During the Stalin and Khrushchev periods, the Leninabadis exercised their delegated power over Tajikistan together with a considerable number of Russians. Even while documenting the extent of Russian influence in the party and administration, Rakowska-Harmstone found that the local cadres had more autonomy than the prevailing wisdom in Soviet studies then allowed.[61] It appears, however, that local educational opportunities expanded significantly in the 1950s, creating a new stratum of professionals who profited from a second wave of indigenization in the early Brezhnev years. Perhaps in response to the rise of potential local competitors, the Leninabadis developed a patronage relationship with Kulabis starting in the 1970s.

There are various accounts of how the alliance between Leninabad and Kulab developed. For many decades the principal cleavage in the republic was simply between Leninabadis (northerners) and southerners. Perhaps in the 1970s the Leninabadi apparatchiks began to delegate administrative power and strong-arm duties to Kulabis. Dudoignon says that patronage relations between the two regions developed because Leninabad processed raw cotton from Kulab.[62] In any case, he claims that Kulabis eventually gained control of the local administration in the south, while the Leninabadis controlled the party apparatus, republican administration, and most economic assets belonging to Union Ministries.

The Kulabi elites took advantage of this position to engage in a variety of underground activities. Their "mafia" was particularly active and included violent enforcers. One of the most prominent such enforcers was the "career criminal" Sangak Safarov, who later became the leader of the Popular Front that won the civil war in 1992. He mysteriously transformed decades of experience as a murderer and prison inmate into a position as beloved leader and savior of the country in a matter of months. Yaqub Salimov, reputed head of the Kulabi mafia groups in Dushanbe, who had served five years in prison for racketeering, became Minister of the Interior in the post-civil war government.[63] Their previous duties may also have enjoyed a quasi-official character. But with the dissolution of the Soviet institutions that enabled the Leninabadis to exercise social control, the Kulabi underworld's ability to mobilize violence became crucial. Kulabis thus fit the prototype of a conservative impoverished group attached to an old regime by the small share of power it gave them and resistant to a new order that might displace them. Dudoignon refers to the Tajik *mezzogiorno*, comparing southern Tajikistan to the poor, mafia-ridden areas of southern Italy that kept the Christian Democratic elite in power in Rome for so many years.

Garmis, on the other hand, especially those resettled in Kurgan Tiube, turned into an energetic diaspora group. Excluded from official position, they seized new opportunities in education and the market: they can be compared with the Tamils of Sri Lanka or Caucasians in Russia, or Jewish and Asian immigrant groups in the US.[64] They vigorously exploited the private plots of land they received in their settlements in Kurgan Tiube as well as the opportunities to invest in private activities such as silk raising. They controlled much of retail sales.[65] Questions about the Garmis in Kurgan Tiube invariably evoke stereotypes of hardworking, studious people who knew how to get ahead.[66]

Garmis also flooded into the new institutions of higher education in the Tajik language that opened or expanded in the 1950s and 1960s, forming a new generation of the intelligentsia in Dushanbe and provincial schools. Together with a large group of the young intelligentsia from Mastchah, they constituted a successor generation that challenged the dominant position of Samarqandi émigrés and Khujandis in the Tajik intellectual world. Economically, they supported the free enterprise many of their families were engaged in and opposed the kolkhoz directors of Kurgan Tiube, who were often Kulabis or Uzbeks.

Garmis, however, did not control any administrative or economic units the assets of which could create the basis for organizing as a cohesive "clan." Their places of origin in the regions of Qarategin, Wakhiha, and Darwaz were divided into small raions under the control of Kulabis and Leninabadis; in Kurgan Tiube they were under the control of a Kulabi-dominated administration. Consequently, they had relatively little stake in Union institutions and a great one in both the principal institution of national cultural identity—the academy of sciences—and the emergent market economy. Given their weak institutional base in the Soviet system itself and the administrative fragmentation of the areas of their origin, only the formation of political parties—the DPT and IRP—enabled Garmis to find a framework for collective action at the republican and regional levels.

Pamiris were also particularly prominent in the arts and in the Academy of Sciences. In addition, when Andropov headed the KGB, they had been recruited to the republican KGB and Ministry of the Interior. Their role was to act as watchdogs over both the Leninabadi apparat and the Kulabi underworld. They also played an important role in the war in neighboring Afghanistan, where their fellow Isma'ilis supported the government against the devoutly Sunni *mujahidin*.

State breakdown, mobilization, and intervention

The conflicts that developed into the Tajikistan civil war began as part of all-Soviet politics.[67] As elsewhere, technocrats initially allied with elements of the intelligentsia to support perestroika against an entrenched party apparat. In Tajikistan, this meant that Khujandis were split along ideological and functional lines. These same technocrats took advantage of new and rather vague laws on the autonomy of enterprises to engage in nomenklatura privatization, turning themselves into businessmen.

The alliance of technocrats and nationalist intellectuals underlay the early activities of Rastokhez and other cultural nationalist movements. A series of events including violent riots in February 1990 and the emergence of more radical nationalist and Islamic politics in the IRP and DPT pushed the old intelligentsia and the technocrats back into an alliance with the apparat. This reunited the Khujandis, but in the subsequent struggle, with the dissolution of the Communist Party of the USSR, the apparatchiks lost power to the economic managers among the Khujandis. The Khujandi Prime Ministers of post-civil war Tajikistan have all come from this background; the first two (Abdullajonov and Samadov) were both known as wealthy businessmen, while the third, Jamshed Karimov, is a respected technocrat. All had been associated with pro-Gorbachev measures.

As social controls broke down in the aftermath of the Soviet breakdown and mass politics emerged, patronage networks based on regionalism became key to political mobilization. The DPT and IRP made use of the ties of members of the intelligentsia to their places or origin and also networks of mullahs, small "businessmen," and brigade or kolkhoz leaders.[68] Since the Khujandis had no forces in the south to counter the mobilization of Garmis and Pamiris by the DPT and IRP, they called on the Kulabis (as when President Nabiev distributed Kalashnikov rifles to Sangak Safarov's followers in May 1992).

The descent into civil war mainly resulted from the breakdown of social control due to the dissolution of Soviet institutions. In the resulting insecurity, competitive mobilization led to escalation of conflict among patronage networks defined by the contours of elite recruitment in Soviet Tajikistan. But the loss of Union subsidies channeled through the Khujandi nomenklatura, combined with political and military mobilization for the civil war in southern Tajikistan, shifted the center of power to the south for the first time since the 1920s.

Iran, as well as *mujahidin* in northern Afghanistan supported by Arab and Pakistani Islamic groups, provided some aid to the opposition. Most decisive, however, was the aid from Uzbekistan and Russia to the restorationist forces. President Islam Karimov's government gave refuge to thousands of Uzbeks fleeing attacks by nationalist opposition forces in Kurgan Tiube; the Uzbekistan KNB (former KGB) armed and organized Uzbek forces from Hissar and Kurgan Tiube, and Uzbekistan's Ministry of the Interior forces participated in the capture of Dushanbe in November 1992.

Ultimately, however, Russia became more closely involved. President Yeltsin made Tajikistan into a test case of Russia's security doctrine in the near abroad. As fighting on the Afghan border continued during the summer of 1993, he announced that the Tajikistan–Afghanistan border was "in effect, Russia's" and rushed thousands of border forces there. Two years later, the 25,000 Russian and other CIS forces are principal political actors in the republic.

Russia also returned to the pattern of subsidizing the republic's budget. While exact figures are not available, various reports indicate that Russian subsidies may comprise over two-thirds of Tajikistan's budget, more than Moscow did during the Soviet period. The external provision of both financial support and military force effectively reduces pressure on the government, dominated by the leaders of the Kulabi mafia/clan, to become more inclusive or accountable.

Conflict resolution: hegemony, balancing, and international organizations

The abrupt dissolution of the Union by Russia in late 1991 probably made some sort of turmoil inevitable in Tajikistan; its proximity and links to Afghanistan made escalation to violence even more likely. President Karimov of Uzbekistan argues that stricter authoritarianism—fewer compromises with the opposition—would have made Tajikistan more stable.[69] However, it is not clear that President Nabiev had at his disposal a sufficiently loyal and powerful security force to carry out such a program. Otherwise, he would not have had to call on the criminal underworld and other countries to wage war against his opponents.

President Karimov sounded an alarm after the opposition coup of September 1992, which led to both a convening of the CIS military leaders and a fact-finding mission to Tajikistan by the UN Department of Political Affairs. Despite the resulting UN activity, it was of course not UN action but military intervention by Russia and Uzbekistan in support of the Popular Front that settled the war's first round.

In 1993, pursuant to a Security Council Resolution, the United Nations began an effort to seek a negotiated solution between the government and the opposition, whose surviving leaders were now virtually all in exile. The secular leadership (mostly from Maschah) was centered in Moscow, while the Islamic leaders (mostly Garmis) fled to Teheran or northern Afghanistan. Some Pamiris went to Moscow, while others were able to stay in Badakhshan, where the local government protected them.

Both the international and domestic political situations have changed since the negotiations began, however, transforming the underlying political configuration. Several political dynamics are affecting the outcome: a shift of political power in Tajikistan away from northerners to southerners and the consequent growth of a "realignment" of the regional coalitions; the debate in Russia over the definition of national interests and the role of the military; the attempts of other Central Asian states to protect their newly won independence; and Uzbekistan's aim of achieving regional hegemony.

Russian involvement in Tajikistan was at first partly motivated by concern for the "abandoned brethren" of the imperial nationality. During the period of opposition rule in Dushanbe, some nationalist leaders (notably DPT President Shodmon Yusuf) threatened the Russians of Dushanbe, warning them they would be hostages for the behavior of Russian troops. This concern seems to have faded, however: of the 388,000 Russians counted in Tajikistan in 1989, at least 300,000 have emigrated, and they harbor no desire to return. Neither they in their new homes in Russia nor the tiny Russian population that remains wield significant political influence. Russians settled in Tajikistan very recently, and they have no historic roots or feeling of belonging there as they do in Ukraine, Kazakstan, or the Baltic states. There is no longer any effective "triadic nexus" of imperial core, nationalizing periphery, and abandoned brethren.[70]

Since at least 1993, Russia's presence in Tajikistan arises out of post-imperial security considerations, complicated by the growing institutional and personal interests of those directly involved. The collapse of a state on the border where the USSR had fought its last war drew in Russia as the latter tried to create a stable periphery around its territory.

The mainstream view of Russian interest in Tajikistan, articulated by President Yeltsin and Foreign Ministers Kozyrev and Primakov, is implicitly based on the reality that the Soviet successor states, including Russia, are not fully demarcated separate states capable of autonomous self-defense. Russia, for instance, has no defensible security borders to the south except the old Soviet ones. This should remind us of Jack Snyder's observation that sets of conventionally structured nation-states are not the only possible successors in the post-imperial space.[71] In President Yeltsin's view, therefore, the Tajikistan–Afghanistan border is "in effect, Russia's."[72] Military access to Tajikistan in order to defend that border is thus seen as vital for Russia, supposedly threatened by Islamic radicalism, terrorism, and the trade in drugs and arms. This view leads to an alliance with a Tajikistan garrison state supported by Russian troops, seen as the least risky way to assure defense of the border.

At the same time, the troop presence has been expensive, the narrow base of the government could destabilize it, and the continued exclusion of the exiled opposition has pushed it further into the arms of international Islamic movements. The rise of the Taliban in Afghanistan intensified this concern. For those concerned primarily with the security of Russia in its present borders, the Russian presence in Tajikistan is a means to an end, not an end in itself. Those with such views are also more concerned with Russia's general international standing and seek international recognition of Russia's peacekeeping role in Tajikistan and throughout the CIS; hence, they have been willing to consider solutions including a political settlement and some form of broader international presence on the border. In return for a political deal with the opposition, Russia might gain such long-sought recognition. After the Russian parliamentary elections of December 1993, however, and the greater visibility of nationalist politics within Russia, Moscow's pressure on Dushanbe for concessions and concern for international recognition of its role seemed to diminish.

Those in Russia with more explicit neo-imperialist agendas, however, viewed the Russian troop presence as a welcome opportunity to reassert Russian hegemony over Central Asia. Some members of the Russian diplomatic and military community in Dushanbe openly espoused such views. On several occasions, hardline statements by Russian military officials in Tajikistan that seemed to contradict official policy created obstacles for the UN negotiations. In addition, some members of the officer corps of the Russian forces and other officials in Tajikistan have developed personal interests in remaining there. Military forces are able to profit from the growing trade in illegal drugs from Afghanistan through Central Asia, and some officials are said to be connected to weapons factories that are selling arms to the Tajikistan government.[73] Thus the quest for a settlement of the conflict has been complicated not only by different national and political interests, but by the lack of institutionalization of both the Russian and Tajikistan states.

Uzbekistan has shifted from calling for Russian involvement to seeking to limit and balance it. If, as Menon and Spruyt argue elsewhere in this volume (see Chapter 6), small powers balance only against each other rather than against great powers, President Karimov must not consider Uzbekistan to be such a small power. In the immediate aftermath of the independence of Central Asia, he did behave as Menon and Spruyt predict. Both the rulers and many observers feared the spread of "Islamic fundamentalism" from the Islamic states of the south (Iran,

Afghanistan, Pakistan). President Karimov was also concerned about the claims of Tajik nationalists on parts of Uzbekistan and their support for his Islamic and democratic opposition. Uzbekistan, rather than Russia, took the initial lead in orchestrating the CIS reaction to the Tajikistan civil war in 1992.

Since then, however, Russia has dealt with Tajikistan bilaterally, treating the other Central Asian states as adjuncts to Russian policy. In May 1993, for instance, Russia and Tajikistan signed a Friendship Treaty with provisions going beyond those in the CIS treaty. Furthermore, the rise of nationalism and imperial irredentism in Russian politics alarmed Central Asian leaders about the future. They came to see the Russian troops in Tajikistan as at least as great a potential threat as "Islamic fundamentalism," which has failed to take root anywhere in Central Asia.

Hence Uzbekistan, Kazakstan and Kyrgyzstan began to co-operate in support of the UN negotiations, even urging the Kulabi government in Dushanbe to consider the opposition's proposals for a coalition government. Uzbekistan went beyond this: in his search for partners, in the spring of 1995 President Karimov welcomed to Tashkent both the US Secretary of Defense and the leaders of Tajikistan's Islamic opposition. In June 1996 he made his first visit to Washington. In this context, realism correctly points out that anarchy leads to balance of power politics but errs in that the relevant actors are not all states. In particular, where states are poorly institutionalized or barely able to exercise sovereignty, international and domestic politics become hopelessly intertwined to the point where it is impossible conceptually or empirically to distinguish them.[74] Furthermore, states seeking to engage in such balancing find international institutions indispensable in solving problems of coordination, communication, and commitment.[75]

Both Russian and Uzbekistan security interests depend above all on control of the southern Tajik area bordering Afghanistan, which can no longer be assured through Leninabadi intermediaries. The agreement to share power between the current government and the opposition that was part of the general accord signed on 27 June 1997 would above all mean a government of southern Tajiks. Such a government would, however, face problems in integrating its Uzbek and Pamiri minorities, as well as Leninabad itself. The future of political order within Tajikistan will depend above all on whether its neighbors and the local hegemon will co-operate in support of the construction with Tajikistan's domestic actors of a more stable, inclusive political order. The alternative is a continuation of the Russian-sponsored garrison state.

Notes

1 Statisticheski Komitet Sodruzhestva Nezavisimykh Gosudartsv (SKSNG), *Itogi Vsesoyuznoi perepisi naseleniia 1989 goda*, vol. 7, *Natsional'nyi sostav naseleniia SSSR*, Minneapolis: East View Publications, 1993, part 2, p. 592. I have defined "Russian speaker" as Russians, Tatars, Ukrainians, Germans, Jews (excluding Central Asian Jews), and Belorussians. Russians alone were 8 percent of the population.

2 On despotic and infrastructural power, see M. Mann, "The Autonomous Power of the State: Its Origins, Mechanisms, and Results," in J.A. Hall (ed.), *States in History*, Oxford: Blackwell, 1986, pp. 109–36.

3 US diplomats claim to have evidence that Iranian intelligence provided support and training for the opposition coup.

4 For an analysis that includes a chronological account, see B.R. Rubin, "The Fragmentation of Tajikistan," *Survival*, Winter 1993–94, vol. 35, pp. 71–91.

5 S. Gretsky, "Civil War in Tajikistan and its International Repercussions," *Critique*, Spring 1995, p. 13; this account by an opposition figure is confirmed by international specialists who are not willing to be cited.

6 Note that in Tajikistan, the organization known as the "Popular Front" was the militia that drove the opposition coalition from power.

7 Kyrgyzstan, which had many of the same economic and regional tensions as Tajikistan, lacked the link to Afghanistan and had a higher degree of political institutionalization.

8 In the 1980s the Soviet Union's complex administrative structure included two principal levels of organization below the republic: oblast and raion. During earlier periods other terms were used; Uzbekistan's districts were first called okrugs, while the local units of the Tajikistan Autonomous Republic retained the Central Asian term vilayet. These administrative units merged and split in a seemingly technical process which reflected power struggles, as described below. I have opted for the more familiar Russified spelling of the names of these areas, for example, Kurgan Tiube rather than Qurghan Teppa, Garm rather than Gharm, with some minor exceptions where the Russian spelling misleads English speakers, e.g. Kulab rather than Kulyab. I use the Tajik spelling Khujand rather than the Uzbek–Russian Khojent.

9 International Monetary Fund (IMF), *Economic Review: Tajikistan*, Washington, DC: IMF, 7 May 1992, p. 2.

10 See for instance V.I. Bushkov, "Tadjikistan, quelques prémisses de la crise," in S.A. Dudoignon and G. Jahangiri (eds), *Le Tadjikistan existe-t-il? Destins politiques d'une "nation imparfaite"*, special edition of *Cahiers d'Études sur la méditeranée orientale et le monde turco-iranien* (CEMOTI), 1994, vol. 18, pp. 15–26. On the general situation in Central Asia, see B. Rumer, *Soviet Central Asia: A Tragic Experiment*, Boston: Unwin Hyman, 1989.

11 P. Mulladjanov, "Réflexions sur quelques effets du passage de génération dans l'intelligentsia contemporaine du Tadjikistan," in *Le Tadjikistan existe-t-il?*, p. 33.

12 SKSNG, *Itogi naseleniia 1989 goda*, vol. 7, *Natsional'nyi sostav*, part 2, p. 610. Central Asian nationalities are defined as Tajiks, Uzbeks, Kyrgyz, Central Asian Jews, Kazaks, and Turkmen. The others represented, in order of magnitude, are Russians, Tatars, Ukrainians, Germans, Jews, Koreans, Armenians, Ossetians, Belorussians, Mordvans, Bashkirs, Azeris, and Chuvash.

13 Bushkov, "Prémisses de la crise," p. 20.

14 S.P. Poliakov, *Everyday Islam: Religion and Tradition in Rural Central Asia*, Armonk, NY: M.E. Sharpe, 1992, edited by M.B. Olcott, provides ample evidence of these phenomena. He attributes them to an ideology of "traditionalism" based on petty commodity production, which his research demonstrated was the predominant form of production in Soviet Central Asia, despite the overlay of Soviet institutions.

15 In the 1950s, smaller state and collective farms with ethnically or regionally homogeneous populations were merged into larger, heterogeneous units (T. Rakowska-Harmstone, *Russia and Nationalism in Central Asia: The Case of Tadzhikistan*, Baltimore: Johns Hopkins University Press, 1970).

16 Ibid.

17 O. Roy, "Le conflit du Tadjikistan est-il un modéle des conflits d'Asie Centrale?" in M.-R. à Djalali and F. Grare (eds), *Le Tadjikistan à l'épreuve de l'indépendance*, Geneva: Institut Universitaire des Hautes Études Internationales, 1995, p. 160. The Laqai and

Arabs maintain their separate identities and dialects in the area, though they were not recognized as separate nationalities by the Soviet state (personal observations, Kurgan Tiube, 1993–4). Though classified as Tajiks by the Soviet census, the Arabs identify more closely with Uzbeks and are usually bilingual, trilingual with Russian. The *basmachi* leader Ibrahim Beg was a Laqai from the area, which was badly damaged during the civil war. Data from Tsentral'noe Statisticheskoe Upravlenie (TsSU) SSSR: Otdel Perepisi, *Vsesoyuznaya perepis' naseleniia 1926 goda* , vol. 15, *Uzbekistan*, Moscow: Izdanie Ts.S.U. Soyuza SSR, 1928, pp. 152–3.

18 In making this calculation, I added the population of the *okrug* of Khojent, part of Uzbekistan in 1926, to that of the Tajikistan ASSR. For details and a rough chronology of the population transfers see Bushkov, "Prémisses de la crise," pp. 20–2.

19 M. Atkins, "Tajikistan: Ancient Heritage, New Politics," in I. Bremmer and R. Taras (eds), *Nations and Politics in the Soviet Successor States*, Cambridge: Cambridge University Press, 1993, pp. 361–83,describes conflicts in this area reported in the Soviet-era press. Comparable areas are the Helmand Valley in Afghanistan and the Gal Oya project of Sri Lanka, where irrigation settlements changed the ethnic or tribal balance contributing to future conflicts over the newly available resources.

20 While this is a common theme in most writings, it was particularly emphasized by O. Roy, "The Civil War in Tajikistan: Causes and Implications," occasional paper, United States Institute of Peace, February 1993; S. Tadjbakhsh, "The Bloody Path of Change: The Case of Post-Soviet Tajikistan," *Harriman Institute Forum*, July, 1993, vol. 6, pp. 1–10; Mullahdjanov, "Réflexions," pp. 27–36; and G. Jahangiri, "Anatomie d'une crise: le poids des tensions entre régions au Tadjikistan," in *Le Tadjikistan existe-t-il?*, pp. 37–72.

21 The definition of nationalism is from E. Gellner, *Nations and Nationalism*, Ithaca, NY: Cornell University Press, 1983.

22 Montstuart Elphinstone, *An Account of the Kingdom of Caubul and Its Dependencies in Persia, Tartary, and India* . . . ., Karachi: Oxford University Press, 1972 [First edition, 1815], vol. 1, pp. 403–4.

23 The inhabitants of Qarategin, Darwaz, and Wakhiha are collectively known as Garmis, after the Garm vilayet (district) of Bukhara and then the Tajikistan Autonomous Republic, which included all three areas. The current Garm raion is smaller. The inhabitants of Gorno-(mountainous) Badakhshan are called Pamiris, after the mountains where they live. On the geography of the *basmachis*, see Rakowska-Harmstone, *Russia and Nationalism in Central Asia*, p. 26. Rakowska-Harmstone also includes Maschah as one of the *basmachi* strongholds; this is one of the "sequestered places" mentioned by Elphinstone in the upper Zarafshan Valley. It ended up in Leninabad oblast after 1929, though previously it was part of the Penjkent vilayet. Its inhabitants were mountain Tajiks with strong local clan institutions, many of whom were later forcibly resettled in the plains. It supplied much of the "democratic" opposition leadership in 1992. On the social structure of Maschah, see Bushkov, "Prémisses," 17, and his Russian references.

24 Iranian languages are divided between Western and Eastern branches. Western Iranian includes ancient Pehlevi and modern Persian, along with its variants, Tajik and Dari, and Baluch. Eastern Iranian languages include ancient Sogdian, its direct descendant Yaghnobi, the Pamiri languages, Pashto, and Kurdish.

25 Gellner, *Nations and Nationalism*.

26 B.G. Fragner, "The Nationalization of the Uzbeks and Tajiks," in E. Allworth (ed.), *Muslim Communities Reemerge: Historical Perspectives on Nationality, Politics, and Opposition in the Former Soviet Union and Yugoslavia*, Durham, NC: Duke University Press, 1994, p. 15.

27 These were the vilayets of Ura Tiube, Penjkent, Hissar, Garm, Kulab, Kurgan Tiube, and Gorno-Badakhshan.

28 Rakowska-Harmstone, *Russia and Nationalism*, pp. 72–3.

29 Jahangiri, "Anatomie," p. 40.
30 The city known in Persian as Khujand and in Uzbek and Russian as Khojent was the core of the eponymous okrug of Uzbekistan. Upon joining Tajikistan it was renamed Leninabad, like the enlarged oblast of which it became the center. In 1989 the city resumed its old name, while the oblast kept the name Leninabad. Confusion reigns in contemporary nomenclature. There are two hotels in the city of Khujand, the Hotel Khujand and the Hotel Leninabad, and my limited personal experience indicates that a taxi driver asked to go to one has about a 50 percent chance of going to the other. The people of the region are now mainly called Khujandis, though some people still say "Leninabadis."
31 These were Ura Tiube (1926 population 21,050), Kanibadam (19,254), and Isfara (8,307).
32 Rakowska-Harmstone, *Russia and Nationalism*, discusses *korenizatsia*. Stéphane Dudoignon, "Une segmentation peut en cacher une autre: régionalismes et clivages politico-économiques au Tadjikistan," in *Le Tadjikistan existe-t-il?*, pp. 73–130, discusses the prolongation of the policy into the contemporary period. The title is a play on words used for warnings at railroad crossings in France, "Un train peut en cacher un autre," one train can conceal another. W.R. Brubaker, "Citizenship Struggles in Soviet Successor States," *International Migration Review*, Summer 1992, vol. 26, pp. 269–91 discusses Soviet ethno-federalism and elite recruitment.
33 This is the predominant approach in Rubin, "The Fragmentation of Tajikistan." For a comparative analysis of the relation between state building and social control, see J.S. Migdal, *Strong Societies and Weak States: State-Society Relations and State Capabilities in the Third World*, Princeton, NJ: Princeton University Press, 1988.
34 For an application of this concept to Afghanistan and a review of the literature, see B.R. Rubin, *The Fragmentation of Afghanistan: State Formation and Collapse in the International System*, New Haven, CT: Yale University Press, 1995.
35 Interviews with participants.
36 Gretsky, "Civil War in Tajikistan."
37 For a brief comparative discussion, see B.R. Rubin, "Contradictory Trends in the International Relations of Central Asia," *Central Asian Monitor*, 1993, vol. 2, no. 6, pp. 11–16.
38 Dudoignon, "Segmentation."
39 Dudoignon, "Segmentation," suggested this periodization.
40 S. Gretsky, "Profile: Qadi Akbar Turajonzoda," *Central Asian Monitor*, 1994, vol. 3, no. 1, pp. 16–24.
41 Interview, Jillikul, Khatlon oblast, Tajikistan, 3 June 1994.
42 The role of regionalism in the war was first emphasized in the West by O. Roy, "Civil War in Tajikistan," and Tadjbakhsh, "The Bloody Path of Change."
43 For one primordialist view of clans, see K. Alimov, "Are Central Asian Clans Still Playing a Political Role?" *Central Asian Monitor*, 1994, vol. 3, no. 4, pp. 14–17.
44 B. Posen, "The Security Dilemma and Ethnic Conflict," *Survival*, 1993, vol. 35, pp. 27–47, depicts post-imperial ethnic relations as an anarchy like that of the international system. While the model is overdrawn and not generally applicable to all post-imperial ethnic relations, it captures one variant of the problem.
45 Daria Fane shared some of her historical research on this point with me, for which I thank her.
46 Roy, "Le conflit du Tadjikistan," pp. 157–61; Dudoignon, "Segmentation," pp. 80–2. I also benefited from discussion of this point with Vitaly Naumkin.
47 J. Snyder, Chapter 1 in this volume. For a general theory, see Posen, "Ethnic Conflict and the Security Dilemma"; for an application to Tajikistan, see Rubin, "Fragmentation of Tajikistan."

48 S.L. Solnick, "The Breakdown of Hierarchies in the Soviet Union and China: A Neoinstitutional Perspective," *World Politics*, January 1996, vol. 48, pp. 209–38.

49 There is an extensive monographic literature on this subject. For a classic study see L.I. Rudolph and S.H. Rudolph, *The Modernity of Tradition: Political Development in India*, Chicago: University of Chicago Press, 1967, Part I.

50 There are, however, groups classified as passport Uzbeks or Tajiks who have, or had tribal groups, such as the Laqai or Arabs.

51 P. Centlivres and M. Centlivres-Demont, *Et si on parlait de l'Afghanistan? Terrains et textes 1964–1980*, Neuchâtel: Éditions de l'Institut d'Ethnologie, and Paris: Éditions de la Maison des Sciences de l'Homme, 1988, contains studies of such groupings among Uzbeks and Tajiks in northern Afghanistan.

52 Ghilzai Pashtuns in Afghanistan say that khans "tie the knot of the tribe" by redistributing resources. J.W. Anderson, "Khan and Khel: Dialectics of Pashtun Tribalism," in R. Tapper (ed.), *The Conflict of Tribe and State in Iran and Afghanistan*, New York: St. Martin's Press, 1984, pp. 119–49.

53 R. Tapper, *Pasture and Politics : Economics, Conflict, and Ritual among Shahsevan Nomads of Northwestern Iran*, London and New York: Academic Press, 1979; O. Roy, "Le double code afghan: marxisme et tribalisme," *Révue française de science politique*, December 1986, vol. 36, pp. 846–61.

54 Poliakov, *Everyday Islam*.

55 Rakowska-Harmstone, *Russia and Nationalism*, p. 164. For various other complaints about such flaws in the Tajikistan party organization, see ibid., pp. 159–61, 172.

56 TsSU SSSR, *Vsesoyuznaya perepis' naseleniia 1926 goda* , vol. 15, *Uzbekistan*, p. 7. Tashkent, Samarqand, Andijan, Kokand, Bukhara, and Margilan were all larger than Khujand. As shown by this list, Uzbekistan's portion of the Ferghana valley alone had three cities larger than Khujand.

57 D. Fane, "Political Elites in Tajikistan," unpublished paper, Columbia University, 1995.

58 Rakowska-Harmstone, *Russia and Nationalism*, pp. 172–3.

59 Ibid., p. 183.

60 Rubin, *Fragmentation of Afghanistan*.

61 Rakowska-Harmstone, *Russia and Nationalism*.

62 Jahangiri, "Anatomie," p. 40.

63 Ibid., p. 66. Salimov was sent to Turkey as ambassador in August 1995 when the government signed a UN-sponsored protocol on a political settlement with the opposition. He had been considered the core leader of the hard-liners among the Kulabis.

64 Garmis were not totally excluded from office; the position of Chairman of the Supreme Soviet of Tajikistan was reserved for a Garmi. This post, however, was quite powerless and did not bring with it control over important personnel decisions or valuable assets.

65 Jahangiri, "Anatomie," pp. 42–3.

66 Personal observation, Kurgan Tiube, various visits, 1993–94; visit to Garm, 1996.

67 Atkins, "Ancient Nation, New Politics"; Dudoignon, "Segmentation."

68 Most of the IRP military commanders seem to be former unofficial mullahs, but the commander of Shartuz, Ali, is variously identified as a businessman or criminal, sometimes both, depending on the speaker's attitude (personal observations, Shartuz). As in the case of Safarov and Salimov, these two categories overlapped considerably in Soviet Central Asia, as in any society where private enterprise fulfills social needs but is illegal.

69 Interview, Uzbekistan Ministry of Foreign Affairs, Tashkent, May 1993.

70 On this term see Alexander J. Motyl, "After Empire: Competing Discourses and Interstate Conflict in Postimperial Eastern Europe," in this volume.

71 Snyder, "Introduction," in this volume.

72 "The Empire Strikes Back," *The Economist*, August 7, 1993, p. 36. See also Chapter 6 in this volume.

73 Interviews with diplomats stationed in Dushanbe.

74 This point is analyzed more fully in B.R. Rubin, *The Search for Peace in Afghanistan: From Buffer State to Failed State*, New Haven, CT: Yale University Press, 1995.

75 Fuller documentation of this assertion through analysis of the actions of the UN, OSCE, ICRC, and other organizations is beyond the scope of this chapter.

8

CONCLUSION
Managing normal instability*

Barnett R. Rubin

The contrast between the apparent stability of the Soviet Union and the long list of open conflicts on the territory of its successor states has given rise to a general impression that this area is destined to be a zone of endemic strife. Perspectives that emphasize the re-emergence of supposedly primordial conflicts after the collapse of Communist repression lead to particularly pessimistic conclusions. Most of the contributions to this volume, however, view these conflicts as the result of the process of imperial breakdown. As the detritus of empire is recombined into new states and a new international system, stability could re-emerge. Indeed, data on the incidence of conflict in the former Soviet territory indicates that stability of a sort is returning, though dangers remain and will continue to threaten the security of the that region's inhabitants for the forseeable future.

These perpectives are only two of the large variety of theories and images of the region. Such a profusion of views is only to be expected in the aftermath of such an epochal and complex set of events as took place since the advent to power of Mikhail Gorbachev. These events included at least three distinct though inter-dependent transformations: the end of the Cold War and thus of strategic bipolarity in the international system; the abandonment of state socialism by the world's first—and still most powerful—Communist-ruled state; and the breakup into sovereign national republics of a multinational state that some have character-ized as the last empire.[1]

These transformations consisted of several distinct, though linked, stages that had different effects. The internal reforms launched by Mikhail Gorbachev led to changes of the political regime and economic system. The domestic reforms—a combination of political liberalization and a degree of democratization with the start of market-oriented economic transformation—were linked to Gorbachev's innovations in foreign policy. These included efforts to reduce tensions with the US and the West and to recast the USSR's relations with Eastern Europe and the Third World. This period reached its peak in 1989, with the first free elections to

* I would like to thank Alexander Cooley for research assistance and Ted Gurr for making data and unpublished papers available. Stephen Burg provided comparative data on Serbia and Russia. Jack Snyder's comments on an earlier draft greatly improved the chapter.

the Supreme Soviet, the fall of the Berlin Wall, and the withdrawal of Soviet troops from Afghanistan.

As early as February 1988, when Gorbachev announced his intention to withdraw Soviet troops from Afghanistan, he predicted a new era of disarmament and conflict resolution based on international co-operation.[2] During the interlude that followed, the Bush administration and, indeed, most Americans concerned with foreign policy, hoped that a more democratic and market-oriented but unified Soviet Union would evolve from a rival into a partner in managing the global system. These two hopes, for a consolidated Soviet partner and for the world order that such partnership could inaugurate, were the themes of two of President Bush's best known, if often criticized, foreign policy speeches: the "Chicken Kiev" speech, where he warned Ukrainians against "suicidal nationalism," and his speech to the United Nations General Assembly during the build-up to the Gulf War, where he spoke, however inadvertently, of a "new world order."[3] The themes of Bush's two speeches were linked: a consolidated but reformed USSR co-operating with the US would enable great powers to co-operate through international organizations to enforce norms such as non-aggression, the territorial integrity of states, and, even, perhaps, human rights. The Gulf War of 1990–1 seemed to validate this model.

Instead, however, the Soviet Union broke up, and conflict spread over much of its territory. Conflicts in other regions of the world, especially Africa, that might once have been attributed to the stresses of post-colonial development or even to the Cold War itself now seemed equally to form part of a "post-Cold War" world characterized by endemic conflicts.

Different perspectives on these conflicts have attributed their apparent spread to different facets of the multidimensional transformation taking place. To some, the fall of Communist repression thawed a frozen history, as ancient hatreds emerged like woolly mammoths freed from the Siberian ice. For others, the end of the Cold War set off a "deregulation" of the international system, as the end of strategic bipolarity weakened hegemonically dominated alliance systems. In this volume, however, the authors have by and large placed the most emphasis on the effect of the third transformation: the breakup of the Soviet Union into independent states. This process required the construction of both new national states and a new international system out of what Jack Snyder calls the "detritus of empire."[4] That this empire's economy, politics, and society had been structured by a Communist Party engaged in the construction of state socialism gave specific characteristics to the process of breakup and reconfiguration. Nonetheless, the end of Communism alone had quite different consequences in the smaller and more ethnically uniform states of East Central Europe.

Gorbachev's reforms had set off consequences that neither he nor most in the West had foreseen. With the loosening of centralized controls, would-be political leaders used a variety of appeals, including ethnic and nationalist ones, to build followings. The economic reforms weakened the command mechanisms before market and legal institutions were established, leading to hyperinflation and a generalized scramble for assets whose ownership was unclear.[5] Similarly, the political reforms weakened authoritarian and imperial mechanisms of social control before the establishment of new institutions for conflict management through state-building, democracy, or international co-operation.

The breakup of the USSR left behind a large regional power, Russia, and a host of smaller ones that now occupied distinct regions (Baltics, Eastern Central Europe, Transcaucasus, Central Asia). The process of dissolution which led, however unintentionally in many cases, to these states' independence, was marked by disorder and violence. Just as the lack of clarity of ownership of economic assets led to disorderly and often criminal competition for wealth, so the lack of clarity about legitimacy, borders, control over security forces, and new inter-state relations led to a disorderly and often criminal competition for power. In both realms, those who already had access to existing levers of power held the advantage: nomenklatura privatization went hand in hand with nomenklatura politicization. This politicization often took the form of appeals to nationalism, especially since the dissolution of the non-ethnic Soviet state left in place only ethnically-defined national republics (most of which also contained ethnically-defined minority regions or republics) as successors.

Some analyses argue that the territory of the former Soviet Union is destined to be an anarchic zone, where the imperial ambitions of one large state, Russia, virtually untrammeled by international norms and, at least to its south, not balanced by any other major powers, will continually stir up trouble in its relations to its smaller neighbors. What order there will be will result from Russian hegemony, it might seem, while the nationalism this hegemony embodies will continue to destabilize a number of states. The ethnic Russians in the near abroad (in particular in Ukraine and Kazakstan) could be important flash points, as rising nationalism leads to ethnic conflict.

Trends in the last few years, however, have already begun to refute views that conflict will necessarily be endemic to these areas, while the role of Russia is far more complex, and mediated by the international environment. The incidence of conflict as measured by numbers of conflicts in the former Soviet space peaked in 1989–1990, though the most violent conflict, that in Chechnya, did not reach its peak of slaughter until after December 1994. The conflicts resulted from the process of imperial collapse unintentionally set off by Gorbachev's reforms. Since 1992, while some conflicts have persisted or even (like Chechnya) become more violent, fewer new ones, and by some counts no new ones, have started. Furthermore, while assertion of a degree of Russian hegemony has been central to the processes of consolidation, the means by which this hegemony has been asserted show the influence of international norms and institutions. Russian ethnic nationalism has not thus far turned out to be nearly as potent a theme in Russian foreign policy as the desire for the Russian state to be recognized as a major world power. The linguistic distinction that exists in Russian between an ethnic Russian—"Russkiy"—and a citizen of the state—"Rossiskiy"—has been borne out in practice. Russia has thus far chosen integration into the international status quo through recognizing the sovereignty of the other former Soviet states rather than risk pariah status through assertive nationalism. Nor does ethnic nationalism appear to be that potent a force in Russian public opinion. The war in Chechnya remains a potent reminder of the worst the Russian state can do, but among its many causes, Russian ethnic nationalism played little if any role.[6]

The present state of the international system, indeed, is far from either polar ideal type of anarchy or world government. States are linked by complex networks of interdependence that limit their freedom of action without subjecting them to the rule of law. In particular, the norm of sovereignty is reinforced by international organizations and agreements that the newly independent states have joined and acceded to. Left alone, the dynamic of former core and periphery analyzed by Motyl might or might not play itself out through irredentism, conflict, and war. In reality, neither entity is so one-dimensionally determined as in his analysis. But in any case, these dynamics do not play out in a vacuum, but in an international environment radically different from what prevailed when the Habsburg, Ottoman, and Czarist Russian empires collapsed.

Indeed, though the process of consolidation has not received nearly the degree of attention as the outbreak of unanticipated conflict, analysis of the incidence and sequence of conflict in the post-Soviet space shows clearly that most of the violent conflicts were by-products of the process of imperial breakup and subsequent state building. After the initial shocks, the incidence of conflict is decreasing as new institutions are created to manage instability. Enough uncertainty and human suffering remains to make continuing demands on our attention and resources, and understanding the dynamics of the continuing transformation will help guide policy in productive directions. But the post-Soviet space is moving toward normal instability.

The incidence of conflict in the (post-) Soviet space

While counting conflicts is always somewhat arbitrary, several different approaches suggest that the incidence of conflict in the post-Soviet space is decreasing. The Minorities at Risk Project, led by Ted Gurr with numerous collaborators, has collected and analyzed perhaps the most complete set of data. It includes data on conflict by ethno-political groups; it therefore excludes purely political conflicts like that between President Boris Yeltsin and the Russian parliament in the fall of 1993, but it captures most of the events relevant to the analysis here. Phase I of the analysis, dealing with the period 1945–89, was coded in five-year increments; Phase III, however, is coded in yearly increments for the period 1985–95, and corresponds to the period under examination here.[7]

The Phase I analysis indeed showed a 1980s upsurge in ethno-political conflict in all regions of the world. In most regions this upsurge was a continuation of postwar trends, but in Eastern Europe and the (post-)USSR, the upsurge was almost unprecedented. Such a general increase continued into the 1990–5 period when viewed as a whole. The yearly data, however, showed that all three forms of conflict tracked by the data (non-violent protest, communal conflict, and rebellion) peaked in the early 1990s and declined thereafter. Gurr and Haxton summarize the trends as follows:

> The former Soviet bloc had virtually no ethnopolitical rebellion from the 1950s through 1970s .... Communal conflict and protest occurred throughout, however, and rose precipitously in the latter half of the 1980s. The increase coincided with the advent of perestroika and glasnost, Mikhail Gorbachev's policies of economic liberalization and political liberalization .... Protest shot up after 1987 and then leveled off after 1989, at which point rebellion rose almost as precipitously as did protest two years before .... Protest and rebellion both began to decline after 1992, communal conflict after 1994.[8]

The number of new conflicts began to decline. Gurr defined "'new' episodes of ethno-protest and rebellion [as] those initiated in 1986–1995 by groups that had no prior history of collective action *plus* those initiated by groups that resumed action after a long period of dormancy or limited action."[9] In the post-Communist states the initiation of new ethno-political protest movements and rebellions peaked in 1989–92 (Table 8.1). Gurr argues:

> Though many experts have warned of the potential for new ethnic rebellions in the post-Communist states, we have identified none that began after 1992. Since ethnorebellion is usually preceded by protest activity, the most likely candidates for future rebellion are to be found among groups that initiated protest activities after 1992. [10]

Table 8.1 New ethno-political protest movements and rebellions in the post-Communist states by year of onset, 1986–95

Year	Protest movements	Rebellions
1986	0	0
1987	2	0
1988	3	1
1989	7	0
1990	6	5
1991	6	3
1992	3	3
1993	3	0
1994	1	0
1995	1	0

Source: Gurr, "Minorities Report (2)," 4, 5.

These include the Roma minorities of Central Europe, who have never engaged in violent protest, and the ethnic Russians in Crimea and elsewhere in Ukraine (mainly the Donbass region of eastern Ukraine).

A less rigorous but more focused analysis of violent ethno-political conflicts in the former Soviet space alone bears out the more general analysis. Table 8.2 presents a list of such conflicts or incidents of conflict in the Soviet space from the advent of Gorbachev until the present, and Figure 8.1 shows the incidence over time of the start of these conflicts. This list, not necessarily exhaustive, includes the best known incidents of violence, as well as the dates when violence started. These incidents include both rebellions and communal conflicts, in Gurr's terms, but exclude peaceful protest movements. They also include riots and incidents of violent repression of protest, including protests by titular nationalities of republics that became independent.

The time profile of these incidents is similar to that of the Gurr data, with a peak in 1991 and no new conflicts beginning after 1992. The first outbreak was in Kazakstan, the December 1986 nationalist riots that hinted at the force of emerging nationalism. In 1988 the Transcaucasus began to explode, with the secession of Nagorno-Karabakh and the anti-Armenian riots in Sumgait, Azerbaijan. Over the next three years conflict spread further in the Transcaucasus with the start of several conflicts in Georgia, including violent repression of a Georgian nationalist demonstration, the start of the secessionist war in Abkhazia, and the secessionist movement in South Ossetia. During the same period there were also further riots in Baku and a violent crackdown against Armenian insurgents in western Azerbaijan. Conflict spread to the Russian Caucasus in 1991, when Dzhokhar Dudaev declared Chechnya independent, leading ultimately to the brutal Russian assault that began in December 1994. Ingush and Ossetes clashed in North Ossetia in November 1992.

In the western Soviet Union, the main violent incidents were the 1991 military assault on demonstrators in Lithuania and the Trans-Dniester secessionist movement backed by Russia's Fourteenth Army under General Alexander Lebed in Moldova. The latter, by the way, seems to be the only violent incident on Soviet (or former Soviet) territory directly linked to the presence of a Russian-speaking population or Russian irredenta.

Central Asia during this period had three brief outbursts of violence—two extremely violent communal clashes in the Ferghana Valley in 1989 and 1990 and riots in Dushanbe in February 1990 that spread to neighboring areas of Uzbekistan. In the immediate aftermath of independence Tajikistan erupted into civil war, after Chechnya the bloodiest of all the conflicts of the Soviet transition.

Of these sixteen cases of violent conflict, nine were riots, communal clashes, or incidents of repression that did not develop into protracted conflicts or rebellions. They ran their course or were stopped. In some cases, the grievances they expressed were met when the republics became independent. Of the remaining cases, while few have reached a final settlement, at this writing none remains a hot war without a settlement, though the fate of the agreement negotiated by Lebed in

Table 8.2 Violent ethnic and nationalist conflicts in the USSR and successor states, 1986–96, by region

Conflict	Start date	Status
East Central Europe		
Lithuania/Soviet Army	January 1991	Single incident; Lithuania became independent
Moldova/Gagauz	August 1991	Autonomy agreement in July 1994
Moldova/Transdniestria	September 1991	Autonomy agreement in July 1996
Transcaucasus		
Azerbaijan/Nagorno-Karabakh	January 1988	Unresolved; ceasefire, April 1994
Azerbaijan/Sumgait riots	February 1988	Single incident
Georgia/Soviet Army	April 1989	Single incident; Georgia became independent
Georgia/Abkhazia	April 1989	Unresolved; ceasefire April 1994
Azerbaijan/Baku riots	January 1990	Single incident
Georgia/S. Ossetia	January 1991	Unresolved; ceasefire June 1992
Azerbaijan/Gestasen insurgency	April 1991	Single incident
Central Asia		
Kazakstan/Almaty riots	December 1986	Single incident; Kazakstan became independent
Uzbekistan/Ferghana riots	June 1989	Single incident
Tajikistan/Dushanbe riots	February 1990	Single incident
Kyrgyzstan/Osh riots	June 1990	Single incident
Tajikistan/civil war	May 1992	Peace agreement, June 1997
Russian Federation		
Chechnya	August 1991	Ceasefire and interim agreement, October 1996
Ingushetia/N. Ossetia	November 1992	Unresolved; violence controlled by Russian army

Sources: I. Bremmer and R. Taras (eds), *Nations and Politics in the Soviet Successor States*, New York: Cambridge University Press, 1993; M.B. Broxup, "The 'Internal' Muslim Factor in the Politics of Russia," in M. Mesbahi (ed.), *Central Asia and the Caucasus after the Soviet Union*, Tallahassee, FL: University Press of Florida, 1994; S. Hunter, *The Transcaucasus in Transition*, Washington, DC: The Center for Strategic and International Studies, 1994; G. Otyrba, "War in Abkhazia," in R. Szporluk (ed.), *National Identity and Ethnicity in Russia and the Western States of Eurasia*, Armonk, NY: M.E. Sharpe, 1994; A. Rashid, *The Resurgence of Central Asia*, London: Zed Books, 1994; B.R. Rubin, "Tajikistan: From Soviet Republic to Russian–Uzbek Protectorate," in M. Mandelbaum (ed.), *Central Asia and the World*, New York: Council on Foreign Relations Press, 1994; L. Fuller, "Yet Another 'Historic' Chechen Ceasefire Agreement," *Open Media Research Institute Analytical Brief (OMRIAB)*, 28 May 1996, vol 1, no. 132; L. Fuller, "The Vagaries of Russia's Abkhaz Policy," *OMRIAB*, 29 March 1996, vol 1, no. 51; D. Ionescu, "Moldovan–Dniester Agreement Ripe for Being Signed," *OMRIAB*, 1 July 1996, vol 1, no. 205; B. Pannier, "Tajikistan's Grim Anniversary," *OMRIAB*, 18 April 1996, vol 1, no. 72.
Note: This table is based on research by Alexander Cooley, whom I would like to thank.

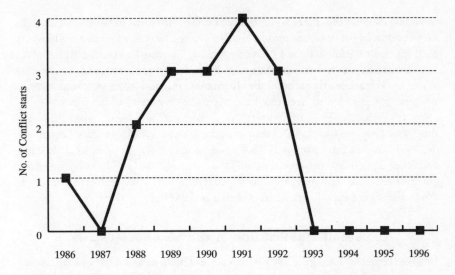

Figure 8.1 Number of violent conflicts initiated per year, USSR and successor states, 1986–96
Source: Table 8.2

Chechnya remains in question, the conflict in Nagorno-Karabakh erupts in violent incidents from time to time, and the Tajikistan power-sharing agreement of 21 February 1997 may not succeed in ending the war.

Of the nine cases of single incidents, three (Almaty in 1986, Tbilisi in 1989, and Vilnius in January 1991) expressed nationalist demands that have now been met with the independence of the republics. Three others were outbreaks of violence in Azerbaijan directly related to the war in Nagorno-Karabakh. The Dushanbe riots, too, originated in rumors related to that war (that Armenian displaced persons were being given apartments ahead of local applicants); the underlying tensions that account for the violence later formed part of the background of the Tajikistan civil war. The two remaining incidents, both in the Ferghana Valley, involved competition over scarce resources (again, including housing and land for housing in the case of Osh), aggravated by the lack of clarity of ethnic and national rights during the transitional period.[11]

Russia is involved in all of the seven ongoing conflicts, sometimes directly and sometimes under the aegis of the CIS, but in all of the seven, the UN or the OSCE (both in the case of Tajikistan) also have some role.[12] In Nagorno-Karabakh, Russian troops police a ceasefire Russia brokered in 1994, and Russian diplomats both compete and co-operate with the OSCE-organized "Minsk group" as mediators. In Abkhazia, a conflict fanned by Russian covert involvement intended (successfully) to pressure Georgia into joining the CIS is now calmed by CIS "peacekeepers" monitored by a UN mission. In South Ossetia the Russian peacekeepers are monitored by a monitoring mission of the OSCE. The OSCE is providing election observers and monitors for the settlement in Chechnya, though its role remains controversial and its head of mission was expelled by the Chechen authorities for stating that the OSCE recognized Chechnya as part of Russia. The OSCE has also established one of its missions of long duration to monitor the situation in Transdniestria, where the Russian army has changed from overtly supporting separatists to re-establishing normality as part of a joint peacekeeping force. In Tajikistan, Russian and CIS "peacekeepers" and border guards uphold the current regime, while a UN envoy convened peace talks, UN military observers deployed around the country try (not always successfully) to monitor a ceasefire and other agreements between the two Tajik sides, and the OSCE both advises the government on its human rights obligations and monitors the treatment of repatriated refugees in field offices turned over to it by UNHCR.

Causes of stabilization of the post-Soviet space

Despite the general image of the former Soviet Union as a tangled web of insecurity and conflict, it is quite striking that no new major conflicts have begun there since the immediate aftermath of the Soviet dissolution. Furthermore, the single potential cause of conflict that is probably most often cited, including by several authors in this volume—the presence of Russians and Russian-speakers outside of Russia in the newly independent states, some of them living in territories to which Russian nationalists (not just Soviet restorationists) lay claim—has so far turned out to be the dog that did not bark. Despite the emergence of Russian protest movements in Estonia, northern Kazakstan, Crimea, and, to a lesser extent, eastern Ukraine, Russia's borders with these neighbors, including the two largest ones, have remained calm. Moldova, which borders on Ukraine rather than Russia, was the only exception.

Note that the Russian communities in Ukraine are the two cases of ethno-protest in the former Soviet Union that Gurr considers as having potential for rebellion. (It is unclear why he does not include the Russians of North Kazakstan.) Motyl concurs in his chapter, arguing that the logic of the post-imperial situation will ultimately dominate, leading to escalating conflict. Casanova, however, argues that the predominantly Russian-speaking regions of Ukraine do not possess a uniform national identity conducive to nationalist mobilization. Rather, linguistic, ethnic, and religious identities overlap unevenly, creating cross-cutting cleavages and a basis for pluralism. These regions have also retained important powers over their economic assets and are able to pursue relations with regions of Russia, especially on economic matters, without raising directly the question of the ethno-nationalist content of state power. The international system now contains space for action not only by national governments, inter-governmental organizations, and the newly recognized entrants, non-governmental organizations, but also for regional and local governments, and cultural groups. The pattern of direct relations among regions has also developed, for instance, in Western Europe.

Even in the most unstable part of Central Asia, Kulab province of Tajikistan and Takhar province of Afghanistan have reached agreements on economic co-operation and are building a new port on the Amu Darya to promote trade. These ties are not leading to any redrawing of borders around a "greater Tajikistan," which interests Tajiks in north Afghanistan as little as rejoining a troubled Mother Russia does the Russians and Russian-speakers of the Donbass. It represents a beneficial form of regional co-operation which the collapse of the centralized empire has in fact made possible for the first time.[13]

Despite its repeated invocation, the issue of the "abandoned brethren" has failed to ignite in Russian domestic politics, and the Russians of the other republics seem to be dealing with their problems by a combination of non-violent protest, usually within the political institutions of the states they inhabit, or emigration.[14] The emigration of Russian speakers is not, however, unique to them; since the independence of the republics, population movements throughout the post-Soviet space have included flows of national return or repatriation by members of all former Soviet nationalities.

The image of the former Soviet Union as a zone of conflict is not totally wrong, of course. While most of the conflicts of the post-Soviet transition are no longer violent, few have actually been resolved to the satisfaction of the parties, and tensions could reignite. Nor can one rule out the possibility that some incident or shock could spark new violence in any of several potential areas of conflict. Chechnya, treated in this volume mainly by Solnick, who sees it as an exception to Russia's generally peaceful evolution toward two-tiered federalism, is the most obvious case of an unsettled, though pacified conflict.

Nonetheless, the largely unremarked fact that virtually no new conflicts have erupted into violence in the post-Soviet period, despite pervasive economic decline and the easy availability of weapons, contains some lessons for how to prevent them in the future. The main processes that have stabilized most of the post Soviet area have been:

1 The building of new states out of the detritus of empire;
2 The construction of a more consistent Russian foreign and security policy toward the other newly independent states and the development of more stable expectations about international behavior in the region.

Both of which have been strongly influenced by:

3 The integration of these new states, including Russia, into an international system, including global and regional organizations, bilateral relations with other states, and relations with a huge range of new international private-sector institutions, ranging from multinational corporations to humanitarian organizations.

These processes have created far more stable expectations about the consequences of actions than existed during the Soviet collapse, which was indeed as sudden and chaotic as Alexander Motyl argues in his contribution.[15]

Building new states

As Snyder argues in the introduction to this volume, the newly independent successor states of the USSR inherited very different institutional parts of the Soviet empire. The distinction was far more complex, however, than is implied by a simple core–periphery dichotomy. Not only different republics, but different regions within those republics (including different regions within Russia) had different relations to the former imperial center. Motyl argues that Russian–Ukrainian relations, for instance, will ultimately conform to a model of revolutionary center and nationalizing periphery. Casanova, however, argues for a more differentiated view of Ukraine, while Menon and Spruyt note that the nationalism of the former periphery can and does take different forms. The relevant units of political action need not be nationality groups—abandoned Russian brethren—but can also include the regional (especially oblast-level) institutions that moved from one system to another with personnel largely intact. Eastern Ukraine, for instance, was in many respects part of the Soviet core, not the periphery. It has been able to use the resulting assets to pursue its interests independently while negotiating the terms of its integration with Ukraine.

The leaders of these regional institutions may at times use ethnic appeals to mobilize support. Solnick demonstrates how the ethnic republics within Russia exploited their unique identity to improve their bargain with the center as the Russian federation was reconstituted along more decentralized lines. There was, however, no ethnic content to their appeals. They used the fact of their having an ethnic identity—what we might awkwardly call "ethnicness"—rather than any ethnic characteristics, which they did not share, as a coordination mechanism for economic bargaining. Such behavior, similar to that of Eastern Ukraine, represents a kind of civic regionalism. The sub-national territorial administrations, which became much more autonomous and openly politicized as a result of the collapse of the imperial control mechanisms, used their resources, including ethnic identity, to bargain peacefully over the terms of their integration into the newly independent states and the new international system of which they were now a part.

At the other end of the spectrum is a kind of "ethnic" regionalism, typified by Chechnya, Abkhazia, Nagorno-Karabakh, Transdniestria, and the regional clans of Tajikistan. In all these cases regions, whether ethnically identified or not, became the basis for violent conflict based on identities reinforced by Soviet administrative institutions. These are the cases of conflict that are still unsettled. By June 1997, even the parties to the Tajikistan civil war reached agreement on an accord, apparently under the impetus of decisions taken in Moscow in response to the September 1996 capture of Kabul by the Taliban movement.

The question which cannot be answered is whether the trend toward integration of the civic regions and the establishment of various forms of coexistence that end overt war even in the absence of a final settlement can endure. Motyl argues that national conflict between center and periphery is simply on a long fuse; as Menon and Spruyt argue, that fuse could be lit or burn faster if an economic crisis overtook Russia or some key states in the region or if Russia turned authoritarian. However, thus far the response to economic decline and painful readjustment has been surprisingly peaceful. In no post-Soviet state except perhaps Belarus have demagogues succeeded in rising to power on a wave of economic resentment. Instead, we see either the consolidation of hegemonic regimes, as in most of Central Asia (and apparently Belarus), or the start of a process of partisan competition and alternance within rules of the game, as in Ukraine, the Baltic states, and, arguably, Russia. A complicating factor in Russia, however, is that the main opposition, the Communist Party, remains an anti-system party, whose commitment to the rules of the game and the market economy remains unclear. Hence system-maintaining protest so far lacks a legitimate vehicle in Russia.

Thus, except for parts of Azerbaijan, Georgia, and Tajikistan, and Chechnya in Russia, regional administrations are being integrated into new states. The states have also established national political institutions of varying types. The new states have also, by and large, been successful in asserting property rights over natural resources and other assets on their territory. At the same time, the inheritance of a transport and communications infrastructure centered on Russia has made it difficult for the newly independent states to exploit these resources on the international market. The well-known problem of pipelines for Central Asian oil and natural gas is only an example of a much wider problem, which has led foreign investors initially to look for raw materials with a high value per unit of weight or size, such as gold or opium.

Indeed, this problematic aspect of post-Soviet state building alerts us to a more general problem. We should not assume that the process of building the institutions of these new states will necessary produce states that fully conform to an ideal type of sovereignty, or that the regional international system of which they are a part will be characterized by anarchic interaction among fully autonomous states that must rely only on their own resources. Rather, while some of the fragments of empire, as well as new structures that are being created, are being combined to form national states, others are being combined to form new types of transnational networks. Russia, for most of the CIS, is emerging as something less than a new imperial hegemon, but something more than simply the largest of a group of equal, sovereign states. We must therefore turn to aspects of Russia's foreign policy to see how international factors contribute to the declining incidence of violent conflict in the former Soviet space.

Russia's foreign policy

It took a certain amount of time for Russia—which despite its inheritance of much of the Soviet state apparatus was also a newly independent state—to elaborate a foreign policy toward the rest of the former Soviet Union, the so-called "near abroad." Russia's complex and still evolving role has not always been a force for stability; indeed, it aggravated or provoked several conflicts. Having largely obtained its main goal, however—integrating the former republics other than the Baltics into a common security system under the aegis of the CIS—Russia has moderated its role.

Motyl argues that Russia's interaction with the newly independent states from the former imperial periphery will be largely determined by a dynamic of nationalism in the periphery versus reassertion in the core. One conflict not analyzed in this volume that fits this model was the secession of Transdniestria from Moldova. After a period of protest against a new language law and several other nationalist measures by the Popular Front government, the Communist leaders of the predominantly Slavic-speaking province of Transdniestria declared independence in September 1991, when it was clear that the USSR would break up. By early 1992, they received overt support from the Russian Fourteenth Army, which came under the command of General Lebed in June of that year. The Russian army assisted the local secessionists in forming armed detachments, which engaged in battles in which almost 500 people died.[16]

The overt nature of the intervention in Transdniestria was unusual, as was its connection specifically to the status of Russians in the near abroad. However, more covert Russian interventions also took place in Abkhazia, and perhaps in Azerbaijan and elsewhere. While it took place within the internationally recognized borders of Russia, the intervention in Chechnya also belongs to this category; the overt military assault seems to have been occasioned by the failure of a clumsily organized "covert" action designed to overthrow the Dudaev government. While at least in Abkhazia the intervention took advantage of a Russian population on the Abkhaz–Russian border, the main motivation of these interventions seems more to have been to pressure the governments into joining the CIS, allowing the stationing of Russian troops or border forces, or some other security goal.[17] Indeed, by most reports, ethnic Russians were the main victims of Russia's devastation of Chechnya.

The behavior of Russia in Transdniestria conformed to the model of cross-border ethnic politics developed by Brubaker and further elaborated by Motyl. Indeed, one can appreciate its generic quality by comparing it to the behavior of Serbia in Bosnia and Croatia at about the same time. Serbia also took up the cause of its abandoned brethren and used the Serbian-dominated Yugoslav National Army to form militias of local Serbs.[18] The interaction between the nationalisms of the former core and former periphery followed the model.

However, Transdniestria turned out to be exceptional in the post-Soviet case, and, in general, Russia's behavior has been quite different from that of Serbia. Even in Transdniestria, starting with the summer of 1992, President Yeltsin made moves designed to defuse the situation. Though in this case Russia was unable to involve multilateral forces, it reached a bilateral peacekeeping agreement with Moldova, and a joint force separated the warring parties. Gradually a solution based on autonomy and language rights seems to be evolving. The more difficult issues seem again to be those connected to international security rather than those connected to nationalism. For the strategic reasons listed above, Russia would like to keep its troops on the Dniester, while the parliament of Ukraine (whose western, more nationalist, region borders Transdniestria) objects to their presence.

Transdniestria, of course, was a minor issue, despite its symbolic importance. The major issues regarding Russians in the near abroad involved Ukraine, the Baltic states, and Kazakstan. In all of these cases, while Russia has used aggressive rhetoric and bargaining at times over issues such as the withdrawal of Russian military personnel, oil pipelines, and the Black Sea Fleet, it has not used military force or direct coercion such as blockades, and all of these tensions seem, for now, to be ebbing rather than increasing.

Some systemic variables may account in part for Russia's more peaceful behavior: Russia was far more powerful in relative terms within the former Soviet Union than was Serbia (even with Montenegro) in Yugoslavia, and the proportion of Serbs living outside Serbia was greater (25 percent, or 41 percent counting Kosovo and Vojvodina) than that of Russians living outside Russia (17 percent), so that the degree of grievance over the "abandoned brethren" was less.[19] But the factors cited by Menon and Spruyt provide some additional explanations for this difference. While Russia still exhibited a number of non-democratic features during this period (a violent near-civil war between parliament and president in 1993, the apparent lack of accountability of some of the security organs), it has clearly moved further toward the democratic portion of the continuum than Serbia. In particular, the media in Russia show much more independence than the still state-controlled ones in Serbia.

Integration with the international system

While it is more difficult to demonstrate, Russia's behavior has also been decisively affected by the Russian Federation's integration into an international system which is now far denser with norms of behavior and wide varieties of interaction than ever before. Indeed the effect on the behavior of states and other political actors of interaction with the full range of transnational actors is an area in need of greater study. Debunking of international institutions often takes the form of illustrating that they are not effective in reaching their stated goals and that states flout international norms and even "laws" with apparent impunity.[20] In arguing that integration with the international system has affected Russian behavior, I do not mean to contend that Russia has fully adhered to international norms or submitted itself to the jurisdiction of international institutions. The war in Chechnya, as much as or more than the war in Afghanistan, was conducted from start to finish in violation of basic rules of humanitarian law. Through covert operations and other means, Russia has repeatedly violated norms of international interaction.

The fact that behavior does not fully comply with norms and laws, however, does not prove that it is the same as it would be if those norms and laws, and the institutions that promote them, did not exist. Most importantly, Russia has become increasingly dependent on external credits to keep its financial system running. Its leaders aspire to build it into a world power, and despite nativistic and autarchic currents, the dominant groups recognize that such power requires Western (and Asian) investment and technology. Threatening behavior by Russia in the security field could jeopardize Russian recovery. Overt actions such as the use of military force to claim territory now belonging to other sovereign states is simply not an option for Russia.

Furthermore, even in some of the most severe conflicts, the existence of international institutions has had a moderating influence. It has made possible strategies that would otherwise have been difficult if not impossible. Ironically enough, the case of Tajikistan supports this claim.

Certainly Russia (and all the other political actors concerned in this struggle) has regularly violated international norms and flouted decisions of international institutions. At the same time, one must wonder why Russia did not follow the easiest and simplest strategy of using force to close off the border with Afghanistan, keep the expelled populations from returning to the country, and building up the victors as uncompromising rulers of the country in order to protect Russian interests.

Part of the answer lies in the estimate by some Russians that such a strategy might not succeed. But Russian foreign policy decision makers, in a variety of interviews, also emphasized that they wished to obtain international recognition and perhaps funding for their peacekeeping role in Tajikistan and elsewhere, and that they recognized that the price of obtaining this type of recognition and status was at least partial adherence to some international norms. Indeed, a sort of "international regime" has developed around the resolution of such conflicts, according to which negotiations among all parties should lead to a mutually acceptable transitional government and new elections, accompanied by a cease-fire, disarmament, the return of refugees and displaced people, with all of these actions carried out or monitored by international institutions.[21] Russia has supported actual implementation of some of these measures, especially the return of refugees. It has been reluctant to accept others, in particular those that would allow the Islamic opposition the opportunity genuinely to contest state power. But the resultant negotiation process with its pressures for elections and other measures has in effect reinforced the legitimacy of the opposition as a political actor and prevented the full consolidation of the victors as a hegemonic government.

One can find other factors that contributed to all these effects, and more research is needed to verify to what extent interaction with institutions and knowledge of the options their existence creates has affected international decision-making in the post-Soviet space and elsewhere. It is clear that these institutions are a complement to, not a substitute for, the power of states. However, that does not mean they have no effect. Indeed, as Miles Kahler argued in comments on an early draft of Snyder's introduction, the present international system is hostile to the reconstitution of imperial structures, providing Russia with considerable incentives to recognize the independence of the other republics and structuring its interactions.[22]

Policy: democracy building and state building

The analyses in this study have focused on the construction or reconstruction of state institutions. Partly in order to redress the balance, we have devoted relatively little attention to the question of regime type, that is democratization, which has been a major focus of policy toward the region. Though democratization is of course an end in itself, its contribution to stabilization and peacemaking in the region has been ambiguous. In general, it appears that consolidated, developed democracies are the most stable states and the least prone to war, at least with each other, but that states undergoing transitions, economic or political, are the least stable and possibly most war-prone. Huntington, of course, made this argument about development in *Political Order and Changing Societies*. Snyder and Mansfield have made an analogous argument about the proclivity to war of different regime types in a series of recent articles.[23] Nor is it clear that policies aimed at democracy building, especially those concentrating on "technical support," can actually build democratic institutions where other institutions are absent, weak, or corrupt. [24]

As Jack Snyder argues in the introduction to this volume, the key problem in the wake of imperial collapse is state building and its concomitant, nation building. Processes of democratization are logically and empirically subordinate to these. Democracy, like any regime type, is a way of regulating the relations between the state and society. Unless the state has the capacity to implement policy formulated by law, the forms of democracy—parties, elections, legislatures—do not constitute means of self-government by a society. Instead they simply provide a mechanism for mobilized social segments to compete over the distribution of state resources, a competition that can easily generate violence, especially when those resources are shrinking.[25] Furthermore, without agreement on the legitimacy of the national unit, it is impossible to specify the subject of democracy—who is the nation that will govern itself?

The dependence of democracy on state building does not mean that state building (and economic development to support it) must come first in a temporal sequence, an argument often used to justify authoritarian rule. The relationship between regime type and processes of state formation is more complex and mutually determined. An authoritarian regime like that of Mobutu in Zaire, to take a recent and extreme example, actively promotes state disintegration; it appears that only some measure of accountability, which could come from some types of democratic institutions, can strengthen basic fiscal and legal institutions. In some countries (Poland, for instance) only governments with democratic legitimacy have had the strength to institute economic reforms that entailed a period of sacrifice before the benefits arrived. Hence the equation of authoritarianism with stability is at least as misleading as the equation of democratization with instability.

The relationship of democracy to state building, however, has implications for policy. That democracy may not immediately and in the short run increase stability does not mean that support for democracy should not be a component of US and Western policy toward the states of the former Soviet Union. But the dependence of democracy on state building for its effectiveness means that we must devote resources to other areas of institution building as well. There are already a number of programs in the vital area of the rule of law. Other important areas are taxation, effective policing that respects rights, local government, regional planning, inter-governmental relations, government contracting, financial institutions, and similar areas. Failures in these areas often undermine public confidence in institutions, as can be seen in the repeated scandals over pyramid schemes in financial institutions.

This agenda is indeed daunting. The processes analyzed in this book, however, while they will undoubtedly produce more conflict, are also producing a more stable environment in which institution building can take place. Nothing guarantees that the war in Chechnya will not resume, that Kazakstan will not slide into civil war, that a new Russian government elected during a massive economic crisis will not try to retake control of Eastern Ukraine, or that segments of a collapsing Russian army may not make a grab for power. However, the domestic and international costs of these or other conflicts are so great that actors seem largely successfully to have found ways of coexisting without violence, even in the absence of agreement. Assistance to the building of key institutions can help consolidate these developments. In the long term, a more stable environment and continued interaction with an international community promoting democratic norms is likely to lower the salience of nationalist and other ethnic demands and promote the development of more civic societies.

Notes

1 On the definition of "empire" and its application to the USSR, see Chapters 1 and 2 in this volume.
2 See the text of Gorbachev's speech where he announced the Soviet decision to withdraw from Afghanistan in *New York Times*, 9 February, 1988.
3 "Remarks to the Supreme Soviet of the Republic of the Ukraine in Kiev, Soviet Union," August 1, 1991, in *Public Papers of the Presidents of the United States: George Bush 1991, In Two Books, Book II – July 1 to December 31, 1991*, pp. 1005–8; "Address to the 46th Session of the United Nations General Assembly in New York, New York," September 23, 1991, ibid., pp. 1199–203.
4 Snyder, Chapter 1.
5 S.L. Solnick, "The Breakdown of Hierarchies in the Soviet Union and China: A Neoinstitutional Perspective," *World Politics*, January 1996, vol. 48, pp. 209–38.
6 V. Tishkov, *Ethnicity, Nationalism and Conflict in and after the Soviet Union: The Mind Aflame*, London: Sage, with International Peace Research Institute, Oslo, and United Nations Research Institute for Social Development, 1997, pp. 246–71. Tishkov asserts the primacy of civic or state over ethnic loyalty in Russia by importing the spelling "Rossia" into English and using the term "Rossians" for citizens of that state.
7 The Phase I analysis is in T.R. Gurr, with chapters by B. Harff, M.G. Marshal, and J.R. Scaritt, *Minorities at Risk: A Global View of Ethnopolitical Conflict*, Washington, DC: United States Institute of Peace, 1993. One report of the Phase III analysis is T.R. Gurr,

"Communal Conflicts and Global Security," *Current History*, May 1995, vol. 94, pp. 212–17. The data and analyses reported here come from T.R. Gurr and M. Haxton, "Minorities Report, 1. Ethnopolitical Conflict in the 1990s: Patterns and Trends," unpublished paper, April 1996, and T.R. Gurr, "Minorities Report, 2. New Contenders, Old Issues: The Rise and Decline of Ethnopolitical Conflict in 1986–95," unpublished paper, May 1996. Both may be downloaded from the Minorities at Risk World Wide Web site at http://www.bsos.umd.edu/cldcm/mar/pubs.htm.

8   Gurr and Haxton, "Minorities Report, 1," p. 18.

9   Gurr, "Minorities Report, 2," p. 3. He notes that these data exclude communal conflicts, where the state is not an actor.

10   Ibid., pp. 6–7. See the analysis of these groups by Casanova in this volume.

11   Y. Ro'i, "Central Asian Riots and Disturbances, 1989–1990: Causes and Context," *Central Asian Survey*, 1991, vol. 10, no. 3, pp. 21–54; Tishkov, *Ethnicity, Nationalism and Conflict*, pp. 135–54.

12   R. Allison, "Peacekeeping in the Soviet Successor States," Chaillot Paper 18, Paris, Institute for Security Studies, Western European Union, 1994; Mark Webber, "Coping with Anarchy: Ethnic Conflict and International Organizations in the Former Soviet Union," *International Relations*, April 1996, vol. 13, no. 1, pp. 1–27.

13   This agreement between the two provinces was described to me by the governor of Takhar, Afghanistan, in Taloqan, the provincial center, in January 1996. I was not able to observe to what extent the agreement was actually functioning.

14   J. Chinn and R. Kaiser, *Russians as the New Minority: Ethnicity and Nationalism in the Soviet Successor States*, Boulder, Co: Westview, 1996; Tishkov, *Ethnicity, Nationalism and Conflict*.

15   Motyl, Chapter 2 in this volume.

16   Chinn and Kaiser, *Russians as the New Minority*, pp. 172–5.

17   Chinn and Kaiser argue that the Transdniestrian intervention also had such goals, at least in part. Keeping the Fourteenth Army in the area provides greater leverage for Russia in the Balkans (ibid., p. 173).

18   See, for example, S.L. Woodward, *Balkan Tragedy: Chaos and Dissolution after the Cold War*, Washington, DC: Brookings Institution, 1995.

19   I would like to thank Stephen Burg for supplying me with these numbers.

20   Mearsheimer, "False Promise."

21   On this regime see Rubin, *Search for Peace in Afghanistan*, Chapter 1.

22   M. Kahler, "Comments/Jack Snyder, Organizing Political Space in the Former Soviet Union," electronic mail, 8 May 1995.

23   S.P. Huntington, *Political Order in Changing Societies*, New Haven, CT: Yale University Press, 1968; E.D. Mansfield and J. Snyder, "Democratization and War," *Foreign Affairs*, May–June 1995, vol. 74, pp. 79–97, and "Democratization and the Danger of War," *International Security*, Summer 1995, vol. 20, pp. 5–38. See also T. Carothers, "The Democracy Nostrum," *World Policy Journal*, Fall 1994, vol. 11, pp. 47–53.

24   For critical studies of democratization as foreign policy, see P.R. Newberg and T. Carothers, "Aiding – and Defining – Democracy," *World Policy Journal*, Spring 1996, vol. 13, pp. 97–108; A. Hadenius and F. Uggla, "Making Civil Society Work, Promoting Democratic Development: What Can States and Donors Do?" *World Development*, 1996, vol. 24, pp. 1621–39.

25   See my chapter on Tajikistan (Chapter 7), where political competition and elections in the context of a failing state helped set off a civil war.

REFERENCES

Author not cited

A Political Portrait of Ukraine. The Results of Four Polls Conducted during the 1994 Election Campaign in Ukraine, Kiev, Democratic Initiatives Research and Educational Center, 1994.

Developments in Crimea. Challenges for Ukraine and Implications for Regional Security, Washington, DC, American Association for the Advancement of Science, 1995.

"Economic Culture of Ukrainian Population," Kiev, Democratic Initiatives Center, 1996.

Evreiskaia Starina, "Iz 'chernoi knigi' russkago evreistva, materialy dlia istorii voiny, 1914–1915," 1918, vol. 10., pp. 231–53.

"How Close is Russia to Breaking Up?" *Current Digest of the Soviet Press (CDSP)*, 25 March 1992, vol. 44, no. 8, p. 1.

Oblastnaia Gazeta, Yekaterinburg, 14 March 1996, translated in FBIS-SOV-96–093-S, pp. 57–63.

"Regions' Heads Feel Threatened by Chechen War," *Current Digest of the Soviet Press*, 1995. vol. 47, no. 3.

"Russia and the Near Abroad," *The Economist*, 18 February 1995, pp. 51–2.

"Social-Political Portrait of Four Ukrainian Cities," Kiev, Democratic Initiatives Research and Education Center, May 1995.

"Ukraine, The Birth and Possible Death of a Country," *The Economist*, 7 May 1994.

"Ukrainian Society 1994–1995: Opinions, Assessments and Living Standards of the Ukrainian Population," Kiev, Democratic Initiatives Center, 1995.

Voennye prestupleniia Gabsburgskoi monarkhii 1914–1917 gg.: Galitskaia golgofa, Trumbull, CT, Peter S. Hardy, 1964.

Authored works

Adams, J., "CIS: The Interparliamentary Assembly and Khasbulatov," *RFE/RL Research Report*, June 1993, vol. 2, no. 26, pp. 19–23.

Adelman, J. R., *Revolution, Armies, and War*, Boulder, CO, Lynne Rienner, 1985.

Agarwala, R., "China: Reforming Intergovernmental Fiscal Relations," *World Bank Discussion Paper 178*, 1992.

Agursky, M., *The Third Rome: National Bolshevism in the USSR*, Boulder, CO, Westview, 1987.

Alimov, K., "Are Central Asian Clans Still Playing a Political Role?" *Central Asian Monitor*, 1994, vol. 3, no. 4, pp. 14–17.

REFERENCES

Allison, R., "Peacekeeping in the Soviet Successor States," Chaillot Paper 18, Paris, Institute for Security Studies, Western European Union, 1994.

Ames, E., and Rapp, R., "The Birth and Death of Taxes: A Hypothesis," *Journal of Economic History*, March 1977, vol. 37, no. 1, pp. 161–78.

Anderson, J. W., "Khan and Khel: Dialectics of Pashtun Tribalism," in R. Tapper (ed.), *The Conflict of Tribe and State in Iran and Afghanistan*, New York, St. Martin's Press, 1984, pp. 119–49.

Anderson, P., *Lineages of the Absolutist State*, London, Verso, 1974.

Arel, D. "Ukraine, The Temptation of the Nationalizing State," in V. Tismaneanu (ed.), *Political Culture and Civil Society in the Former Soviet Union*, Armonk, NY, Sharpe, 1995.

——, "Elite Formation and Elite Conflict," paper presented at the International Conference, "Ukrainian National Security," The Woodrow Wilson Center of the Kennan Institute, Washington, DC, 8–9 May 1997.

Atkins, M., "Ancient Nation, New Politics," in I. Bremmer and R. Taras (eds), *Nations and Politics in the Soviet Successor States*, Cambridge, Cambridge University Press, 1993.

Baechler, J., Hall, J., and Mann, M. (eds), *Europe and the Rise of Capitalism*, London, Blackwell, 1988.

Bahl, R., "Revenues and Revenue Assignment: Intergovernmental Fiscal Relations in the Russian Federation," in C. Wallich (ed.), *Russia and the Challenge of Fiscal Federalism*, Washington, DC, World Bank, 1994, pp. 129–80.

Ball, D., "Arms and Affluence: Military Acquisition in the Asia-Pacific Region," *International Security*, Winter 1993/94, vol. 18, no. 3., pp. 78–112.

Ballentine, K., "The Making of Nations and the Un-Making of the Soviet Union," *The Harriman Review*, December 1995, vol. 8, no. 4, pp. 14–24.

Baranovsky, V., "Conflict Developments on the Territory of the Former Soviet Union," *SIPRI Yearbook*, Stockholm, SIPRI, 1994, pp. 169–203.

Barghoorn, F.C., "Russian Nationalism and Soviet Politics," in R. Conquest (ed.), *The Last Empire*, Stanford, CA, Hoover Institution Press, 1986, pp. 30–77.

——, *Soviet Russian Nationalism*, New York, Oxford University Press, 1956.

Barkey, K., "Consequences of Empire," in K. Barkey and M. Von Hagen (eds), *After Empire*, Boulder, CO, Westview, 1997.

Bates, R., "Modernization, Ethnic Competition, and the Rationality of Politics in Contemporary Africa," in D. Rothchild and V. Olorunsola (eds), *State Versus Ethnic Claims: African Policy Dilemmas*, Boulder, CO, Westview, 1983, pp. 152–71.

Bendix, R., *Kings or People*, Berkeley, CA, University of California Press, 1978.

Betts, R., "Systems for Peace or Causes of War," *International Security*, Summer 1992, vol. 17, no. 1, pp. 5–43.

——, "Wealth, Power and Instability: East Asia and the United States After the Cold War," *International Security*, Winter 1993/94, vol. 18, no. 3., pp. 34–77.

Blackwill, R., and Larrabee, F.S. (eds), *Conventional Arms Control and East-West Security*, Durham, NC, Duke University Press, 1989.

Bociurkiw, B., "The Ukrainian Autocephalous Orthodox Church, 1920–1930: A Case Study in Religious Modernization," in D. Dunn (ed.), *Religion and Modernization in the Soviet Union*, Boulder, CO, Westview, 1977, pp. 310–47.

——, "The Ukrainian Catholic Church in the USSR Under Gorbachev," *Problems of Communism*, November–December 1990, vol. 39, no. 6, pp. 1–19.

——, "The Ukrainian Greek Catholic Church in the Contemporary USSR," *Nationalities Papers*, Special Issue on Religious Consciousness in the Glasnost Era, Spring 1992, vol. 20, no. 1, pp. 16–28.

——, *Ukrainian Churches under Soviet Rule, Two Case Studies*, Cambridge, MA, Harvard Ukrainian Studies Fund, 1984.

Boutros-Ghali, B., *Agenda for Peace*, New York, United Nations Publications, 1992.

Bremmer, I., "Nazarbaev and the North: State-Building and Ethnic Relations in Kazakstan," *Ethnic and Racial Studies*, October 1994, vol. 17, no. 4, pp. 619–35.

——, "How Russian the Russians? New Minorities in the Post-Soviet Regions." paper presented at conference on "Peoples, Nations, Identities, the Russian-Ukranian Encounter," New York, The Harriman Institute, Columbia University, 21–3 September 1995.

Bremmer, I., and Taras, R. (eds), *Nations and Politics in the Soviet Successor States*, New York, Cambridge University Press, 1993.

Brown, B., "Tajikistan: The Conservatives Triumph," *RFE/RL Research Report*, February 12, 1993, vol. 2, no. 7, pp. 9–12.

Broxup, M.B., "The 'Internal' Muslim Factor in the Politics of Russia," in M. Mesbahi (ed.), *Central Asia and the Caucasus after the Soviet Union*, Talahassee, FL: University Press of Florida, 1994.

Brubaker, R., "Citizenship Struggles in Soviet Successor States," *International Migration Review*, Summer 1992, vol. 26, pp. 269–91.

——, *Citizenship and Nationhood in France and Germany*, Cambridge, MA, Harvard University Press, 1992.

——, "National Minorities, Nationalizing States, and External National Homelands," Unpublished paper, 1994.

——, "Rethinking Nationhood," *Contention*, Fall 1994, vol. 4, no. 1, pp. 3–14.

——, "Nationhood and the National Question in the Soviet Union and Post-Soviet Eurasia: An Institutionalist Account," *Theory and Society*, February 1994, vol. 23, pp. 47–78.

——, "National Minorities, Nationalizing States, and External National Homelands in the New Europe," *Daedalus*, 1995, vol. 124, pp. 107–32.

Bushkov, V.I., "Tadjikistan, quelques prémisses de la crise," in S. A. Dudoignon and G. Jahangiri (eds), *Le Tadjikistan existe-t-il? Destins politiques d'une "nation imparfaite"*, special edition of *Cahiers d'études sur la méditerranée orientale et le monde turco-iranien* (CEMOTI), 1994, vol. 18, pp. 15–26.

Carnes, T., "Measuring Anti-Semitism in Russia," paper presented at the Annual Meeting of the Association for the Sociology of Religion, Washington, DC, 19 August 1995.

Carothers, T., "The Democracy Nostrum," *World Policy Journal*, Fall 1994, vol. 11, pp. 47–53.

Carrère-d'Encausse, H., *The Great Challenge*, New York, Holmes and Meier, 1992.

Casanova, J., "Las enseñanzas de la transición democrática en España," *Ayer*, 1994, no. 15, 1994

——, *Public Religions in the Modern World*, Chicago, University of Chicago Press, 1994.

Celik, Z., *The Remaking of Istanbul*, Berkeley, CA, University of California Press, 1986.

Centlivres, P., and Centlivres-Demont, M., *Et si on parlait de l'Afghanistan? Terrains et textes 1964–1980*, Neuchâtel, Editions de l'Institut d'Ethnologie, and Paris, Editions de la Maison des Sciences de l'Homme, 1988.

Chinn, J., and Kaiser, R., *Russians as the New Minority: Ethnicity and Nationalism in the Soviet Successor States*, Boulder, CO, Westview, 1996.

Chlamtacz, M., *Lembergs politische Physiognomie während der russischen Invasion*, Vienna, R. Lechner, 1916.

Cholodecki, J.B., *Lwow w czasie okupacji rosyjskiej, 3 wrzesnia 1914–22 czerwca 1915*, Lwow, Nakladen Towarzystwa Milosnikow Przeszlosci, 1930.

Cholovskii, A., *L'vov vo vremena russkago vladychestva*, Petrograd?, 1915.

Colton, T., and Tucker, R. (eds), *Patterns in Post-Soviet Leadership*, Boulder, Westview, 1995.

Conolly, V., "The 'nationalities question' in the last phase of tsardom," in E. Oberlaender, (ed.), *Russia Enters the Twentieth Century, 1894–1917*, New York, Schocken Books, 1971.

Coonrod, R.W., "The Duma's Attitude toward War-time Problems of Minority Groups," *American Slavic and East European Review*, 1954, vol. 13, pp. 30–8.

Crow, S., "Russia Promotes the CIS as an International Organization," *RFE/RL Research Report*, March 1994, vol. 3, no. 11, pp. 33–8.

Danto, A., *Narration and Knowledge*, New York, Columbia University Press, 1985, pp. 257–84.

Dave, B., "Cracks Emerge in Kazakhstan's Government Monopoly," *Transition*, October 6, 1995, vol. 1, no. 18, pp. 73–5.

David, S., "Explaining Third World Realignment," *World Politics*, January 1991, vol. 43, no. 2, pp. 233–56.

Dawisha, K., and Parrott, B., *Russia and the New States of Eurasia*, New York, Cambridge University Press, 1994.

Deak, I., *Beyond Nationalism: A Social and Political History of the Habsburg Officer Corps, 1848–1918*, Oxford, Oxford University Press, 1990.

Della Cava, R., "Jews and Christians of Russia and Ukraine Speak about Anti-Semitism: Notes from a Travel Journal, May–June 1995," unpublished manuscript, 1995.

Diamond, L., *Promoting Democracy in the 1990s: Actors and Instruments, Issues and Imperatives*, New York, Carnegie Commission on Preventing Deadly Conflict, December 1995.

Dmitrieva, O., "Political Games Around the Budget," *Moskovskie Novosti*, 1993, no. 28, pp. 8–9.

Doyle, M., "Liberalism and World Politics," *American Political Science Review*, December 1986, vol. 80, no. 4, pp. 1151–69.

——, *Empires*, Ithaca, NY, Cornell University Press, 1986.

Dudoignon, S., "Une segmentation peut en cacher une autre: régionalismes et clivages politico-économiques au Tadjikistan," in S. A. Dudoignon and G. Jahangiri (eds), *Le Tadjikistan existe-t-il? Destins politiques d'une "nation imparfaite"*, special edition of *Cahiers d'études sur la méditerranée orientale et le monde turco-iranien* (CEMOTI), 1994, vol. 18, pp. 73–130.

Easton, D., *The Analysis of Political Structure*, New York, Routledge, 1990.

Edelman, R., *Gentry Politics on the Eve of the Russian Revolution: The Nationalist Party, 1907–1917*, New Brunswick, NJ, Rutgers University Press, 1980.

Eisenstadt, S.N., *The Political Systems of Empires*, New York, The Free Press, 1963.

——, "Center-Periphery Relations in the Soviet Empire," in A.J. Motyl (ed.), *Thinking Theoretically about Soviet Nationalities*, New York, Columbia University Press, 1992.

Elazar, D.J., "International and Comparative Federalism," *PS: Political Science and Politics*, 1993, vol. 24, no. 2, pp. 190–5.

Elphinstone, M., *An Account of the Kingdom of Caubul and Its Dependencies in Persia, Tartary, and India*, Karachi, Oxford University Press, 1972 [first edition, 1815].

Emerson, R., *From Empire to Nation*, Boston, Beacon, 1960.

Esman, M., and Telhami, S. (eds), *International Organizations and Ethnic Conflict*, Ithaca, NY, Cornell University Press, 1995.

Evlogii, Archbishop, *Put' moei zhizni: Vospominaniia Mitropolita Evlogiia*, izlozhennyia po ego rasskazam T. Manukhinoi, Paris, YMCA Press, 1947.

Evtoukh, V., "Ethnische Minderheiten der Ukraine, Zwischen Realitäten und Politik," paper presented at conference on "Peoples, Nations, Identities, the Russian-Ukrainian Encounter," New York, The Harriman Institute, Columbia University, 21–23 September 1995.

Fane, D., "Political Elites in Tajikistan," unpublished paper, Columbia University, 1995.

Fedyshyn, O.S., *Germany's Drive to the East and the Ukrainian Revolution in World War I*, New Brunswick, NJ, Rutgers University Press, 1970.

——, "The Germans and the Union for the Liberation of the Ukraine, 1914–1917," in T. Hunczak, (ed.), *The Ukraine, 1917–1921: A Study in Revolution*, Cambridge, MA, Harvard University Press, 1977, pp. 305–22.

Ferro, M., "La politique des nationalités du gouvernement provisoire, fevrier–octobre 1917," *Cahiers du monde russe et sovietique*, 1961, vol. 2.

Fleischhauer, I., *Die Deutschen im Zarenreich: Zwei Jahrhunderte deutsch-russische Kulturgemeinschaft*, Stuttgart, Deutsche Verlags-Anstalt, 1986.

Florinsky, M.T., *Russia: A History and an Interpretation*, New York, Macmillan, 1953.

Foye, S., "End of CIS Command Heralds New Russian Defense Policy?" *RFE/RL Research Report*, July 1993, vol. 2, no. 27, pp. 45–9.

Fragner, B.G., "The Nationalization of the Uzbeks and Tajiks," in E. Allworth (ed.), *Muslim Communities Reemerge: Historical Perspectives on Nationality, Politics, and Opposition in the Former Soviet Union and Yugoslavia*, Durham, NC, Duke University Press, 1994.

Frenkin, M.S., *Russkaia armiia i revoliutsiia 1917–1918*, Munich, Logos, 1978.

Friedberg, A., "Ripe for Rivalry, Prospects for Peace in a Multipolar Asia," *International Security*, Winter 1993/94, vol. 18, no. 3, pp. 5–33.

Fuller, E., "Azerbaijan's June Revolution," *RFE/RL Research Report*, August 13, 1993, vol. 2, no. 32, pp. 24–9.

——, "The Karabakh Mediation Process: Grachev versus the CSCE?" *RFE/RL Research Report*, June 1994, vol. 3, no. 23, pp. 13–17.

——, "The Vagaries of Russia's Abkhaz Policy," *Open Media Research Institute Analytical Brief*, 29 March 1996, vol. 1, no. 51.

——, "Yet Another 'Historic' Chechen Ceasefire Agreement," *Open Media Research Institute Analytical Brief*, 28 May 1996, vol. 1, no. 132.

Geertz, C., *The Interpretation of Cultures*, New York, Basic Books, 1973.

Gellner, E., *Nations and Nationalism*, Ithaca, NY, Cornell University Press, 1983.

——, "Nationalism in the Vacuum," in A.J. Motyl (ed.), *Thinking Theoretically about Soviet Nationalities*, New York, Columbia University Press, 1992, pp. 243–54.

——, "The Price of Velvet: Tomas Masaryk and Vaclav Havel," in *Encounters with Nationalism*, Oxford, Blackwell, 1994, pp. 114–29.

Gerschenkron, A., *Economic Backwardness in Historical Perspective*, Cambridge, MA, Harvard University Press, 1962.

Gerus, O.W., "The Ukrainian Question in the Russia Dumas, 1906–1917: An Overview," *Studia Ucrainica*, 1984, vol. 2, pp. 165–6.

Gessen, I.V. (ed.), *Arkhiv russkoi revoliutsii*, vol. 19, Berlin, Terra, 1928.

Gillette, P.S., "Ethnic Balance and Imbalance in Kazakstan's Regions," *Central Asia Monitor*, 1993, vol. 2, no. 3, pp. 18–22.

Gilpin, R., *War and Change in World Politics*, Cambridge, Cambridge University Press, 1981.

Given, J., *State and Society in Medieval Europe*, Ithaca, NY, Cornell University Press, 1990.

Golovakha, E.I., and Panina, N.V., "The Development of a Democratic Political Identity in Contemporary Ukrainian Political Culture," in R.F. Farnen (ed.), *Nationalism, Ethnicity, and Identity: Cross National and Comparative Perspectives*, New Brunswick, NJ, Transaction Publishers, 1994, pp. 403–25.

Golovin, N.N., *Voennye usiliia Rossii v mirovoi voine*, Paris, T-vo obedinennykh izdatelei, 1939, vol. 1.

Goltz, T., "The Hidden Russian Hand," *Foreign Policy*, Fall 1993, no. 92, pp. 92–116.

Gottmann, J. (ed.), *Centre and Periphery: Spatial Variation in Politics*, Beverly Hills, CA, Sage, 1980.

Graf, D., "Military Rule Behind the Russian Front, 1914–1917: The Political Ramifications," *Jahrbücher für Geschichte Osteuropas*, Neue Folge, Band 22, 1974.

Grebing, H., "Österreich-Ungarn und die 'Ukrainische Aktion' 1914–18," *Jahrbücher für Geschichte Osteuropas*, N.F., vol. 8, no. 3, Munich, Priebatsch's Buchhaldlung, 1959, pp. 270–96.

Greenfield, L., *Nationalism: Five Roads to Modernity*, Cambridge, Cambridge University Press, 1992.

Gretsky, S., "Profile: Qadi Akbar Turajonzoda," *Central Asian Monitor*, 1994, vol. 3, no. 1, pp. 16–24.

——, "Civil War in Tajikistan and its International Repercussions," *Critique*, Spring 1995, pp. 10–19.

Gronskii, P.P., "The Effects of the War on the Central Government Institutions of Russia," unpublished manuscript, Hoover Institution Archives, n.d.

Gurko, V.I., *Features and Figures of the Past: Government and Opinion in the Reign of Nicholas II*, Stanford, CA, Stanford University Press, 1939.

Gurr, T.R., *Minorities at Risk: A Global View of Ethnopolitical Conflict*, Washington, DC, United States Institute of Peace, 1993.

——, "Communal Conflicts and Global Security," *Current History*, May 1995, vol. 94, pp. 212–17.

——, "Minorities Report, 2. New Contenders, Old Issues: The Rise and Decline of Ethnopolitical Conflict in 1986–95," unpublished paper, May 1996.

Gurr, T.R., and Haxton, M., "Minorities Report, 1. Ethnopolitical Conflict in the 1990s: Patterns and Trends," unpublished paper, April 1996.

Hadenius, A., and Uggla, F. "Making Civil Society Work, Promoting Democratic Development: What Can States and Donors Do?" *World Development*, 1996, vol. 24, pp. 1621–39.

Halecky, O., *From Florence to Brest, 1439–1596*, Rome, Sacrum Poloniac Millennium, 1959.

Hall, J., *Powers and Liberties*, Berkeley, CA, University of California Press, 1985.

Hannum, H., *Autonomy, Sovereignty, and Self-Determination: The Accommodation of Conflicting Rights*, Philadelphia, University of Pennsylvania Press, 1990.

Hardin, R., "Why a Constitution?," in B. Grofman and D. Wittman (eds), *The Federalist Papers and the New Institutionalism*, New York, Agathon, 1989, 100–20.

Harris, C.D., "Ethnic Tensions in Areas of the Russian Diaspora," *Post-Soviet Geography*, April 1993, vol. 34, no. 4, pp. 233–8.

Hechter, M., "Nationalism as Group Solidarity," *Ethnic and Racial Studies*, October 1987, vol. 10, no. 4, pp. 415–20.

Herbst, J., "The Creation and Maintenance of National Boundaries in Africa," *International Organization*, Autumn 1989, vol. 43, no. 4, pp. 673–92.

——, "War and the State in Africa," *International Security*, Spring 1990, vol. 14, no. 4, pp. 117–39.

Hill, F., and Jewett, P., *Back in the USSR: Russia's Intervention in the Internal Affairs of Former Soviet Republics and the Implications for United States Policy Toward Russia*, Cambridge, MA, Harvard University, Strengthening Democratic Institutions Project, January 1994.

Himka, J.P., "The Greek Catholic Church and Nation-Building in Galicia, 1772–1918," *Harvard Ukrainian Studies*, December 1984, vol. 8, pp. 426–52.

——, "Ukrainians, Russians, and Alexander Solzhenitsyn," *Cross Currents, A Yearbook of Central European Culture*, 1992, vol. 11, pp. 193–205.

Holton, R.J., *Cities, Capitalism and Civilization*, London, Allen and Unwin, 1986.

Hont, I., "The Permanent Crisis of a Divided Mankind: 'Contemporary Crisis of the Nation State' in Historical Perspective," *Political Studies*, 1994, vol. 42.

Hough, J.F., Davidheiser, E., and Lehmann, S.G., *The 1996 Russian Presidential Election*, Washington, DC, Brookings, 1996.

Huber, K., "The CSCE and Ethnic Conflict in the East," *RFE/RL Research Report*, July 1993, vol. 2, no. 31, pp. 30–6.

Hughes, J., "Regionalism in Siberia: The Rise and Fall of the Siberian Agreement," *Europe-Asia Studies*, 1994, vol. 46, no. 7, pp. 1133–61.

Hunter, S., *The Transcaucasus in Transition*, Washington, DC, The Center for Strategic and International Studies, 1994.

Huntington, S.P., *Political Order in Changing Societies*, New Haven, CT, Yale University Press, 1968.

Iakhontov, A.N., *Prologue to Revolution: Notes of A.N. Iakhontov on the Secret Meetings of the Council of Ministers, 1915*, trans. and ed. by M. Cherniavsky, Englewood Cliffs, NJ, Prentice-Hall, 1967.

Institute for National Strategic Studies, *Strategic Assessment 1995*, Washington, DC, Institute for National Strategic Studies, 1995.

——, *The Military Balance, 1994–1995*, London, International Institute for Strategic Studies, 1995.

International Monetary Fund, *Economic Review: Tajikistan*, Washington, DC, IMF, 7 May 1992.

Ionescu, D., "Moldovan-Dniester Agreement Ripe for Being Signed," *Open Media Research Institute Analytical Brief*, 1 July 1996, vol 1, no. 205.

Jackson, R., *Quasi-States: Sovereignty, International Relations, and the Third World*, New York, Cambridge University Press, 1990.

Jahangiri, G., "Anatomie d'une crise: le poids des tensions entre régions au Tadjikistan," in S.A. Dudoignon and G. Jahangiri (eds), *Le Tadjikistan existe-t-il? Destins politiques d'une "nation imparfaite"*, special edition of *Cahiers d'études sur la méditerranée orientale et le monde turco-iranien* (CEMOTI), 1994, vol. 18, pp. 37–72.

Janusz, B., *293 dni rzadow rosyjskich we Lwowie*, Lwow, Nakladen Towarzystwa Milosnikow Przeszlosci, 1915.

——, *Dokumenty urzedowe okupacyi rosyjskiej*, Lwow, Nakladen Towarzystwa Milosnikow Przes-zlosci, 1916.

——, *Odezwy i rozporzadzenia z czasow okupacyi rosyjskiej Lwowa, 1914–1915*, Lwow, 1916.

Kaiser, R., *The Geography of Nationalism in Russia and the Soviet Union*, Princeton, NJ, Princeton University Press, 1994.

Kappeler, A., *Russland als Vielvoelkerreich*, Munich, C.H. Beck Verlag, 1992.

Kennedy, P., *The Rise and Decline of the Great Powers*, New York, Vintage, 1987.

Keohane, R. (ed.), *Neorealism and Its Critics*, New York, Columbia University Press, 1986.

Khmelko, V., and Arel, D., "Russian Factor and Territorial Polarization in Ukraine," Paper presented at the Conference on "Peoples, Nations, Identities, the Russian–Ukrainian Encounter," at The Harriman Institute, Columbia University, 21–23 September 1995.

Khomchuk, O., "The Far Right in Russia and Ukraine," *The Harriman Review*, July 1995, pp. 40–4.

Klebnikov, P. "Tinderbox," *Forbes*, 9 September 1996, pp. 158–64.

Knox, A., *With the Russian Army, 1914–1917*, London, Dutton, 1921, I.

Kohl, H., *Deutschlands Zukunft in Europa*, Herford, Busse und Seewald, 1990.

Korganoff, G., *La Participation des Arméniens à la Guerre Mondiale sur le Front du Caucase, 1914–1918*, Paris, Massis, 1927.

Krasner, S. D. (ed.), *International Regimes*, Ithaca, NY, Cornell University Press, 1983.

Krawchenko, B., "Ukraine, The Politics of Independence," in I. Bremmer and R. Taras (eds), *Nation and Politics in the Soviet Successor States*, Cambridge, Cambridge University Press, 1993, pp. 75–98.

Kreps, D., and Wilson, R., "Reputations and Imperfect Information," *Journal of Economic Theory*, August 1982, vol. 27, pp. 253–79.

Kupchan, C., *The Vulnerability of Empire*, Ithaca, NY, Cornell University Press, 1994.

Kupchan, C.A., and Kupchan, C.A., "Concerts, Collective Security, and the Future of Europe," *International Security*, Summer 1991, vol. 16, no. 1, pp. 114–61.

Kuzio, T., and Wilson, A., *Ukraine, Perestroika to Independence*, New York, St. Martin's Press, 1994.

Labunka, M., and Rudnytzky, L. (eds), *The Ukrainian Catholic Church 1945–1975*, Philadelphia, St. Sophia Religious Association, 1976.

Laitin, D., "The National Uprisings in the Soviet Union," *World Politics*, October 1991, vol. 44, no. 1, pp. 139–77.

Lapidus, G.W., Zaslavsky, V., and Goldman, P., (eds), *From Union to Commonwealth: Nationalism and Separatism in the Soviet Republics*, Cambridge, Cambridge University Press, 1992.

LeHouerou, P., "Decentralization and Fiscal Disparities Among Regions of the Russian Federation," Internal Discussion Paper (IDP-138), The World Bank, January 1994.

Levi, M., *Of Rule and Revenue*, Berkeley, CA, University of California Press, 1988.

Levyts'kyi, K., *Istoriia politychnoi dumky halyts'kykh ukraintsiv 1848–1914*, 2 vols, L'viv, published by author, 1926.

Lewis, B., *The Emergence of Modern Turkey*, 2nd edn, London, Oxford University Press, 1968 [first edition 1961].

Lijphart, A., *Democracy in Plural Societies*, New Haven, CT, Yale University Press, 1977.

——, *Democracies: Patterns of Majoritarian and Consensus Government in Twenty-One Countries*, New Haven, CT, Yale University Press, 1984.

——, "Democratic Political Systems: Types, Cases, Causes and Consequences," *Journal of Theoretical Politics*, 1989, vol. 1, no. 1, pp. 33–48.

Lincoln, W.B., *Passage through Armageddon: The Russians in War and Revolution*, New York, Simon & Schuster, 1986.

Linz, J.J., "Staatsbildung, Nationbildung und Demokratie," *Transit*, 1994, vol. 7, pp. 43–62.

——, "Plurinazionalismo e Democrazia," *Revista Italiana di Scienza Politica*, 1995, vol. 25, pp. 21–50.

Linz, J.J., and Stepan, A., "Political Crafting of Democratic Consolidation or Destruction, European and South American Comparisons," in R.A. Pastor (ed.), *Democracy in the Americas. Stopping the Pendulum*, New York, Holmes & Meier, 1989, pp. 41–61.

——, *Problems of Democratic Transition and Consolidation. Southern Europe, South America, and Post-Communist Europe.*, Baltimore, The Johns Hopkins University Press, 1996.

Little, D., *Ukraine, The Legacy of Intolerance*, Washington, DC, United States Institute of Peace Press, 1991.

Litvack, J., "Regional Demands and Fiscal Federalism," in C. Wallich (ed.), *Russia and the Challenge of Fiscal Federalism*, Washington, DC, World Bank, 1994.

Loewe, H.D., *Antisemitismus und reaktionäre Utopie: Russischer Konservatismus im Kampf gegen den Wandel von Staat und Gesellschaft, 1890–1917*, Hamburg, Hoffmann und Campe Verlag, 1978.

Luckyj, G.S.N., *Literary Politics in the Soviet Ukraine, 1917–1934*, New York, Columbia University Press, 1956.

Magocsi, P.R. (ed.), *Morality and Religion, The Life and Times of Andrei Sheptyts'kyi*, Edmonton, Canadian Institute of Ukrainian Studies, 1989.

Mandelbaum, M. (ed.), *Central Asia and the World*, New York, Council on Foreign Relations, 1994, p. 7.

Mann, M., "The Autonomous Power of the State: Its Origins, Mechanisms, and Results," in J.A. Hall (ed.), *States in History*, Oxford, Blackwell, 1986, pp. 109–36.

——, *The Sources of Social Power*, Cambridge, Cambridge University Press, 1986.

Mansfield, E. D., and Snyder, J., "Democratization and the Danger of War," *International Security*, Summer 1995, vol. 20, pp. 5–38.

——, "Democratization and War," *Foreign Affairs*, May–June 1995, vol. 74, pp. 79–97.

Markus, V., "Religion and Nationality, The Uniates of the Ukraine," in B. Bociurkiw and J. Strong (eds), *Religion and Atheism in the USSR and Eastern Europe*, London, Macmillan, 1975, pp. 101–22.

——, "Religion and Nationalism in Ukraine," in P. Ramet (ed.), *Religion and Nationalism in Soviet and East European Politics*, Durham, NC, Duke University Press, 1984.

Martin, D., *A General Theory of Secularization*, New York, Harper & Row, 1978.

Martyniuk, J., "Religious Preferences in Five Urban Areas of Ukraine," *RFE/RL Research Report*, 9 April 1993, vol. 2, no. 15, pp. 52–5.

——, "The State of the Orthodox Church in Ukraine," *RFE/RL Research Report*, 18 February 1994, vol. 3, no. 7, pp. 34–41.

McClure, C., "The Sharing of Taxes on Natural Resources and the Future of the Russian Federation," in C. Wallich (ed.) *Russia and the Challenge of Fiscal Federalism*, World Bank, 1994, pp. 181–217.

McNeil, W., *The Pursuit of Power*, Chicago, University of Chicago Press, 1982.

Menon, R., "In the Shadow of the Bear, Security in Post-Soviet Central Asia," *International Security*, Summer 1995, vol. 20, no. 1, pp. 139–56.

Menon, R., and O'Neal, J.R., "Explaining Imperialism: The State of the Art as Reflected in Three Theories," *Polity*, Winter 1986, vol. 19, no. 2, pp. 169–93.

Meyer, S.M., "Yeltsin's Military Bluff, Mr. Doubtfire," *The New Republic*, 14 March 1994, pp. 11–12.

Migdal, J.S., *Strong Societies and Weak States: State-Society Relations and State Capabilities in the Third World*, Princeton, NJ, Princeton University Press, 1988.

Milgrom, P., and Roberts, J., "Predation and Entry Deterrence," *Journal of Economic Theory*, August 1982, vol. 27, pp. 280–312.

Morrison, J., "Pereslayav and After: The Russian–Ukrainian Relationship," *International Affairs*, 1993, vol. 69, no. 4, pp. 677–703.

Motyl, A.J., *Will the Non-Russians Rebel?*, Ithaca, NY, Cornell University Press, 1987.

——, *Sovietology, Rationality, Nationality: Coming to Grips with Nationalism in the USSR*, New York, Columbia University Press, 1990.

——, "Concepts and Skocpol: Ambiguity and Vagueness in the Study of Revolution," *Journal of Theoretical Politics*, January 1992, vol. 4, no. 1, pp. 93–112.

——, "From Imperial Decay to Imperial Collapse: The Fall of the Soviet Empire in Comparative Perspective," in R.L. Rudolph and D.F. Good, (eds), *Nationalism and Empire*, New York, St. Martin's Press, 1992, pp. 15–43.

——, *Dilemmas of Independence. Ukraine after Totalitarianism*, New York, Council on Foreign Relations, 1993.

——, "Imperial Collapse and Revolutionary Change," in J. Nautz and R. Vahrenkamp (eds), *Die Wiener Jahrhundertwende*, Vienna, Bohlau, 1993, pp. 813–19.

——, "Reform, Transition, or Revolution?," *Contention*, Fall 1994, vol. 4, no. 1, pp. 141–60.

——, "Structural Constraints and Starting Points, Postimperial States and Nations in Ukraine and Russia," paper presented at the conference on "Post-Communism and Ethnic Mobilization," Cornell University, 21–23 April 1995.

——, "How Empires Rise and Fall: A Conceptual Enquiry with Some Implications for Theory," unpublished paper.

Newberg, P.R., and Carothers, T., "Aiding – and Defining – Democracy," *World Policy Journal*, Spring 1996, vol. 13, pp. 97–108.

Nolte, E., *Die faschistischen Bewegungen*, Munich, Deutsche Taschenbuch Verlag, 1966.

North, D., *Institutions, Institutional Change and Economic Performance*, Cambridge, Cambridge University Press, 1990.

Offe, C., "Capitalism by Democratic Design? Democratic Theory Facing the Triple Transition in East Central Europe," *Social Research*, 1991, vol. 58, pp. 865–81.

Olson, M., *The Logic of Collective Action*, Cambridge, MA, Harvard University Press, 1965.

Ordeshook, P., "Constitutional Stability," *Constitutional Political Economy*, 1992, vol. 3, no. 2, pp. 137–75.

Otyrba, G., "War in Abkhazia," in R. Szporluk (ed.), *National Identity and Ethnicity in Russia and the Western States of Eurasia*, Armonk, NY, M.E. Sharpe, 1994.

Pannier, B., "Tajikistan's Grim Anniversary," *Open Media Research Institute Analytical Brief*, 18 April 1996, vol 1, no. 72.

Parker, G., *The Military Revolution*, New York, Cambridge University Press, 1988.

Petrovych, I., *Halychyna pidchas rosiis'koi okupatsii: serpen' 1914–cherven' 1915*, L'viv, Politychna Biblioteka, 1915.

Pipes, R., *The Formation of the Soviet Union*, Cambridge, MA, Harvard University Press, 1964 [first edition 1954].

Plokhy, S., "Kyiv vs. Moscow: The Autocephalous Movement in Independent Ukraine," *The Harriman Review*, Spring 1996, vol. 9, nos. 1–2, pp. 32–7.

Polanyi, K., *The Great Transformation*, New York, Farrar and Reinhart, 1994.

Poliakov, S. P., *Everyday Islam: Religion and Tradition in Rural Central Asia*, Armonk, NY, M.E. Sharpe, 1992.

Politychnyi Portret Ukraine, Kiev, Democratic Intitiatives Research and Education Center, May 1994; May 1995; February 1996.

Polner, T.I., Obolenskii, V. and Turin, S.P., *Russian Local Government During the War and the Union of Zemstvos*, New Haven, CT, Yale University Press, 1930.

Posen, B.R., "The Security Dilemma and Ethnic Conflict," *Survival*, Spring 1993, vol. 35, pp. 27–47.

——, "Nationalism, the Mass Army, and Military Power," *International Security*, Fall 1993, vol. 18, no. 2, pp. 80–124.

Powell, W.W. and DiMaggio, P.J. (eds), *The New Institutionalism in Organizational Analysis*, Chicago, University of Chicago Press, 1991.

Przeworski, A., *Democracy and the Market, Political and Economic Reforms in Eastern Europe and Latin America*, New York, Cambridge University Press, 1991.

Przeworski, A. *et al*, "What Makes Democracies Endure?" *Journal of Democracy*, January 1996, vol. 7, pp. 39–55.

Przysiecki, F., *Rzady rosyjskie w Galicyi wschodniej*, Piotrkow, Wiadomosci Polskich, 1915.

Rakowska-Harmstone, T., *Russia and Nationalism in Central Asia: The Case of Tadzhikistan*, Baltimore, Johns Hopkins University Press, 1970.

Rashid, A., *The First Book of Demographics for the Former Soviet Union*, Shady Side, MD, New World Demographics, 1992.

Rashid, A., *The Resurgence of Central Asia: Islam or Nationalism?*, London, Zed Books, 1994.

Rejai, M., and Phillips, K., *Leaders of Revolution*, Beverly Hills, Sage, 1979.

Rempel, D., "The Expropriation of the German Colonists in South Russia during the Great War," *Journal of Modern History*, 1932, vol. 4, pp. 49–67.

Riker, W., *Federalism: Origin, Operation, Significance*, Boston, Little, Brown and Co., 1964.

Ripets'kyi, S., *Ukrains'ke sichove strilets'tvo: Vyzvol'na ideia i zbroinyi chyn*, New York, 1956.

Ro'i, Y., "Central Asian Riots and Disturbances, 1989–1990: Causes and Context," *Central Asian Survey*, 1991, vol. 10, no. 3, pp. 21–54.

Roeder, P., "Soviet Federalism and Ethnic Mobilization," *World Politics*, January 1991, vol. 43, pp. 196–232.

Rogger, H., and Weber, E. (eds), *The European Right*, Berkeley, CA, University of California Press, 1966.

Rothschild, J., *East Central Europe between the Two World Wars*, Seattle, University of Washington Press, 1974, pp. 73–135.

Roy, O., "Le double code afghan: marxisme et tribalisme," *Révue française de science politique*, December 1986, vol. 36, pp. 846–61.

——, "The Civil War in Tajikistan: Causes and Implications," occasional paper, United States Institute of Peace, February 1993.

——, "Le conflit du Tadjikistan est-il un modèle des conflits d'Asie Centrale?" in M. Djalali and F. Grare (eds), *Le Tadjikistan à l'épreuve de l'indépendance*, Geneva, Institut Universitaire des Hautes Études Internationales, 1995.

Ruben, D.H. (ed.), *Explanation*, Oxford, Oxford University Press, 1993.

Rubin, B.R., "Contradictory Trends in the International Relations of Central Asia," *Central Asian Monitor*, 1993, vol. 2, no. 6, pp. 11–16.

——, "The Fragmentation of Tajikistan," *Survival*, Winter 1993–1994, vol. 35, no. 4, pp. 71–91.

——, "Tajikistan: From Soviet Republic to Russian-Uzbek Protectorate," in M. Mandelbaum (ed.), *Central Asia and the World*, New York, Council on Foreign Relations Press, 1994, pp. 185–204

——, *The Fragmentation of Afghanistan: State Formation and Collapse in the International System*, New Haven, CN, Yale University Press, 1995.

——, *The Search for Peace in Afghanistan: From Buffer State to Failed State*, New Haven, CT, Yale University Press, 1995.

Rudolph, L.I., and Rudolph, S.H., *The Modernity of Tradition: Political Development in India*, Chicago, University of Chicago Press, 1967.

Ruggie, J., "Peacekeeping and U.S. Interests," *The Washington Quarterly*, Autumn 1994, vol. 17, no. 4, pp. 175–84.

Rumer, B., *Soviet Central Asia: A Tragic Experiment*, Boston, Unwin Hyman, 1989.

Rumer, E.B., "Will Ukraine Return to Russia?," *Foreign Policy*, 1994, no. 96, pp. 129–44.

Rupert, J., "After Survival, Revival for Ukraine's Jews," *The Washington Post*, 30 March 1995.

Russett, B.M., *Grasping the Democratic Peace*, Princeton, NJ, Princeton University Press, 1993.

Sachs, J., *Poland's Jump to the Market Economy*, Cambridge, MA, MIT Press, 1994.

Sagan, S., "1914 Revisited: Allies, Offense, and Instability," *International Security*, Fall 1986, vol. 11, no. 2, pp. 151–175.

Sakwa, R., *Russian Politics and Society*, London, Routledge, 1993.

Salmon, M.H., "Explanation in the Social Sciences," in P. Kitcher and W.C. Salmon (eds), *Scientific Explanation*, Minneapolis, University of Minnesota Press, 1989, pp. 384–409.

Sartori, G., "Guidelines for Concept Analysis," in G. Sartori (ed.), *Social Science Concepts*, Beverly Hills, CA, Sage, 1984, pp. 15–85.

Schweller, R., "Tripolarity and the Second World War," *International Studies Quarterly*, March 1993, vol. 37, pp. 73–104.

Selten, R., "The Chain Store Paradox," *Theory and Decision*, 1978, vol. 9, pp. 127–59.

Sheehy, A., "The CIS: A Shaky Edifice," *RFE/RL Research Report*, January 1993, vol. 2, no. 1, pp. 37–40.

Shevchuk, Y.I., "Dual Citizenship in Old and New States," unpublished manuscript, Political Science Department, New School for Social Research, New York, n.d.

Shirk, S., *The Political Logic of Economic Reform in China*, Berkeley, CA, University of California Press, 1993.

Skocpol, T., *States and Social Revolutions*, Cambridge, Cambridge University Press, 1979.

——, "Social Revolutions and Mass Military Mobilization," *World Politics*, January 1988, vol. 40, no. 2, pp. 147–68.

Slezkine, Y,. "The USSR as a Communal Apartment, or How a Socialist State Promoted Ethnic Particularism," *Slavic Review*, Summer 1994, vol. 53, no. 2, pp. 414–52.

Slider, D., "Federalism, Discord, and Accommodation: Intergovernmental Affairs in Post-Soviet Russia," in J. Hahn and T. Friedgut (eds), *Local Politics in Post-Soviet Russia*, Armonk, M. E. Sharpe, 1994, pp. 239–69.

——, "Privatization in Russia's Regions," *Post-Soviet Affairs*, 1994, vol. 10, no. 4, pp. 367–96.

Smirniagin, L., "Political Federalism versus Economic Federalism," *Segodniia*, 25 June 1993, p. 2, FBIS-USR-93-089, pp. 54–7.

——, "The Federation: Processes from Below," *Rossiiskie Vesti*, 26 June 1993, p. 2, FBIS-USR-93-090, pp. 17–19.

Smith, W.D., *The Ideological Origins of Nazi Imperialism*, New York, Oxford University Press, 1986, p. 53.

Snyder, J., *The Myths of Empire*, Ithaca, NY, Cornell University Press, 1991.

——, "Nationalism and the Crisis of the Post-Soviet State," *Survival*, Spring 1993, vol. 35, pp. 5–27.

Snyder, J. and Ballentine, K., "Nationalism and the Marketplace of Ideas," *International Security*, Fall 1996, vol. 21, pp. 5–40.

Solchanyk, R., "Russia, Ukraine, and the Imperial Legacy," *Post-Soviet Affairs*, October–December 1993, vol. 9, no. 4, pp. 337–65.

Solnick, S.L., "The Breakdown of Hierarchies in the Soviet Union and China: A Neoinstitutional Perspective," *World Politics*, January 1996, vol. 48, pp. 209–38.

Sosa, E., and Tooley, M. (eds), *Causation*, Oxford, Oxford University Press, 1993.

Spruyt, H., *The Sovereign State and Its Competitors*, Princeton, NJ, Princeton University Press, 1994.

Starovoitova, G., "Democracy in Russia after Chechnya," *The East & Central Europe Program Bulletin*, May 1995, vol. 5, no. 4.

Statisticheski Komitet Sodruzhestva Nezavisimykh Gosudartsv, *Itogi Vsesoyuznoi perepisi naseleniia 1989 goda*, vol. 7, *Natsional'nyi sostav naseleniia SSSR*, Minneapolis, East View Publications, 1993.

Stone, N., *The Eastern Front, 1914–1917*, London & Sydney, Hodder and Stoughton, 1975.

Stoner-Weiss, K., "Local Heroes: Political Exchange and Governmental Performance in Provincial Russia," Ph.D. Dissertation, Department of Government, Harvard University, 1994.

Stourzh, G., *Vom Reich zur Republik*, Vienna, Edition Atelier, 1990.

Suny, R., *The Baku Commune, 1917–1918: Class and Nationality in the Russian Revolution*, Princeton, NJ, Princeton University Press, 1972.

——, *The Revenge of the Past*, Stanford, CA, Stanford University Press, 1993.

——, "Ambiguous Categories: States, Empires and Nations," *Post-Soviet Affairs*, 1995, vol. 11, pp. 185–96.

Swietochowski, T., *Russia and Azerbaijan*, New York, Columbia University Press, 1995.

Szporluk, R., "Reflections on Ukraine after 1994: The Dilemmas of Nationhood," *The Harriman Review*, March–May 1994, vol. 7, nos. 7–9, pp. 1–9.

Taagepera, R., "Patterns of Empire Growth and Decline: Context for Russia," unpublished paper, March 1995.

Tadjbakhsh, S., "The Bloody Path of Change: The Case of Post-Soviet Tajikistan," *Harriman Institute Forum*, July, 1993, vol. 6, pp. 1–10.

Tapper, R., *Pasture and Politics : Economics, Conflict, and Ritual among Shahsevan Nomads of Northwestern Iran*, London and New York, Academic Press, 1979.

Taylor, B.D., "Russian Civil-Military Relations After the October Uprising," *Survival*, Spring, 1994, vol. 36, no. 1, pp. 3–29.

Teague, E., "North-South Divide: Yeltsin and Russia's Provincial Leaders," *RFE/RL Research Report*, 26 November 1993, vol. 2, no. 47, pp. 7–23.

——, "Russia's Difficult Road Toward Elections," *RFE/RL Research Report*, 15 October 1993, vol. 2, no. 41, pp. 3–4.

——, "Center-Periphery Relations in the Russian Federation," in R. Szporluk (ed.), *National Identity and Ethnicity in the New States of Eurasia*, Armonk, NY, M.E. Sharpe, 1994, pp. 21–57.

Terletskyi, O., *Istoriia ukrainskoi hromady v Rashtati*, Kiev-Leipzig, Ukrainska Nakladnia, 1919.

Tiander, K., *Das Erwachen Osteuropas: Die Nationalitätenbewegung in Russland und der Weltkrieg*, Vienna and Leipzig, Wilhelm Braumuller, 1934.

Tilly, C. (ed.), *The Formation of National States in Western Europe*, Princeton, NJ, Princeton University Press, 1975.

——, "War Making and State Making as Organized Crime," in P. Evans, D. Rueschemeyer, and T. Skocpol (eds), *Bringing the State Back In*, Cambridge, Cambridge University Press, 1985.

——, "How Empires End," in K. Barkey and M. Von Hagen (eds), *After Empire*, pp. 1–11.

Tishkov, V., *Ethnicity, Nationalism and Conflict in and after the Soviet Union: The Mind Aflame*, London, Sage, with International Peace Research Institute, Oslo, and United Nations Research Institute for Social Development, 1997.

Tolz, V., "Thorny Road toward Federalism in Russia," *RFE/RL Research Report*, 3 December 1993, vol. 2, no. 48, pp. 1–8.

Touval, S., "Why the U.N. Fails," *Foreign Affairs*, September 1994, vol. 73, no. 5, pp. 44–57.

Tsentral'noe Statisticheskoe Upravlenie SSSR: Otdel Perepisi, *Vsesoyuznaya perepis' naseleniia 1926 goda*, vol 15, *Uzbekistan*, Moscow, Izdanie Ts.S.U. Soyuza SSR, 1928.

Tsereteli, I.I., *Vospominaniia o Fevral'skoi revoliutsii*, Paris and The Hague, Mouton and Co., 1963.

Verdery, K., *National Ideology under Socialism: Identity and Cultural Politics in Ceausescu's Romania*, Berkeley, CA, University of California Press, 1991.

——, "Nationalism and National Sentiment in Post-socialist Romania," *Slavic Review*, Summer 1993, vol. 52, no. 2, pp. 179–203.

Walt, S.M., *The Origins of Alliances*, Princeton, NJ, Princeton University Press, 1987.

Waltz, K., *Theory of International Politics*, New York, Random House, 1979.

Webber, M., "Coping with Anarchy: Ethnic Conflict and International Organizations in the Former Soviet Union," *International Relations*, April 1996, vol. 13, no. 1, pp. 1–27.

Wehler, H.U., *The German Empire, 1871–1918*, Leamington Spa, Berg, 1985.

Weingast, B., "Constitutions as Governance Structures: The Political Foundations of Secure Markets," *Journal of Institutional and Theoretical Economics*, 1993, vol. 149, no. 1, pp. 286–320.

——, "The Political Foundations of Democracy and the Rule of Law," manuscript, February 1993.

Weinthal, E., "The Politics of Redistributing Resources in the Aral Sea Basin," paper delivered at the MacArthur Consortium Workshop on the Politics and Economics of Development Policy and Institutional Innovation, University of Wisconsin, March 1996.

Wheeler, G., *The Modern History of Soviet Central Asia*, Westport, CT, Greenwood Press, 1975.

Wildman, A., *The End of the Russian Imperial Army*, Princeton, NJ, Princeton University Press, 1987.

Wilson, A. "Ukraine as a Nationalising State: Will the 'Russians' Rebel?," paper presented at conference on "Peoples, Nations, Identities, the Russian-Ukrainian Encounter," New York, The Harriman Institute, Columbia University, 21–23 September 1995.

Wlasovsky, I., *Outline History of the Ukrainian Orthodox Church*, 2 vols, New York, Ukrainian Orthodox Church of USA, 1974–1979.

Woodward, S.L., *Balkan Tragedy: Chaos and Dissolution after the Cold War*, Washington, DC, Brookings Institution, 1995.

World Bank, *Statistical Handbook: States of the Former USSR*, Washington, DC, 1992.

Zenkovsky, S.A., *Pan-Turkism and Islam in Russia*, Cambridge, MA, Harvard University Press, 1967, pp. 123–9.

Zipperstein, S.J., "The Politics of Relief: The Transformation of Russian Jewish Communal Life During the First World War," in J. Frankel (ed.), *The Jews and the European Crisis, 1914–21*, vol. 4 of *Studies in Contemporary Jewry: An Annual*, Oxford, Oxford Univeristy Press, 1988.

Zolotarev, A.M., *Zapiski voennoi statistiki Rossii. Tom I: Teoriia statistiki. Obshchee obozrenie Rossii. Vooruzhennye sily*, St. Petersburg, A.E. Landau, 1885.

INDEX